THE EDUCATION OF
KEVIN POWELL

THE EDUCATION OF
KEVIN POWELL

A Boy's Journey into Manhood

KEVIN POWELL

ATRIA BOOKS

NEW YORK   LONDON   TORONTO   SYDNEY   NEW DELHI

ATRIA BOOKS

An Imprint of Simon & Schuster, Inc.
1230 Avenue of the Americas
New York, NY 10020

Poems excerpted throughout this book were first published in the author's poetry collections *No Sleep Till Brooklyn* (Soft Skull Press, 2008) and *recognize* (Writers & Readers, 1995).

First Atria Books hardcover edition November 2015

ATRIA B O O K S and colophon are trademarks of Simon & Schuster, Inc.

For information about special discounts for bulk purchases, please contact Simon & Schuster Special Sales at 1-866-506-1949 or business@simonandschuster.com.

The Simon & Schuster Speakers Bureau can bring authors to your live event. For more information or to book an event, contact the Simon & Schuster Speakers Bureau at 1-866-248-3049 or visit our website at www.simonspeakers.com.

Interior design by Kyoko Watanabe
Jacket design by Kerry DeBruce

Manufactured in the United States of America

10 9 8 7 6 5 4 3

Library of Congress Cataloging-in-Publication Data is available.

ISBN 978-1-4391-6368-9
ISBN 978-1-4391-6421-1 (ebook)

For my mother, Shirley Powell, the first teacher and leader I ever met. Ma, I love you forever—

"How I got over/How I got over/Oooh, my soul look back and wonder/How I got over"
—CLARA WARD/THE FAMOUS WARD SINGERS

"I think that somehow, we learn who we really are and then live with that decision."
—ELEANOR ROOSEVELT

"Wanting to be someone else is a waste of the person you are."
—KURT COBAIN

"People think just because you were born in the ghetto that you are going to fit in."
—TUPAC SHAKUR

CONTENTS

PART II

living on the other side of midnight

Intro

FISTS POUNDED my face from every angle. *I am so stupid for coming out into this hallway,* I thought. *I should've known they'd be out here waiting for me.* I wanted to scream, but I resolved to take the beating as punishment for my life. As the blows torpedoed my nose, my eye sockets, my temples, and my ears, my mind staggered toward the possibility that I could die, and I imagined the damage: the deviated septum, the detached retina and the loss of vision, the loudness of sudden deafness, garbled speech. I saw my body days later—swollen, with lumpy clots around the gashes—being found in a park, decomposed and fed upon by bloated, fanged street rats. My mother would come to the hospital to identify me and scream—the kind of cry every ghetto mother saves for the day when it is her son who has died prematurely. I could hear my mother's anguished voice: "Lawd, I knew he would end up this way. He was always walkin' the wrong path."

Dang, what a way to go out! Beat down by some pissed-off Black men. I wasn't with that. I squirmed and ducked enough head blows to fold my bony frame into a ball the way they'd taught us in that Jersey City P.A.L. karate class—but the kicks and punches blasted through anyway. Blood—thick, bitter clumps of it—oozed between my teeth and gums. My eyes had swollen into puffy balloons, so I couldn't make out the faces through the slits, but the voices sounded familiar:

"We should kill this kid for that ISH!"

"Man, later for that! I ain't tryin' to get no murder rap."

"Stop being a punk, yo! Who gonna tell?"

I wanted to say to those voices, "Yo, brothers! Don't y'all know who I am? I'm that kid from around the way. . . ." But they could not have cared less. I was just another Black boy who had played the wrong game and needed a good butt-kicking—

Once the men had planted me solidly on the tiled floor, I faked like I was out cold, hoping to get some mercy. "Get up, boy, you ain't dead yet!" Sturdy, leathery hands yanked me by my feet, and I was dragged down the hallway stairs, out of the building, into the parking lot next door. An electric-like current jolted my body, and I could feel my flesh frying atop the friction and heat of the pavement. *Does anyone see any of this?* I thought as heavy shoes and work boots pummeled my chest and rib cage.

For the first time I bawled loud and long—like an abandoned baby. *Aaaah! These dudes are going to kill me!* Flat on my back, I cupped the night's pitch-blackness in my outstretched hands and prayed silently—and I wondered if I were going to heaven or hell. *The Lord is my shepherd; I shall not want . . .* My mother told me to say that whenever I was in deep trouble. Maybe I had used up too many prayers. But the men, reeking of alcohol and now exhausted, hurled their legs and arms into me a few more times, then floated backwards to admire their work. As they turned away, I could hear them smacking palms and each other's backs, muttering, "Dang, we beat that kid down. . . ."

PART I

trapped in a concrete box

1

My mother

Dear Lawd,

Ah ain't mean't to do dis Lawd. It wuz uh accident, God. But God,

Ah done had de baby now an' it ain't

Nothin' Ah kin do but t' raise it.

But God, how cum dat damn Cunningham done disown his chile?

Oooh Jee-zus! He 13 years older dan me an' he should know bedder.

Lawd, Ah swear, if Ah known dat he was gonna do dat,

T' m, t' leeve me an' dis chile

Ah sho wouldn't had never let him touch me.

Ahm ashame Lawd 'cause dis baby ain't got no daddy.

Ah donno where t' turn. Ah kin't go back down South

'Cause dey'll call me a *heffa*.

Oh God! *Pleeze* show me de way 'cause dis

Ain't gonna be eazy.

All Ah ask Lawd is dat you give me de strength

T' take care of dis chile 'til he grown

Enuf t' do fo' hisself.

An' Lawd, when dat boy gits t' be uh man-size, if he ever run int'

His daddy, let him make his daddy pay fo' what he done did.

Ahm sorry, Lawd, fo' sayin' it lak dat but dat's de way Ah feel God.

Ah-man.

M Y MOTHER ripped me away from the fire-hot radiator as I screamed in agony. "Maaaaa! Maaaaa! Aaaaah! Maaaaa!"

I was somewhere between two and three years old, captivated by the hissing of this thing that both warmed us in the dead-cold winter, and also made the kind of noises that lured a child as a familiar toy would. While my mother looked elsewhere, I stared at it, sized it up, and then I raised my right hand, as if saluting it, and I touched it—

Pain knotted my fingers and I couldn't let go of the radiator. It ricocheted through my hand, up my wrist, and shocked my entire right arm into submission. I was stuck and all I could do was scream.

"Maaaaa! Maaaaa! Aaaaah! Maaaaa!"

My mother suddenly appeared and with one mighty tug freed me from that radiator.

"Oh, Jee-zus! Boy, what you done did now?"

I was crying hysterically, snot festering in my nose. My mother cradled me in her arms and wiped the tears from my face as I bawled. She moved to release me for a moment and I screamed again.

"Maaaaa! Maaaaa! Aaaaah! Maaaaa!"

"Boy, I ain't goin' nowhere 'cept to get a cold cloth to put on yo' hand. Now stop all that crying for a minute."

I continued to wail, standing frozen in our dingy apartment as my mother ran cold water in the kitchen sink. When she returned, I attempted to run away, but she grabbed me by the hand that was burned.

"Boy, stop actin' like a fool and sit still!"

When she applied it to my hand, the iciness of the wet cloth seemed to make the burn hotter. But after a few minutes, I felt some relief. My mother held me again in her arms. I was still crying, but somewhere in the far-off horizon of my mind, I began to paint the sky black and dot it with the tiny white holes they call stars, and I fell asleep.

◆

After I got burned on that radiator, the pictures of my life sharpened.

I lived with my mother and my Aunt Cathy and my cousin Anthony in Jersey City, New Jersey. Aunt Cathy and Anthony shared a bed in the living room, and my mother and I shared a bed in the bedroom. Anthony was born three days before me on Thursday, April 21, 1966. I was born in the wee hours of Sunday morning, April 24, 1966, at 4:15 A.M., at the Margaret Hague Maternity Hospital. As Anthony's mother was leaving the hospital with him, my mother was wheelchaired in to deliver me.

My mother and my aunt were sisters. Anthony and I played together every day, and we fought nearly every day, too. Sometimes I bit Anthony when I got angry, and my Aunt Cathy would beg my mother to make me stop, but my mother never said anything to me. I laughed a lot, but I was also mad a lot. I didn't know why. I loved cartoons. I loved milk. And I loved to run, to play.

One day my mother told me we were going to get my picture taken.

"What is that, Ma?"

"A man is going to shoot you while you sit still."

"A man is going to shoot me?"

That same fear and terror I felt when I burned my hand on the radiator reasserted its grip over my mind and body.

"I do not want to go, Ma! I'm scared!"

"Boy, hush with all that fool talk. We goin'."

We boarded the Bergen Avenue bus. It was orange and round and crowded with people. When we arrived at the place where the man was going to shoot me, I refused to go in. My mother looked at me sympathetically but then said, "Boy, get your fool self in here. This man ain't got all day for you."

I was wearing what my mother called a shorts set. She told me it was like a military uniform. The man taking my picture had wrinkled skin, and his color was different from my mother's and mine. It was what she later told me was white, that he was a White man. I did not understand.

The man asked me to sit on a bench and explained to me why he was going to shoot me.

"I am going to take your picture. It is not going to hurt. All you have to do is look into this camera, into this box, and smile, or laugh, or both. Can you do that, sonny?"

I was confused. My mother told me my name was Kevin and this man called me "sonny." I looked at my mother. She gave me that look she always gave me when she needed me to do something, whether I wanted to do it or not.

I nodded uneasily. The man went behind the box, and his head disappeared beneath a black towel.

"I'm shooting now, sonny! Just look into the box."

I did what he told me to do because I did not want to be beaten by my mother for disobeying.

The man raised his head from the black towel and came over to me.

"Sonny, you have to move your left arm from behind your back. It looks like you only have one arm."

The man tried to tug at my arm and I screamed: "Nooooo!!!!"

He looked at my mother.

"Kevin, get your arm where this man wants it or—"

Not even the threat of a beating from my mother persuaded me to move my arm from behind me. I was frozen and the arm kept me propped up. I knew this, but my mother and the man did not know this. I shook my head.

"Okay, miss, he ain't gonna budge. I will do the best I can with what he is giving me."

The man's head disappeared again behind the black towel, and the clicking sounds from the box continued. I laughed once. I did not know why. I just did. Otherwise I was staring into the box as this man aimed it at me. Again and again and again. Click. Flash. Click. Flash.

◆

One day, when I was three years old, my mother told me she was going to "teach" me.

"You are going to learn how to count. Then you are going to learn the alphabet. Then you are going to learn your name and your address. Do you understand?"

I nodded my head.

My mother then sat me down, and we spent what felt like the entire day counting numbers and repeating the alphabet and my name and my address.

"You are going to college. You are going to get a good education," my mother said to me. "You have to go farther in school than I did. Do you understand?"

I did not understand her at all, but I said yes anyway.

"I want you to be a lawyer or a doctor. Somebody important. Get you a good education and you can get you a good job. You can be somebody. Be like Abraham Lincoln or somebody."

"Who is Abraham Lincoln, Ma?"

"He was president of the United States."

"What is president of the United States, Ma?"

"He the man that run everything."

"Run everything like what, Ma?"

"Run everything, the government."

"The what?"

"The government."

I did not understand what my mother was saying, but from the way she was saying it, I knew the president must be important.

I took what my mother was teaching me and I counted and said my alphabet every single day. She told me I was learning how to read, and she gave me words to read. I felt my mother was the smartest person in the world because of all the things she was teaching me. I wanted to make my mother happy, so every time she told me something, I would say it back to her, over and over. She liked how I said these things back to her, and she told me I was "smart." I did not know what smart meant. I just knew I wanted to make my mother happy.

◆

I was terrified of fire. Every time I heard the word, fear wracked my body and my heart leapt inside my chest. From the conversations I overheard between my mother and Aunt Cathy, I knew that "fire" was responsible for big people and little boys like me "dyin' in their sleep."

"They was sleepin' and that fire came like a thief in the night," my mother would say.

"Humph! That's why it ain't good to sleep hard in the North. You just might sleep through your own death," Aunt Cathy declared.

"Yeah, chile, them fire escapes even ain't no good. *The Jersey Journal* said that family over there on Bergen Avenue made it out of the apartment, and was waitin' for the firemen on the fire escape, and then the fire escape gave out. They dead now," my mother concluded, dread filtering through her voice.

Then my mother grew quiet and stared into space, and Aunt Cathy, too, fell silent.

"That's why I don't want to live in no projects. It's too high up," my mother eventually said.

Aunt Cathy nodded her head in agreement.

One frigid winter night while we were sleeping, an odd smell brushed against my nose and awakened me. I could hear a rat prancing in the kitchen area, and I thought that perhaps another rat had died and had left a sour odor. But no, this was not the smell of a dead rat. I opened my eyes slowly, and as I focused, I could see, in the black of night, the narrow wavy lines of smoke. My mind raced. Smoke? Where had I heard that word before? On television? From my mother or aunt? On the block where we lived? And what was connecting that word to the terror that was climbing up my spine? I could not recall.

I desperately wanted to wake my mother, but her back was to me and she was in a deep sleep, her snoring blending in time with the late-night shouts and screeching cars outside. I was so frightened I lost the capacity to speak; so I edged in closer to my mother, and gently snuggled my head into her bosom. That closeness made me feel warm and protected.

Temporarily comforted, I tried to go to sleep. However, smoke stormed back into my thoughts. I had figured it out: smoke comes from fire, and I remembered my mother saying that if you scream when you see smoke, then that scream would make the fire speed toward you. Now I was crippled with fear. *What do I do? If I wake my mother, she will be mad at me and she might beat me. But if I do not wake her, and Aunt Cathy and Anthony in the front room, will we die because of this smoke?*

"Ma," I whispered.

My mother snored on.

"Ma, I smell smoke. Ma, ma, ma," I said as I poked my mother with my index finger.

"Huh? What you want, boy?"

"Ma, I smell smoke," I said.

"Boy, be quiet. Ain't no smoke in here."

Silence. And the inhaling and exhaling of my mother's breath. Abruptly, the vibration of my mother's breathing halted and I started to cry. I thought she was dead because of the smoke. Then in one full motion, my mother jumped from the bed.

"Oh, Lawd! This dang building is on fire! Cathy! Wake up! Get up, Kevin! Put on your robe!"

My mother stumbled in the shadows, cursing as she kicked her feet into her slippers and donned her robe.

"Cathy!" she screamed again. "Girl, don't you hear me? I think the building is on fire." My mother snapped on the lamp and grabbed me by the arm.

Now in the living room, the four of us, cold and afraid, stood trembling as fire-engine sirens whistled below our windows. *Why aren't we leaving the apartment?* I wondered. *If there is a fire, shouldn't we try to get out? Or at least stick our heads from a window and let the firemen know we are up here? Or are we just going to die?* I looked at my cousin Anthony. Both scared, we clung tighter to our mothers. The two women spoke in hushed tones.

"What we gonna do?" Aunt Cathy asked.

"I donno," my mother said. "The fire might be in the hallway. We can't run through it. And I ain't gettin' on no fire escape. It might give out."

A decision had been made: we were not going to yell for help; we were not going to leave through the entrance to the apartment; we were not going out to the fire escape; and we were not returning to our beds. No. We would face whatever awaited us together. So we stood, the four of us, in the corner of the front room, near the hissing radiator, waiting. We heard fire engines come up the block. We heard voices, female, male, and children's, crying, screaming, pleading. We heard dogs barking. We heard the long, painful shrieks of an old woman: "Lawd Je—sus! Please take me, don't take my grandbabies, Lawd. They ain't never hurt nobody!" And we heard the palpitations of our hearts, the heavy sounds of our breathing.

But the fire never came to us. We stayed up the entire night, standing in that corner by the radiator. When dawn came, my mother put on her street clothes and left the apartment. She returned a few moments later. Anthony and I were sitting at the kitchen table munching Frosted Flakes while Aunt Cathy washed dishes. My mother was in a somber mood.

"The building next door burned down. They said some people died."

My mother looked at us, then at the kitchen floor. I followed my mother's eyes. A big, furry gray rat scurried past her feet and headed toward the refrigerator. My mother took off her shoe and threw it in the direction of the rat.

"We gotta move," my mother said, defeat in her voice. "It ain't good to live next to a building that burned down. All kind of spirits is over there and our building could be next."

Aunt Cathy nodded her head in agreement. My cousin Anthony and I sat, emotionless, digging our spoons into our cereal. My mother retrieved her shoe and left the kitchen.

A few weeks later, we moved from Bostwick Avenue to our new apartment building, at the corner of Bergen and Orient. But we only stayed there for a short period until moving again, this time to 116 Bergen Avenue, directly across from Audubon Park.

And it was at 116 Bergen Avenue, in a cluttered first-floor apartment at the back of the building, that Jersey City, where I was born and where I would spend the first eighteen years of my life, began to disrobe itself, fascinating me, annoying me, and tempting me simultaneously. Each event, each moment, outside and indoors, I held on to tightly, afraid that if I let go, then that event, that moment, would be gone forever:

Like the rapture of playing on the black-and-gray gravel of Audubon Park: climbing the monkey bars, coasting hands-free down the sliding board, or kicking my feet toward the clouds as my mother pushed me on the swings.

Like the worldliness of regular Saturday afternoon rides with my mother on the crowded orange-and-white Bergen Avenue bus.

Like the longing for adventure induced by the teenage boys who scrambled after a bus to grab hold of the back window and ride for blocks until the police chased them off.

Like the bewilderment I felt when rain smeared the bright red bricks of 116 Bergen Avenue into a dull, purplish hue.

Like that fleeting taste of nature from the tiny green leaves of a bush that my cousin Anthony and I tossed into each other's mouths.

Like the experience of death—without dying ourselves—whenever a mutt or an alley cat was struck by a passing car or bus, then lurched and moaned pitifully on the sidewalk before going still on the ground.

Like the peculiar sensation of watching a drunk or junkie tilt toward the earth, only to right himself, piss on himself, curse himself or the nearest neighbor, then march, dignified, down the block.

Like the hostile paranoia I felt whenever my mother and I trekked Jackson Avenue, past the empty, boarded-up buildings, past the garbage-strewn lots, past the stinking, unshaven men with their pocket-size bottles of liquor.

Like the naive assumption that Jersey City was splitting in half whenever I saw a new crack in the concrete leading to my building.

Like the nostalgia whenever I spotted yet another pair of grimy sneakers dangling from the electric wires overhead.

Like the titillation of ice-cream truck music caroming in my ears and in the ears of all us ghetto children, who would sprint toward the truck.

Like the unsolicited pity of observing pigeons as they battled over a scrap of bread.

Like the cryptic sense of great expectations when I angled my head skyward and snared snowflakes on the rim of my bottom lip.

Like the apocalyptic sound of thunder and sight of lightning that propelled my mother and Aunt Cathy to snatch off the lights, unplug all the electrical appliances, and forbid Anthony and me from speaking or moving, until that sound and that sight had expended themselves.

Like the surge of power I savored when I trapped a cockroach with a plastic top and mocked its maneuvers to free itself.

Like the hot panic in my throat whenever I heard the bustling feet of rats in the walls.

Like the musty air of predictability from the white rice my mother served with every dinner.

Like the ungovernable hunger I had whenever my mother baked a thickly crusted sweet potato pie and set it in the refrigerator to cool.

Like the magical appearance of dust rays as the sun lapped the windows of our apartment.

Like the budding selfishness of my cousin Anthony and me any time we would hide our toys from each other.

Like the sudden and inexplicable happiness that rocked me when Mister Rogers invited me into his neighborhood.

Like the rage that engulfed me when our black-and-white television set succumbed to age and a fat black line fixed itself on the screen.

Like the possibilities that accompanied those quiet moments when my mother asked me to recite the alphabet, to say a new word, to repeat my full name and street address, or to count higher than I had before.

Like the private satisfaction of seeing faces and bodies in the patterns of the cheap, brown-and-beige kitchen chairs.

Like the muffled hope and myth of better times ahead, every New Year's Day when my mother prepared the Southern dish of "hoppin' john"—black-eyed peas and rice—for good luck.

And like the sheer delight and obscure passing of tradition when my mother taught me to do "the jerk," "the mashed potato," or "the twist," or when she belted the lyrics to Smokey Robinson and The Miracles' "Shop Around" or Marvin Gaye's "Pride and Joy."

Jersey City, my Jersey City, held me up with its arthritic hands, as the moon touched my baby-oiled face and baptized me a native son.

2

That little boy

i was born a year after Malcolm was blown away, two years before a rifle stifled MLK, and five years before Tupac would step, flippin' the bird, onto the stage. i am the only child of a young single Geechee woman who greyhounded it from a shotgun shack to a northern tenement.

THAT LITTLE boy is drunk!" exclaimed a plump, boisterous woman wearing a yellow flower-patterned blouse and hip-hugging jeans that flared outward at the ankles. "He ain't but a baby and he drinkin' already. God bless his soul! He wanna be a man!"

At four years old, I did not know what the word "drunk" meant. But I did know that the entire apartment, which belonged to my mother's older sister, Aunt Birdie, was rotating; I could barely hold on to the sofa arm where I was sitting and watching "the big people," as I called grown-ups back then: some drank from cans and glasses, some smoked miniature white sticks, and some jerked their heads, arms, and legs to the rhythms spewing from the record player in the corner. Some of the men's and women's bodies were pressed tightly together, and their faces dissolved into one another.

I was having fun because the big people were having fun. If one of them told me to get up and dance, then I got up and danced. If one of them told me to say a word, any word, then I said that word. And if one of them offered me more to drink, then I sipped from their can or glass. Each time I carried out a command, "the big people" laughed from the hidden pockets of their stomachs, and that laughter excited me, egging me on to the next crowd-pleasing performance.

My mother had brought me to the party because she did not have a babysitter. At one point, while she was engrossed in conversation with some loudmouthed man with a big afro, my mother had left me with my Aunt Birdie, and someone handed me a beer to drink. The beer had a bitter taste, somewhat like the cold medicine my mother gave me when I was sick. I scrunched my mouth into a pout and mimicked the big people's dance steps. My Aunt Birdie cracked up, her large white teeth taking up most of her face.

A tall, rail-thin man with a mass of curls on his head told me, "Boy, don't ever drink and *not* eat," so I munched on cake and potato chips. I went about the business of enjoying myself, particularly since I was the only little boy at the party and everyone seemed to be enjoying me. That is, until I became so light-headed that I could barely stand. Without warning, the faces of the big people split in half and spiraled to the ceiling, and my stomach began to expand and contract rapidly. A foul flavor scraped the base of my throat, and then the beer, cake, and potato chips gushed from my mouth, onto my chest and then the floor.

The music played on, but the big people stopped laughing and dancing and looked at me with pity. I was sick, but was that such a bad thing that it could stop the party? Would my mother be mad that I had thrown up on myself? Hadn't the big people given me the drinks and cake and potato chips? A woman I couldn't see said, "His momma gonna be mad y'all gave him all that beer."

Someone summoned my mother from the kitchen, where she had been talking, and she saw me standing in the puddle of vomit. I tilted my head to the right, as I had seen a man do on television, and beamed proudly at her. My mother's body grew taut, and she rushed over to me, furious, grabbed me by the arm, stripped the belt from my waist, and beat me hard on the back and backside as the big people watched. I tried to wring myself free of her grip and I did, but only for a moment. As I moved to run away, I slipped on my vomit and landed facedown in the puddle. Rather than help me up, my mother brought the full force of the belt down on me. I screamed, but that only infuriated her more. The lashing seemed endless, but she finally stopped.

By that time, the big people had returned to their activities, paying no attention at all to my mother and me. My mother asked me if I was *ever* going to drink beer again, and I could not answer her, because I did not understand what beer was. She grabbed me by the neck of my shirt and pulled me to my feet and into the bathroom to wash, as best she could, the vomit from my clothes. As my mother scrubbed me with a washcloth, I felt the stinging welts on my arms, my back, and my legs. I grew angry with my mother and writhed when she tightened her grip.

"Stay still, Kevin!" she yelled. "How can I clean this stuff off you if you ain't gonna stay still? Huh?"

Sulking, I stood motionless and silent. A second later I attempted another getaway. My mother clamped her left hand around my right arm and smacked me across the mouth with the open palm of her right hand. The force of her open palm swung my head from left to right. Tears flooded my eyes. She looked at me and asked, "You gonna be good?"

I could neither answer nor look at her. I nodded my head yes. Once she was done, my mother told me that we would be leaving soon and led me back to the sofa.

"Don't do nothin', you hear? Don't move, don't talk. Nothin'!" she barked, her eyes boring into me as she returned to her conversation in the kitchen.

I was now terrified of my mother, so I didn't dare move or speak—even when some of the big people approached me. This was not the first time my mother had beaten me, but for some reason *this* beating stayed with me for many years. Humiliated that my mother had lashed me in public, I wondered why no one had come to my rescue. I slouched low in the sofa, rage boiling, and stared at the gyrating bodies.

I yearned to be outside playing in the streets, or chasing a sponge ball, or foot-racing against other little boys, or tossing mud pies at my cousin Anthony. I also yearned for my mother's affection, for her to hold me, for her to regret beating me in front of the big people. Most of all, I yearned to move and to talk, but my mother had forbidden me to do anything. So I sat, defiant—and waited—resolving that one day I, too, would be one of the big people and able to do as I pleased. Eventually I fell asleep.

◆

One day my mother and I were out shopping in an area in Jersey City called Journal Square, when an old White woman stopped my mother, grabbing her by the arm and saying, "That little boy is so cuute!"

Then my mother did something I had never seen her do before. She giggled like a child herself, and her body seemed to contort and bend at the waist as the old White woman spoke.

"Thank you so much!" my mother said. "He real smart, too. He know his alphabet and can count and everything."

My mother shoved me forward and gave me the signal to speak. I said my alphabet, then counted until I ran out of numbers. Then I stepped behind my mother and hooked my fingers to her trousers, peeking at the White woman with a hump in her back and a patch of gray hair on her head. But when this old White woman looked at me, I fixed my eyes on the pavement, afraid to make eye contact with her.

I could feel her examining me, her ocean-blue eyes sweeping across my body from head to toe. It made me tense and uncomfortable, but I did not know why. She then pulled a piece of peppermint candy from her purse and gave it to me.

"Boy, you keep doing what your mother tells you to do and you will be a credit to your race."

I did not understand what the old White woman meant, but I looked up at her and nodded. Then she walked away. As soon as she was out of sight, my mother swung around to me, the mother I knew.

"Kevin, if a White person says you cute, then you know it must be true. They don't just be saying that to anyone."

There was a level of unmistakable pride in my mother's words, loaded with energy and meaning that I could not grasp at that moment. But those words stayed with me. "If a White person . . ."

Who are these White people? I wondered, then pushed the thought from my mind. I was just happy that we were going to get some Kentucky Fried Chicken.

I said nothing. My mother shook me.

"You deaf, boy? You hear me talkin' to you? You gonna run away again? Huh?"

I looked down at the concrete. "No, I ain't gonna run away no more."

A short while later we arrived at Public School Number 14. My chest pounded and my worst fears were realized: parents, mostly women, chased frightened little boys and girls in the hallways. One boy, with dried-up, green snot beneath his nose, sobbed pathetically as a doctor begged him to return to his office. The doctor waved an assortment of brightly colored lollipops inches from the boy's eyes, but he did not budge. I was doomed.

Moments later, Anthony and I were in the doctor's office separated by a curtain and told by a nurse to take off our shirts. I was baffled by the huge jars filled with cotton balls, Q-tips, and Band-Aids, and the machines with the funny knobs and handles and big words could not read. And yikes—the needles! I was startled by a pudgy in in a white jacket with a reddish knot on the top of his bald head. was a doctor.

"Hi, young man. What is your name?"

looked at the floor.

Hey, you, there," the doctor said, waving his arms. "I bet you a piece of candy, don't you?"

he doctor reached into a pocket of his white jacket and pulled handful of Mary Janes—my favorite.

mile swept across my face and the doctor seized the moment. hought so! How about we do a trade? You let me give you these nd I'll give you the candy? That's fair, right?" the man said, his inkling.

-huh," I said, slowly.

d. So let's get started. This will take no time at all and it won't t."

her trusted nor believed him and leapt from the table. The ught me by the arm before I got to the exit.

3

Going to school with Martin Luther King, Jr.

even my mother, southern warrior that she is, cannot scrape the tinted windows off that child's imagination

ONE DAY, when I was nestled at the feet of our black-and-white television set, my mother announced that I was going to school in September.

"But I already went to school, Ma," I said.

"That wasn't school, that was nursery school," my mother said.

"So what kinda school do I have to go to now?" I asked.

"Kindergarten," my mother said. "You gonna be in school until you turn eighteen, then you will go to college, and then to law school and be a lawyer like Abraham Lincoln."

I scratched my head. "For real, Ma? But wait—Ma, Abraham Lincoln, the president?"

"Yes. He was a great man, he was a lawyer, and then he was president of these United States. And he was real smart, like you," my mother said.

"For real, Ma? So I'ma be like him?"

"That's right."

My mother smiled at me and that made me feel good. But then her manner changed.

"Me and Cathy gotta get you and Anthony some school clothes. We gonna get y'all five shirts and five pairs of pants for every day of the week. Y'all gotta look nice for school."

What was so bad about getting new clothes? I had no problem with that.

"And y'all gotta get shots."

Shots? I knew what shots were! I had gotten them before.

"Ma, I don't want no shots."

"You gotta get 'em or they ain't gonna let you go to school."

"Why I gotta go to school?"

"'Cuz you got to."

"But why, Ma?"

"'Cuz I said so. Now, shut the hell up with all them fool questions!"

My dreams became a singular, sorrowful nightmare: I am lying in the bed, alone, while an extra-long, sharp needle, suspended from the ceiling directly above me, pursues me whenever I move to one side or the other. I attempt to climb from the bed, but a fence, raised from the floor, traps me. My hands and feet are chained to the bed. Finally, the needle is released and plunges straight down into my face and my head explodes.

I vowed that I would run away on the day Anthony and I were due to get our shots. I told my cousin Anthony about my plan.

"I ain't gettin' no shots," I said stubbornly.

"Why not?" Anthony asked.

"'Cuz I don't want to. They hurt."

"But we have to," Anthony said.

"I don't have to do nothing."

I obeyed my mother that morning of the doctor's appointment: I ate breakfast; she bathed and dressed me; I brushed my teeth; she tied my shoes for me, greased my hair, smeared my chest with baby powder, and rubbed Vaseline—lots of it—on my face.

There, I thought. *I have done everything she wants of me. Now* my escape! *When we hit the pavement outside, I will run. Where? I do* *But I'm gonna run as fast as I can to get away from my mother.* Tha the plan. As our mothers adjusted our clothes one final time mirror, I nodded to Anthony. He didn't get it.

No matter. When the four of us stepped outside into t spring breeze, I walked slightly ahead of my mother. Witho ing, I darted down Bergen Avenue toward Wegman Parkv street. My mother ran after me, screaming: "Ke—vin! T fool! Hey! Stop him! My son! Stop that little boy!"

I turned the corner at Wegman Parkway and ran righ a tall, bespectacled man wearing a white hat with a feath and a long, mint-green leather coat. The man's weigh backwards to the ground. My mother was upon me.

"Thanks, sir, for stopping my son for me. He w away," my mother said, panting.

"Oh, it's alright ba—by," the man drawled, his the tip of his hat. "You know a foxy mama like you a man around to keep this boy in check."

My mother's face flamed with indignation.

"Humph! Ain't nobody gonna try and shack put no ring on my finger, you hear?"

"See, that's the problem with you single gov-ment done give y'all a little welfare and y for a brother."

The man looked my mother up and dow adjusted his hat, then stormed off, mumbl

My mother yelled after him, "Go to good nigga!"

The man, over his shoulder, yelled why that little bad boy is just like his training."

My mother turned to me. "The n I'ma beat the devil out of you, you h

"Where do you think you're going? Would your mother like it if you ran away?"

I thought about that but did not respond.

The doctor hoisted me by my armpits back onto the table, reached for cotton balls and rubbing alcohol, and then examined a long needle he removed from a case. Horrified, I wanted to run but was frozen with the thought of what would happen should I make a break. There was nothing else to do except close my eyes. So I did.

The doctor rubbed a moist cotton ball against my right arm, holding it tightly, the way my mother did whenever she whooped me. A pinching sensation. Another one. And another. A few minutes later, it was over.

"Now, that wasn't so bad, was it, young man?" the doctor asked, his smile a sea of yellow teeth.

I shook my head.

The man handed me the candy, picked up a folder, and made strange markings on it.

"Kevin Powell? That's your name, right? Can you spell your name?"

I could and I did. The doctor looked impressed. I was now bored and wanted to leave.

"Wow, you're a smart little boy. As a matter of fact, you're smart like another little boy from Jersey City who was a student at this very school. He's real famous today. Do you know who that is?" the doctor asked.

I was clueless, and shook my head no.

"Flip Wilson! That's right, young man. You know who Flip Wilson is, don't you?"

I'd seen him on television. Sometimes he wore a suit and sometimes he wore a dress. And when he wore a dress he called himself Geraldine. *He* was from Jersey City? He was on *television*. My mother said that people who were on television made lots of money. So that meant that Flip Wilson was rich. Now I liked the doctor. He had basically told me I, too, could be rich. I had to figure out how to get on television!

Excited, I hopped off the table, hurriedly put on my shirt, and joined my mother and Aunt Cathy, who were still waiting for Anthony. I told my mother about Flip Wilson. I was disappointed that she already knew that Flip Wilson had been born in Jersey City. And so it seemed did everyone else lurking in the hallways. No one welcomed my newfound information— not even Anthony (yes, he knew, too). I was astonished that I was the last to know of Flip Wilson's humble Jersey City roots.

◆

On an early September morning in 1971, my mother, Aunt Cathy, Anthony, and I walked along Bergen Avenue to Public School Number 41. Finally, we were off to kindergarten. On this monumental day Anthony and I had no idea that P.S. 41 would be the first of four different grammar schools we would attend, as our mothers moved us from grimy building to grimy building, and as they fought constantly to get us a quality education. Anxious, I pushed my fingers deeper into my mother's hand.

"Ma, I don't wanna go to school. Not by myself," I said.

"You ain't goin' to school by yourself. Anthony goin' with you."

"But, Ma—"

"Hush, Kevin. I ain't got time for no fussin'."

When the four of us arrived at the entrance to P.S. 41, a throng of boys, girls, and mothers were crowding the sidewalk as a man stood at the top of a ladder speaking through a round object, which made his voice loud. On one side of the dirty, beige-colored building was a local police precinct and on the other side Henry Snyder High School, where the teenagers went to school.

"If we can please have two lines, one for the kindergartners and one for returning students, then we will let everyone in. In order!"

The crowd charged ahead and the man scowled and waved his arms.

"Again, no one is getting in until two lines are formed!"

My mother looked at Aunt Cathy and rolled her eyes.

"We can't never do nothin' right," my mother said, disgusted.

Aunt Cathy nodded her head, pulled a Kleenex from her purse, and bent down to wipe excess Vaseline from Anthony's face. My mother did the same to me.

A while later, two lines formed and Anthony and I were on our way to kindergarten.

I was assigned to Mrs. Stallworth's class. I gasped as Anthony was led by his mother to another class. We were being separated.

"Ma," I said, barely holding back my tears.

"Boy, hush. You gotta get use to it sooner or later. You can't be with me all the dang time."

With that my mother said goodbye and left me in a classroom with Mrs. Stallworth and twenty-five or so boys and girls I had never seen before. Panic, shame, and paranoia flooded me. When Mrs. Stallworth began asking students for their names, I sank in my chair, hoping to fall through the floor, to China, just like in a Bugs Bunny cartoon.

"What is *your* name?" Mrs. Stallworth asked me. Her voice could have belonged to an angel.

My head rose cautiously, and I gaped at Mrs. Stallworth, instantly aware of how beautiful she was, and embarrassed by the fact that I liked the way she looked.

My God, she is so pretty, like the women on television. Her skin is like a satin sheet. Her lips are so full. Her lashes are so long. Her perfume is in my nostrils, teasing me. I will smell her now and dream of her tonight. I wonder if she will marry me.

I quickly turned my eyes away. But as I did, I noticed her plaid miniskirt and the thickness of her smooth brown legs and, suddenly, my insides heated up. Something was happening in the lower part of my body and I was horrified. What if Mrs. Stallworth found out what I was thinking and what my body was doing? I would be in trouble. My chin pressed against my chest, I sat, immobilized.

"Are you shy?" Mrs. Stallworth asked, bending my chin upward with one of her soft hands.

I would not say a single word that day. Nor did I get up when it was time for recess. I was ashamed, although I could not say for sure what I was ashamed of. Mrs. Stallworth asked me several times: *Do you like me? Do you like school? Do you miss your mother? Do you want to go home?* I did not answer that day or for months afterward.

My mother was called to school. She had no explanation for my silence. I did my schoolwork, and as my mother would tell me, one of the tests that I had taken prior to the school year said I was able to do the work of a third-grader. I heard one of the grown-ups tell my mother, "He is a very bright boy." No matter, I would not speak. It would be a few months before I became moderately at ease in school.

One day, Mrs. Stallworth told the class that we were going to watch a movie about a great man named Martin Luther King, Jr. I had no clue who he was, but I did love movies. Mrs. Stallworth brought a projector and screen into our room.

I assumed that we were about to watch yet another presentation about numbers or the alphabet, taught by this Martin Luther King, Jr. But Martin Luther King, Jr., appeared before us talking in a cartoon film. When he said, "I have a dream," I daydreamed of Jackie, the charming, ponytailed girl who sat to my right, two seats over.

Abruptly, the narrator's voice turned cold, and I refocused on the screen: Martin Luther King had been shot. The animated image of him lying on the balcony of a hotel in Memphis was far too much for me to bear. I was so terrified that I wanted to cry and bolt from the classroom, but I was afraid that the fate of the man on the screen would be mine if I dared to move from my chair. I heard in my head my mother and Aunt Cathy talking about death:

"Girl, you can mess with the dead, but they will come back and haunt you," my mother would say.

"Yes, Lawd, 'specially if you treated them bad when they was alive," Aunt Cathy would say.

"Remember Down South, how some of them ghosts scared people so much them people killed themselves tryin' to get away?" my mother would ask.

"Humph! That's why it ain't good to treat people bad. They might come back to get you after they dead," Aunt Cathy would say.

They would also discuss other, startling things, like "hags risin'"—

spirits or ghosts of dead people taking over our bodies as we slept. My five-year-old mind didn't quite understand what they meant, but I did experience the rising of hags or spirits. I cannot say exactly when it began, but it frightened me: I'd be in bed sleeping next to my mother when some *thing* would cross my body, settling over me so that I could not move. This hag would pin me to the bed, and the more I fought to rid myself of it, the greater it weighed upon me. I learned that the best way to rid myself of the hag was to relax and allow it to think that it had won. Then, I would push forward—hard!—and the hag would be gone—until the next time one decided to pass through my body.

My God! I thought. *Will the ghost of Martin Luther King, Jr., visit me tonight? What if his ghost is here in this room, right now?* I slumped low in my chair and buried my head in my arms.

When Mrs. Stallworth clicked off the projector and turned the lights back on, all of the students clapped, except me. I heard Mrs. Stallworth's footsteps marching toward me.

"What is the matter, Kevin?" she asked.

I could not respond. She asked again. Silence. Finally, Mrs. Stallworth asked if the short cartoon film about Dr. King had bothered me. I couldn't raise my head, or my voice. Mrs. Stallworth sighed, sensing I had returned to my shell. Once again my mother was summoned to school, and I heard grown-ups say things like "He is antisocial" and "He is emotionally underdeveloped." My mother defended me, telling anyone who listened that I was "smart, as smart as any of these other students." I just blotted out the big people's opinions and did what was asked of me.

At the end of the school year, in June 1972, I was promoted to the first grade, as was my cousin Anthony. I was so relieved to be away from *that* classroom. My fear of Martin Luther King, Jr., would be rekindled each January for years to come. I always found it difficult to watch television specials about his life, because I was consumed by his death, and by his haunting words, "I've been to the mountaintop."

4

My grandfather and the American South

those thick glasses distract from the tobacco-stained teeth. tingling
carolina stench braid coarse charcoal hair.

O NE DAY in the summer of 1971—the summer before Anthony
and I started kindergarten—our mothers told us, "We are going
Down South." Anthony and I looked at each other, clueless.

Our mothers hurriedly gathered items for the trip to Ridgeland,
South Carolina—their hometown—via a Greyhound bus. They
packed clothes, underwear, baby oil, Vaseline, lotion, and baby powder into suitcases. Then they fried chicken for the trip, carefully po-
sitioned the pieces on slices of white Wonder Bread smeared with
hot sauce, and wrapped them neatly in aluminum foil. The chicken
would be washed down with cans of soda.

Then they did a curious thing: they put our luggage in thick, black
garbage bags and carried them on the Bergen Avenue bus to Journal
Square. They didn't remove the luggage from the garbage bags until
we got to Newark Penn Station.

"Ma, how come we did that with the suitcases?"

"'Cuz we don't need nobody knowin' we goin' away for a while. People see you leavin' and soon as you gone they break into your apartment through your kitchen window. Or they pick the lock on your front door."

"For real, Ma?"

"Yeah, Bubba. Can't trust these no-good niggas where we live."

My mother often called me "Bubba." I didn't like that nickname, but she used it all the time, so I grudgingly accepted it. I frequently heard Black people calling each other "niggas" as a little boy, too, or referring to themselves that way, and I accepted the word as part of everyday conversation.

Soon enough, the Greyhound bus arrived. A long line of people, every last one of them Black, noisily lurched feet and bags forward in single file to take the ride "Down South." A Black man in a cap and bluish uniform that read "Greyhound Lines" stood right outside the entrance to the bus and punched holes in our tickets with a silvery metal device.

I could no longer contain my excitement, and asked, "Mister, are we going Down South?"

"That's right, young fella. I'm your driver—"

Before I could ask any more questions, my mother shot me *that* look and propelled me up the bus steps with the meaty palm of her right hand. Anthony sat with his mother in the row in front of my mother and me. Then we were off. Every seat on the bus was occupied, and apparently, everyone had brought the same food that we did. The alluring aroma of fried chicken filled the bus end to end, welcoming but overwhelming.

Anthony and I pressed our faces against the windows, staring in wonder at the panorama on the other side of the glass. The Greyhound bus driver pointed out places alien to us:

The New Jersey Turnpike
Wilmington, Delaware, and the Delaware Memorial Bridge
Baltimore, Maryland

Washington, DC
Richmond, Virginia
Rocky Mount, North Carolina

Then there were several stops in South Carolina, including places like:

Yemassee
Hardeeville
Walterboro

Finally, Ridgeland. Since there was no bus station in Ridgeland, we had to pull the string for the driver to stop and let us off on the side of the road. I was overjoyed when my mother allowed me to pull the string.

Once off the bus, there we were—two mothers and two sons—in a place with more space and open road than I had ever seen in my life. Soon, a car drove up and a young man with a sunny smile climbed out. My mother and Aunt Cathy told Anthony and me that this was our "Uncle Lloyd," who they also called "Jabba."

"Shirley and Cathy! Look at these boys y'all didn't tell us about! They ain't babies! They big!"

"Hush, Jabba!" my mother barked shamefacedly while Aunt Cathy stood silently.

"Well, I'm sho glad to see y'all. Real glad y'all finally came back home. Let me get your bags and get y'all to Wagon Branch."

Wagon Branch? I did not know what that was. Uncle Lloyd maneuvered the car down a main highway, turned onto one road, then onto another, until we reached an all-dirt road. He blew the horn several times, which frightened me.

Uncle Lloyd cackled like a chicken.

"Oh, don't be scared, boy. We blows the horn here in Wagon Branch just to let other cars know we comin' so ain't no car crashes around here. And also to warn the stray dogs that be runnin' around without lookin'. Listen at me good, ya hear? You boys ain't scared of dogs or snakes or big flying bugs or anything, is you?"

I gulped as I recalled my mother's tales of this place called Down South, stories of ghosts and spirits visiting without warning; of relatives struck down by lightning because they were too near a tree; of tragic car accidents involving cousins driving across the Savannah River; of the White people who employed my mother and her family; of how poor they were living in a "shack" home; of the days of eating syrup for dinner; of the girls taking turns going to school because there weren't enough clothes for each to wear; of my mother picking cotton at age eight, along with other children and adults, as the scalding southern sun whipped their bent tar-black, coffee-colored, and high-yellow torsos and wrung pounds of sweat from them; of hard work not being a choice but a requirement for their very survival; and of my Uncle Lloyd, the youngest and the lone boy, being the sole Powell kid to graduate from high school as each girl, one by one, dropped out of school to toil in the fields, or to clean and cook in the homes of the White people.

My uncle edged the car into a big open yard. Sandy-brown dust leapt from the earth and licked the windows and sides of the automobile. In front of us stood an unpainted, grubby wooden house with a porch and with several chickens scampering around. I had never seen live chickens before and found myself both fascinated and terrified.

An old man and woman emerged through the front door, looking like images in a worn old photo album. The man, very dark-complexioned, was squat, had a straw hat fixed on top of his head, and wore blue overalls. The woman, fairer in skin tone, a buttery hue, was tiny, had thick, horn-rimmed glasses planted on her nose, and wore a plain checker-patterned dress and stockings on her pole-like legs. When we got out of Uncle Lloyd's car, the man and the woman stared at us in disbelief.

"Who dem little boys belong ta?" the old woman finally asked, in an accent that I could barely understand.

The man said nothing, only shook his head, eyebrows stitched together, his mouth drooped downward in an upside-down letter U.

"This our children, Lottie," my mother said. "One belong to me and one belong to Cathy."

My mother and Aunt Cathy had not told this old man and old woman, their father and mother, about Anthony and me. They had decided to let our arrival be the introduction. They called their parents by their first names, not Mother or Father, Ma or Daddy. Anthony and I were told that this man and woman were our grandparents, Pearlie Powell and Lottie Burrison Powell.

At that moment, another person came out of the rusted front-screen door—Pearlie Mae Powell, my mother's and my Aunt Cathy's oldest sibling and sister. There were five Powell children: Pearlie Mae, Birdie Lou, Shirley Mae, Catherine, and Lloyd, born in that order. Something seemed very different about Aunt Pearlie Mae as she gaped at the sight of Anthony and me. She was uncoordinated, cautious, and looked exactly like our grandfather Pearlie, except that she was a woman. I remembered that my mother and Aunt Cathy had often referred to Aunt Pearlie Mae as "slow" long before I met her.

"Dem sho is some pretty chillin' y'all got dere, Shirley and Cathy. We sho ain't known 'bout 'em. Y'all done kept it secret all dese years. But here dey is."

With that, Anthony and I began to meet other relatives who we'd never known existed. Later I heard adults whisper about "babies with no daddies" and "welfare," but I did not understand what any of that meant. Anthony and I had our own agenda. As we did back home in Jersey City, we played, fought, and played some more. Our grandfather Pearlie showed us where the chickens lived and also where the "outhouse" was, and told us that if we needed to use the bathroom, the outhouse was it. He told us to carry a stick with us "if ya walk up da road apiece, just ta protect ya self" from snakes and wild dogs. Anthony and I decided then and there never to venture too far from this wooden house—or from our mothers.

The chickens captivated me, especially the way my grandmother fed them every morning by calling out, "Heeeeerre chick-chick-chick!!! Heeeeerre chick-chick-chick!!!" But my grandfather put an end to my fascination with these strange creatures one afternoon when he decided to teach Anthony and me how to "ketch and kills a chicken."

As he walked among them, the chickens pecked about his feet. Suddenly, he lunged forward, grabbed one of the animals with his wide, rubbery hands, and tore its head off. I was shocked. My grandfather twisted its neck, just as I would twist the cap on a soda bottle and pull it off. Headless, blood spurting from its neck, the bird darted across the yard a few feet and collapsed, dead. For years, I could not look at another chicken without downloading that memory.

On our first nightfall Down South, I was paralyzed with fear. We had no electric lights or streetlights, just a "kerosene lamp." Aunt Pearlie Mae told Anthony and me that we were "city boys" and needed to get accustomed to being Down South. But the blackness around us and the sounds of creatures whistling, crying, and screaming like an orchestra of Halloween spooks and goblins convinced us that going to sleep would be a fatal mistake.

That first night, Anthony fell asleep. I could not—I refused. I do not know how many days and nights we spent in that wooden shack, but I do know I never shut my eyes for more than a few minutes at a time. In my five-year-old mind, I resolved that if death were to come, I would meet it eyeball to eyeball, wrestling it, biting it, kicking it, whatever I had to do to defeat it. Death was not going to drag me from my bed.

◆

We returned to Jersey City, and a year or so later, my mother announced, with barely any emotion, that my grandfather had died, and that we were going back to South Carolina. I was so frightened by this news that it felt like only a few minutes had expired between my mother sharing it and our arrival at my grandfather's funeral.

The South Carolina sun was oppressive that day. Heat rays felt like pitchforks piercing holes in our clothing as we perched on thin planks that passed for pews. My mother, Aunt Cathy, cousin Anthony, Aunt Birdie (and her new baby girl Monique), Aunt Pearlie Mae, Uncle Lloyd, his new wife Zennie Ree, and Chrissy (their first child) huddled together in the sweltering church.

I saw cousins everywhere, new ones and some I had met on that first trip to Ridgeland. Some were from my grandfather's family, who had come from Philadelphia and Georgia, but most were from my grandmother Lottie's side.

In the middle of the funeral service, I was so bored that I began to mutter to myself. My mother was distant, so my Aunt Birdie shot me a glare that said, "Shut the hell up, boy!"

When it was time for the family to view my grandfather's body one last time, I shuffled past the casket and stopped dead in my tracks.

That is not him! That ain't him! Who is this man pretending to be my grandfather? Where is my real grandfather?

Yes, a dark-skinned Black man with close-cropped hair was resting peacefully in that casket. Yes, there was some resemblance to my grandfather. But this man, this person in the casket, was coated with makeup, part of his face swollen and puffy, part flattened. Yet, like my grandfather, his life was gone. Forever.

My mother nudged me to keep moving. My grandmother Lottie stood before the casket. She had been crying throughout the service, but now she let loose an earsplitting cry, one so long and deafening that it sounded as if it were traveling with my grandfather to that heaven in the sky the preacher had preached about minutes before.

People stood around my grandmother. When she lunged forward, they lunged with her. When she fell backward, they caught her. This dance of despair went on for several minutes. At one moment, my grandmother acted as if she wanted to climb into the casket with my grandfather. Her life was intertwined with his in the wild holler of his name: "Pear-leee! Pear-leee! Sweet Jee-zus! Why ya gots ta take my husband right now, Lawd! Pear-leee! Help me, Jee-zus! Help me, Lawd! What Ahs 'spose ta do now, Lawd? Aaaaaaah! Catch me, Lawd! Catch me! Pear-leee!"

With that, my grandmother nearly passed out, and the entire church echoed with other mourners' wails and shrieks and tears of anguish and loss. I felt nothing. I looked around and saw that neither my mother nor Aunt Cathy shed one tear. They stared vacantly into space.

We went outside into the baking sun to stand at the gravesite. Men dug into the earth with shovels, and my grandfather's casket was carried to the hole, and slowly lowered into the gaping cavity. Again, my grandmother Lottie screamed out my grandfather's name. "Pear-leee!" Again people around my grandmother swayed with her to and fro as she refused to let go of her husband.

Once in the ground, the casket was slowly covered with dirt until it disappeared. The grown-ups sang a song that seemed familiar. It was a song about life, a song about death, a song about the world after this one. The heaviness of the emotions in the voices pulled my spirit into the grave with my grandfather, into the earth with him. I became deathly afraid. I had felt this feeling of death before, of belonging to this world but also belonging to another. I inched my frail body closer to my mother's, hoping for protection.

Many years later, I would learn more about my grandfather from the conversations and stories of "the big people." I began to hear, feel, and see my grandfather, for the first time.

Pearlie was born in the year 1900, the son of former slaves. His father, Benjamin Powell, was a chef and had owned four hundred acres of land in the Low Country of South Carolina, the same place where my mother and her sisters and brother would be born. A Black man whose land was wanted so badly by the White men of this area, Benjamin was found dead one day with food stuffed in his mouth. His wife, my great-grandmother, was told that he choked on his own food. These White men then forced my grandfather's mother, my great-grandmother, to sell 397 of the 400 acres of land for one penny each. She, a widow, was left to raise my grandfather and his siblings alone in an area known as "Shoe Hill." The land that was taken was called the Powell Property. The White men who took it did not bother to change the name for years.

Decades later, my mother was born, in the early 1940s, and, as a little girl, she would pick cotton on this land owned by the men who had stolen it and the life of Benjamin Powell. My grandfather, Pearlie Powell, could only read at a second- or third-grade level, but he traveled a good deal in his younger life and was married once before he wed my grandmother. He so hated White people that he called the rich ones "bukras" and the poor ones "crackers," just as other Blacks of his day did.

Pearlie was defiant. He hated being called "boy" or "nigger" or "uncle." He hated the fact that he could not vote freely. And he did not care what White people thought of him. He would set his bathtub out in the front yard, get in, and sit naked in broad daylight, this deep-chocolate Black man, while White people passed and shook their heads, and Black people—including his wife and children—hung their heads in shame.

My grandfather was a mean man and a proud man and a violent man. They said he had Native-American blood; that he could have done something with his life; that he was a farmer; that he had worked for his mother and was drafted to fight in World War I before she stopped him from going because she did not want him to die in war.

◆

But my grandfather died in other kinds of wars. He died one day when he did not like something my grandmother Lottie said and he knocked her out with a single punch. He died the day he kicked her and threw a bucket of water on her to wake her up. He died when he would beat my mother and her sisters and brother with mule whips and soda bottles. He died a tragic, slow death eating foods that gave him diabetes and high blood pressure because they were the only foods available to him. In the final days of his life, with his mind mostly gone, my grandfather was put to sleep so doctors could cut off one of his legs to stop the damage diabetes had done, but he died right before the surgery.

I didn't spend much time with my grandfather, but I felt as though I knew him completely, because his life and story were with me wherever I ventured. That old man in the overalls standing on the washed-out wooden porch staring and squinting at me in the heat of a South Carolina day—

5

My cousin Anthony

and you raised anthony
the best way you knew how
just like my mother raised me
and anthony grew and i grew
with our frustrated imaginations

ANTHONY AND I were playing peacefully in the living room, two little boys, two cousins, doing what children do to entertain themselves, while our mothers made dinner in the kitchen. Then, Anthony asked me, "Kevin, why did you take that toy?"

"Because it is mine."

"No, it's not. It's mine."

"Nope."

"Yes."

"No!"

Anthony reached and tugged the miniature red, white, and blue truck we had been rolling back and forth between us. I refused to let go. The more Anthony pulled, the more a small flame in my mind grew into a violent fire of anger. I socked Anthony in the mouth. His eyes swelling with tears, he balled his right fist and he hit me back.

In short order, we swung wildly at each other, landing, missing, ducking, and dodging. We grabbed and ripped each other's shirt and tussled to the hardwood floor. One moment Anthony was on top, his hands around my throat; the next I was on top biting his left arm. I refused to let go as Anthony hooted in agony.

"Ow! Ma!"

Aunt Cathy and my mother sprinted into the living room. Aunt Cathy was disgusted that my teeth were stuck in Anthony's arm and yanked mightily to get me off of him. When I finally let go, a blood clot had formed on Anthony's left bicep, and he was puking tears and mucus. I was crying, too, but I felt victorious.

"Shirley! You gotta do somethin' 'bout that boy. You can't be lettin' him bite Tony like that all the time!"

My mother eyed my Aunt Cathy sympathetically, but she said nothing.

"Shir-ley! Please make Kevin stop doing that! He as crazy as *you*!"

Aunt Cathy's tone ignited a heat in my mother's eyes.

"Don't tell me how to raise my chile, ya hear! You hef-fa!"

"You a heffa, Shirley!"

My mother and Aunt Cathy began using words that Anthony and I did not understand, but we could sense their viciousness. They were lobbing insults back and forth like grenades, yelling until my mother scrambled to the kitchen, grabbed the broom, and threatened to clobber Aunt Cathy with it. Aunt Cathy cowered in submission, panting, fear in her eyes, her hands up to protect her face. My mother withdrew, satisfied that she had won another battle.

Aunt Cathy attended to Anthony, then he and I returned to playing silently, and my mother and Aunt Cathy returned to the kitchen. My mother didn't stop me from fighting or biting Anthony. And she never stopped fighting my Aunt Cathy.

◆

Growing up, no one could unglue my cousin Anthony and me. Anthony was my playmate, my sparring partner, and my best friend.

From the time we could walk and talk, we did everything together, sharing a one-bedroom apartment the first nine years of our lives.

When Anthony got new school clothes, I got new school clothes. Whichever school Anthony attended, I was right there with him. Oftentimes when Anthony went to the bathroom to piss, I would be right there, too. When Anthony went out to play, I went out to play. When Anthony was at the babysitter's, I was there, too. When Anthony rode to the YMCA after-school program in that little van, I went with him. When our mothers thought we were too old at age seven to share beds with them any longer, they went out to buy small folding beds for us. Anthony's cot was placed next to his mother's, and mine next to my mother's.

Anthony and I made Audubon Park our personal backyard. There we would run hard and fast, until we could not breathe, our chests heaving in and out. We scaled fences, launched ourselves down sliding boards, and held on to the swings as one pushed the other. Our mothers would sit on a park bench, quietly, stoically. Random pages of *The Jersey Journal* served as thin barriers between them and the filthy bench. Anthony and I would run by our mothers again and again. And when our fathers bought us our first bikes, we would ride laps around our mothers, again and again.

Yes, we had fathers. Anthony's father was John Gamble, and mine was Elize Cunningham. We did not see them much. Our fathers bought Anthony and me our first bicycles and our first watches, because our mothers asked them to, and very little beyond that. The only steady male figure Anthony and I had in our lives was each other. Everyone else around us were women. Most had lots of children—except for our mothers.

"These heffas stay pregnant," my mother said.

"They sho do," my Aunt Cathy said, nodding her head in agreement.

"They act like da welfare gon last forever. One day they gon cut welfare and then them womens in real trouble with all them kids," my mother muttered.

They were both silent for a moment, drifting off into the lonely and difficult parts of their own lives.

"Once you wobble you can't fall down," my mother finally said, meaning that she and Aunt Cathy should never have more children.

Anthony and I had each other. And our mothers had each other— and us. As young as Anthony and I were, we knew this to be truth. And there was something safe, something magical, in the individual scenes of our lives.

Like the ecstasy that Anthony and I felt as we watched one Bruce Lee movie after another. Lee's gymnastic leaps and kicks were a getaway to a freedom mad distant from our lives.

Like those long Sundays that Anthony and I spent on the telephone once our mothers got their own apartments. Chatting away on the first home phones our mothers ever had, we drank in one football game after another as if the future of the world depended on our not missing a single play.

Like the great shame, physical stimulation, and crude emotions that Anthony and I attempted to contain when our mothers took us to films with titles like *Shampoo* and *Foxy Brown*, unintentionally exposing us to sex education in the darkness of a movie theater.

Like our shared wisdom in resisting the little rascal with the dirty hands and the ashy face who tried and failed to convince Anthony and me to stick our fingers into an exposed electric socket.

Like the pride we felt as our mothers put us to work—at age eight—bagging groceries at a local market.

Like the glee we shared every single time we saw a Richard Pryor movie or an episode of *Benny Hill*.

And like the super-size egos and rivalries that we swapped yearly, especially as new teenagers.

By the time Anthony and I were thirteen years old, he had shot up in height and his voice had deepened, while I remained miniature and sounded like a young Michael Jackson. Our bond shattered one chilly fall day in the eighth grade, when we were new to Public School Number 20 on Danforth Avenue. Whenever two boys were set to fight after school, the word wafted through the hallways like the funk of an uncovered sewer hole. This kid Tyrone was going to scrap with the boy known as "Stretch"—my cousin Anthony. Anthony had grown so tall so fast that he had picked up that nickname a couple years back. I did not know Tyrone personally, but I recalled that he had a large family. I had to be there in case Tyrone and his relatives tried to jump my cousin!

In the courtyard, Anthony and Tyrone prepared to rumble. I did not know what the beef was over, but that did not matter. When boys in our neighborhoods called you out for a fight, you had to do it, whether you wanted to or not, whether you were terrified or not. You had to know how to maneuver with your hands, your feet, your legs, and even your head and mouth when necessary. Losing was not an option. Losing meant you would be the joke of your school and your community pretty much for the rest of your life—or at least until you moved.

There was a crisp breeze that day and everyone was wearing a jacket of some sort. I held Anthony's for him. Tyrone brought an army of boys and a few admiring girls. Anthony and Tyrone stepped inside a circle created by all of us, looked each other up and down, and then it was on.

Tyrone was a few inches shorter than Anthony, but he scored first. Bam! Right to Anthony's right cheek. Anthony shook off the blow— and pow!—took a shot at Tyrone's mouth. The two boys were egged on by the swollen crowd around them, several screaming for Tyrone because they did not know Anthony.

My cousin did not care. He landed a succession of blows—to Tyrone's temples, to his cheeks, to his chin. Anthony's arms were giraffe-long and lean, rapidly shooting back and forth from their shoulder sockets the way a snake's tongue zips out and in. Tyrone did not know that, in addition to worshipping Bruce Lee and studying the martial artist's every move, Anthony had convinced his mother to let him take free karate classes after school. This would be the big test of Anthony's warrior skills!

Even though my cousin was clearly winning this fight, doom and dread weighed on me like a barrage of bricks. I kept feeling that I had to help my cousin, to help him now. I tried to ignore the feeling, burying my hands in my pants pockets and turning my head and body away from the brawl. But that feeling spun me back around, and I could not stop myself. I plunged into the middle of their fight, clutching Tyrone as Anthony was fighting him. Anthony hock spit an ugly gob of disgust to the ground. Tyrone was amused. So was his massive posse, which quickly pushed me away. Soon after, some adults came from the building and the fight was officially over.

Angry and embarrassed, Anthony refused to speak to me on our terribly slow return home. He mumbled a few times that I should have minded my own business, and that he had the fight won. I realized that I had taken a necessary victory from him, especially since he—we—were new to that school. The way you made a name for yourself in a foreign environment was to win a fight, especially against someone as popular as Tyrone. Anthony felt I had betrayed him.

For the next five years—our last five living in Jersey City with our mothers—the gap between Anthony and me grew. We continued to talk, to play sports together, to hang on our block and street corners together, to be on the same track teams in high school, but our old bond was effectively gone. I felt abandoned. This rejection by Anthony was made more painful when I heard whispers, from mutual teenage friends, that Anthony thought that I was "crazy" and that was the reason he kept his distance. Whenever I thought of my cousin Anthony, I felt like a sad, empty Coke bottle getting kicked down Jersey City pavements. And there was nothing I could do about it. Nothing.

6

The ghetto

dead like a ghetto baby
slurping the dust from
his crack mother's nipples
dead dead like the drug
dealer harvesting crops
on this concrete plantation

A S A CHILD, I did not know that we lived in the ghetto, and
I'm not sure when I first heard the term. But I began to see myself, my mother and Aunt Cathy, my cousin Anthony, and the
people around us—our neighborhood—as different from the families
and places on television. On *The Brady Bunch*, on *The Partridge Family*, on *Eight Is Enough*—each and every TV show presented "White
families" and their lives, which were unlike mine.

With that recognition of being different, of being "other," I began
to look at myself and my family with a new set of eyes. I began to feel
with a bruising numbness that our lives were doomed, that we were
poor—*very, very poor*—as was everyone around us.

Yes, we had roaches all over the place, but didn't our neighbors,
too? Our mothers covered every single piece of food in plastic or

pieces of aluminum foil to keep them out. But sometimes that did not work. An uneasy laughter would balloon from my belly whenever we turned the lights on in a room—especially in the kitchen—and exposed hundreds of roaches. Indeed the roaches were so powerful and so present in our lives that I came to regard them as a part of who we were. I chased them, fanned them off our kitchen table with my scrawny hands, and sometimes even played with one, using the plastic lid of a 25-cent toy I had bought from a corner-store machine to trap and tease it.

But I was terrified of rats. I was scared stiff while awake and even while I slept. In all of our apartments—like 116 Bergen Avenue, like 232 Dwight Street—we routinely heard rats scampering across our floors and in the walls of our apartment. A lightning bolt of horror would rocket through my body, and I would freeze in my tracks—breathless—certain the rodent would kill me with its fangs in the way I'd heard that a baby up the block had been eaten alive by a rat.

But my mother was my hero and protector. She was daring and did not fear rats. My mother would rear back with her broomstick, and the full weight of her fury would come down on the rat—BLAM!—killing it before it could race back to one of the many cracked, open entrances in our walls. Or my mother would rise in the middle of the night, leaving me scared in bed, as she went to the kitchen to clean up and dispose of a bloody rat that had run itself straight into our old refrigerator.

We were often cold in the winter. Heat made a guest appearance only when it felt like it. The cranky radiator would wind up every couple of hours like a car engine—sputtering, hissing, shooting steam upward—as water dribbled down from its valve. As soon as the radiator had gotten good and started, it shut off again, and I would lie in bed shivering beneath the thin, wool blanket.

Showers were no different. I would be standing in the shower allowing the hot water to caress me when, without fail, it would instantly convert into ice water. The first time that happened, I nearly slipped and fell backwards from the cold, cruel downpour on my young body. But eventually I figured it out. I learned to time the water's mood swings and to predict exactly when it would switch from hot to cold, and I would step in and out at the right moment, proud to defeat it.

Everywhere we lived, paint chipped from the walls and fell from our ceilings. Anthony and I played with the paint chips on the walls and imagined them falling from the ceiling into our mouths. Tempting as they were, we dared not eat them. But we *were* hungry.

Our mothers ignored our cries of hunger because they knew what we would eat and when: cereal for breakfast, a baloney sandwich with mustard or mayonnaise to take to school for lunch, and some kind of meat with rice for dinner. On special occasions like holidays, we would get potato salad or macaroni and cheese. On weekends we ate grits and bacon, or sausage and scrambled eggs. I always put ketchup on my eggs, and loved hot sauce with pretty much everything else.

Yet I was eternally hungry. I did not like vegetables of any kind, and I was so skinny that my mother would stitch my pants in at the waist to keep them from falling to my feet. I looked like a fishing pole with a head and big ears, draped with material that passed for clothes. To offset my hunger fits, I did what every other child in my 'hood did: I ate lots and lots of candy, potato chips, cookies, and cupcakes, and often begged my mother to give me ice cream, soda, and those cheap 25-cent juices in different flavors. I ate and drank so much of this stuff that I frequently saw spots before my eyes, and often got dizzy from the sugar in my bloodstream. Eventually I started daydreaming, seeing things—people, animals, moving objects—in the patterned designs of our kitchen chairs, living-room curtains, or the paint chips that fell like confetti from the ceilings.

There were lines for us everywhere. "Lines for poor people," someone said. On the first day of every month, there was the welfare line at the Shop-Rite on Grove Street in Downtown Jersey City. Before heading to the store, my mother and Aunt Cathy waited patiently, along with the other mothers in our building, for the mailman to come, anticipating his time of arrival. When he finally appeared, all the mothers surrounded him as he shoved mail into each of the boxes. Before he had finished, hands of assorted sizes reached around, over, under, and through him to grasp their welfare checks. Every month or so I would hear the sorrowful groan of a mother whose welfare check had not come, whose check had been stolen, or who surmised that "the government" had cut her off for this reason or that.

In the devil's heat of summer and in the wicked witch's cold of winter, mothers and children stood in the welfare line to cash their checks. We had no other choice, and we also had no other choice but to receive "food stamps," which my mother told me were like money. Money was green, but food stamps came in a variety of colors. My mother said that food stamps helped poor people like us to buy food, and that without them many people—maybe even our family—would starve.

Food stamps, and the boxes of cheese we received, came from the government. The boxes had long words on them and even longer numbers that made no sense to me. The cheese lasted an extremely long time and was rock hard, but it allowed us to enjoy foods we loved, like grilled cheese, ham and cheese, and macaroni and cheese.

The other line that I was always in—usually during the summer—was the "free lunch" line for poor kids. White people in white T-shirts came to Audubon Park to set up tables. They had cheerful smiles and beaming eyes, and told us to stand one-behind-the-other while they handed Anthony and me baloney sandwiches with mustard. We also received some fruit and tiny cartons of milk, but I longed for something special like McDonald's or Kentucky Fried Chicken.

My mother and Aunt Cathy did their best to keep Anthony and me off Jackson Avenue—the main artery for shopping and criminal activity in our neighborhood. But I was fascinated by "the Ave," as some folks called it. Elsewhere, liquor stores and churches were on virtually every street, sometimes right next to each other. Church was where you went if you wanted to "get right with the Lawd." The liquor store was where you went "if you ain't right with the Lawd." I was far more captivated by the liquor store. Not only could you buy every kind of alcohol there, but you could cash checks, "play the numbers" (or the official lottery games), and buy cigarettes. Outside the liquor store the men, mostly, talked about their lives in slurs while they sipped their Jack and Bacardi.

> *ahma be rich one day—you wait and see*
> *man shoot, ahm tired of bein poor*
> *tired of sellin these incense and these oils*
> *been workin too hard, you know?*
> *use to own my own business, couple of 'em, matter of fact*
> *maybe ah just didn't have the right formula though*
> *swore ah'd be rich by now*
> *but ahm gonna make that million, you watch—*
> *either ahm gonna be rich or ahm gonna be dead. . . .*

When our mothers left Anthony and me at the house of a babysitter, who we called "Miss Sue," we would escape to the corners of Jackson Avenue to eavesdrop on these men. They leaned against boarded-up, piss-stained buildings, sat on sunken milk crates they treated like royal thrones, and played checkers, chess, or dominoes like Americans and Russians battling for world supremacy.

"Nigga, ain't I told you Nixon was nothin' but a goddamn liar?"

"Nah, nigga, you ain't told me nuthin'. I told you. Just like I told you we ain't had no business in that there Vietnam. We need to mind our biz-ness for once."

"Y'all hear this cat who can't even read his own name? Act like he done been reading the newspapers and whatnot."

"Your momma, man! I can read! Went to the fourth grade, more than you ever done."

"Yeah, but I got more money than you and get way more womens than you ever could even smell."

The men saw Anthony and me standing outside their court, little boys listening keenly and inhaling every word like drug addicts—I had seen too many drug addicts—sucking on marijuana sticks.

"Come here, boys!" one man called to us.

We were beyond shy and wanted to run away from these men. But we inched forward, in spite of ourselves.

"You boys want a drink?"

Anthony and I shook our heads furiously left and right. Our mothers had told us many times to never taste liquor, never smoke a cigarette, and never do drugs. Those were the ways of the devil, paving the way to hell for both of us, they said.

"Good! You young niggas don't wanna be like us," one man said and beamed, his eyes a grotesque shade of yellow, crisscrossed by thin, red lines.

"But I know what these young fellas will like, just like us," another said mischievously.

Anthony and I edged closer out of curiosity.

"You boys want to grow hair on your face one day, right?"

We nodded our heads in ready approval.

The man shifted on his crate, straightened his back, and cocked his wrinkled neck in our direction.

"Then y'all need to learn how to taste a woman just right. Not only will that put hair on your top lip and all over your face, but that there will grow hair on your chest as well."

The men went back to their games and ignored us. Anthony and I kept walking along Jackson Avenue. Our mothers would soon be to Miss Sue's to pick us up, but we weren't worried about getting back.

As we walked, I saw the same things I had always seen: a purplish velvet drawing of a man named James Brown, who they called "the Godfather of Soul." A picture of a little beige man wearing a hat that looked like an upside-down pot, named Elijah Muhammad, the word "Messenger" always by his name. Jackson Discount, where our mothers bought our school clothes each year, on layaway, putting a little down each visit until the clothes were ours. They did the same to pay for our beds, television sets, kitchen set, and all our furniture. I came to believe that layaway was the only option for purchasing anything.

Pretty much every single store we passed on Jackson Avenue had the word "LAYAWAY" posted prominently in its window.

There were also barbershops, beauty salons, pawnshops, and several laundromats, including one called Sluggo's. Sluggo was a real person who owned the laundromat and was also a preacher. Next door was a hole-in-the-wall candy store where my mother and Aunt Cathy "played the numbers."

Whenever my mother or Aunt Cathy had a dream, or someone gave them a number, they would play it. Every now and again, word would get around that someone in our neighborhood "hit the number big," cashed out, and bought something they had always wanted, like a new car. One time my Aunt Cathy hit and purchased a brand-new record player.

As much as we loved record players and television sets, I learned that being on welfare meant we were not supposed to have those things. Often, someone called a "social worker" would show up at our apartment at 116 Bergen Avenue to check on the four of us. My mother and Aunt Cathy said it was because "they did not want poor people having nice things." Our mothers somehow knew the knock of a social worker, and would tell Anthony and me to get the extra bed sheets to cover our televisions and our record players. We put our food away. We hid our clothes. Then, and only then, would my mother or Aunt Cathy open the door and allow the person to enter.

Every social worker would walk purposefully around the apartment, staring down my mother, Aunt Cathy, Anthony, and me. Our mothers were always polite and would smile a lot, their demeanors different with the social worker than with anyone else. It was as if these people exerted supernatural power over them.

Social workers worked for "the government" and were connected to our welfare checks and food stamps. Anthony and I looked at the floor and said nothing when the social worker tried to make small talk with us. We feared that if we spoke, the social worker might do something to our mothers or, worse, they might take us away, like the other children in our neighborhood who never came back.

cry, oh how I would cry—as that boy must have cried when his life was taken without remorse by the knife that pierced his heart and stole it—

"A hero ain't nothin' but a sandwich. . . ." These words echoed throughout my neighborhood. Maybe they came from a book, from a movie, or from both, or maybe someone just made them up. But I knew that I was no hero. No one around me was. I did not know what I was, and I did not know who we were. We were just there. In this place called "the ghetto" where I felt trapped forever. In my child mind I began to call the ghetto a concrete box. We lived in, and were trapped in, a concrete box. There was no escapin' this. This was as good as it would ever get. I was born here. I would live here. I would die here. It would only be a matter of time—

7

Puerto Ricans

the way Tito Puente got soul
the way James Brown got soul
the way every afro-familia . . .
with a relative named Malik Rodriguez or Maria Jackson
got a little rican and a little soul, nahmean?

T STARTED when I was about four years old with the PBS shows *Sesame Street* and *The Electric Company*. I was sitting dutifully in front of our rickety black-and-white television set, my face as close to the screen as I could get, watching the many characters. But one day, first on *Sesame Street*, then immediately after on *The Electric Company*: I heard a language I had never heard before—

Uno dos tres cuatro cinco . . . The TV people said it was "Spanish," and I was mesmerized. First they would count—one to ten—in English, and then they did so in Spanish. I found myself repeating the words, spellbound. Next they did the same with the alphabet, and I repeated every single letter exactly as they said it. I also found myself learning basic words: *Hola* meant "Hello." *¿Cómo estás?* meant "How are you?"

I said aloud the numbers, the alphabet, the words, the phrases—

in English and in Spanish—all around our apartment over and over again. My mother never told me not to, but she certainly had made some pretty nasty comments about Puerto Ricans.

"Boy, don't be trustin' them Puerto Ricans. They ain't no good. They eat they rice and beans with all that garlic, they breaths stink, and they always talkin' fast in Spanish. They need to speak English, damn Mira Miras!"

My eyes and ears were tagged—like graffiti on a ghetto wall—by an entirely different image of Puerto Ricans. Maybe it was the way the smell of Spanish rice and beans with chicken, *arroz con pollo*, would seep through the walls of our apartment. Maybe it was the way our cardboard-thin walls, ceiling, and floor would reverberate to the sounds of *salsa y merengue*—vibrant rhythms—a festive holler of "*¡Wepa!*" coming from our neighbors as they sang or danced to the percussion-driven beats. Maybe it was the way I befriended Diana and Daisy Noriega in grade school, twin Puerto Rican girls who were so beautiful with their matching manes of long and flowing black hair. They were also smart, and had the coolest little brother who they called "Flaco," one of the best stickball and baseball players in the world (or at least in Jersey City).

Oh, how I wanted to be a part of their family. At least in these Puerto Rican clans there seemed to be a lot of hugging, kissing, and affection for each other; lots of togetherness, with phrases like *Te amo* and *Primo* being used even if they did not know each other. I noticed their various skin colors—some were Black like me; some had an olive tint or tan and could pass for Native American or Arab; others were as white as White people. They also seemed to intermingle quite easily, whereas Black people and White people in Jersey City typically stayed far apart.

Maybe it was those trips to Downtown Jersey City—the first of each month—when I realized that single Puerto Rican mothers and children were on the welfare lines with us. In Downtown Jersey City, most residents were Puerto Ricans. Although I didn't realize it, enormous love and interest in the language, culture, and people bloomed inside me.

But my mother had a long-running, ugly feud with Hector, the super at one of our tenement buildings, because he was "a foreigner" and different from us. One day—when I was in my early teens—I had a chat with Hector, trying to reconcile the animosity between the two of them. When I dared to share that with my mother, she broke down crying.

"I cannot believe you talked to that no-good man! He not like us, he don't like us. He hate us, that damn Mira Mira! Boy, I cannot believe you did that to me. All I done for you and you do this to me. You let that man talk to you about me!"

I had never seen my mother cry like this. Her leathery, chocolate-brown face morphed into that of a little girl, tears tumbling like a torrential rain. She paced to and fro and smashed the palms of her hands together.

The notion that I had somehow betrayed my mother by attempting to be a bridge-builder both frightened and saddened me deeply. I watched this giant figure in my life slump into her living-room chair and sob uncontrollably for what felt like an hour. From that point on, I kept to myself my love and appreciation of Puerto Ricans, and any conversations I had with other Latinos who were from dreamy settings like Peru, the Dominican Republic, Cuba, and Mexico. Each exchange, each new Spanish word or phrase that I picked up, and each new Latin tempo, fed my imagination, allowing me to live not only in Jersey City, but also in God-kissed, tropical lands thousands of miles away from the misery and loneliness of my youth.

8

Church

dreamer Will
you mind if I tell you I
believe in god but it
just might not be the
god you believe in

GOD WAS with us there in the ghetto from the very beginning. I know he was. He would not just let us suffer through the poverty and misery and depression alone, would he?

I thought about this question practically every single day, perhaps because my mother and Aunt Cathy spoke that much about how poor we were. My cousin Anthony and I heard a lot of talk about death and dying and heaven and hell, at home and outside on the streets of Jersey City. My mother reminded us so often that God would never let us fall even when things were at their worst and we were scraping the floor of the bottom that we'd clearly hit.

That's why we went to church. In church there was God, and a preacher, and answers to our prayers and fears. All our eyes were watching God, and God was watching us, too. We had to worship God, praise God, and be with God, and so we attended two churches, because we desperately needed as much God as we could get. One of the churches was in Newark, New Jersey, and the other in New York City. (Why we never—*never*—attended church in Jersey City I do not know.)

The church in Newark was called the Deliverance Evangelistic Center. Sometimes we'd go there for regular Sunday service and sometimes we'd go on a Tuesday night—if we needed "special prayers." It made no difference if Anthony and I had to get up early for school the next day.

Anthony and I did not have suits like some other little boys. Nonetheless, our mothers prepared us as best they could. We had to be very clean for God. We scrubbed much harder than usual; we showered far longer than usual; we shellacked our skins with baby oil; we dumped white talcum powder inside our shirts, which crawled up our chests to our necks; and we spread a generous helping of Vaseline on our faces—making us glow like the spit-clean job of a shoeshine man.

We took the Bergen Avenue bus to Journal Square and the PATH train from Jersey City to Newark Penn Station. One Newark bus took us to Broad and Market; the next took us to Clinton Avenue and South 10th Street in the heart of the inner city. The preacher of the Deliverance Evangelistic Center was Arturo Skinner, a middle-aged man with an elastic, honey-coated face, a short-cut afro with a razor-sharp part chiseled in on the left side, and a river-wide grin that felt fatherly and protective. Arturo wore stylish—but conservative—suits, bright-colored neckties, and he always kept a piece of cloth that matched his tie in the upper-left pocket of his suit.

The adults did not call him "Reverend" or "Pastor," but "Apostle," and they said that he was a man of God, a healer with supernatural powers. He once had lived a life of the devil, a fast life with women and liquor and drugs, in a place called "show business." God spoke to him one day—halted him dead in his tracks—when he was about to kill himself shortly after his mother had died, and God gave him the choice to go with him or to go with the devil. He chose God and his life was magically changed. He gave up everything that had to do with show business. All he had left was his mother's Bible—"the Word" they called it—when he took to a hotel room—for about a month—to be with God. Him and God. God spoke to him and he spoke to God, and it was good. God had executed a healing on Arturo Skinner. God had lifted him up like a newborn baby—to the heavens—and given him the gift of ministry, of healing, so that he could heal others. And it was so.

In this church led by Apostle Arturo Skinner, two thousand seats were filled with Black people from Jersey City, Newark, Irvington, East Orange, Hillside, and from parts of New York City. Apostle Skinner was from Brooklyn and also had a church like this there. Deliverance Evangelistic had once been a synagogue and was shaped like those old colosseums with gargantuan pillars seen in movies. Inside, the ceiling featured a stained-glassed skylight. I wished I could fly up to kiss that skylight.

My mother, Aunt Cathy, Anthony, and I would sit in church, completely still and quiet. We rose when we were told to rise. We sat when we were told to sit. We listened to speakers proclaim "the word of God." Whenever we were there, I felt a gush of energy in my scrawny body. I dared not show even the slightest emotion, because my mother didn't show any, and I feared that she would beat me.

Behind the church altar stood a choir of men and women of all sizes and ages, all in black robes. At a black organ on the right sat an elder Black woman in a black dress and a black wig with a small white price tag dangling from it on a small white string. A round black man with stick-like legs—also in a black robe—would come out to stand before the choir, his back to those of us in the church seats. Everyone became silent. Slowly, the round man would raise his hefty arms to the Lawd and sound roared from the choir. I felt as if I would be ejected from my seat—straight up through that stained-glass skylight to the heavens—to be seated at the bare-white feet of God himself. I felt both overjoyed and utterly terrified. I thought of heaven, of hell, of life, of death, of "living in sin," as they said continually. With each vocal climax, each distortion of a phrase or biting off of a word, this choir sang to me . . . to us, to the church, to the block, to the neighborhood, to the entire world, to a place where we no longer knew poverty or misery or depression. All around us people leapt from their seats, jumping as if they could touch that gleaming skylight, shamelessly, effortlessly—

"Yes, sweet Je-sus!"

"Lawd, sing! Let 'em sing through ya, Lawd!"

"Heal me God! Heal me!"

At first a few would stand, then a few more, until before long the entire church was standing—including us. However, we were not doing what others about us were doing. Our mothers stared straight ahead, their stiff postures and dead silences acknowledging and accepting that this is where they were supposed to be—to get right with God—no matter how cursed and doomed our lives seemed to be. Anthony and I would look at each and giggle hysterically.

The organ lady played with a gusto that I had never before seen. Sweat flowed down her face as she rocked with the choir, wig lopsided, her shoes kicked off to reveal stockings with a yawning hole near the right ankle. The round man would start to dance, then start running back and forth on the stage. He had what my mother told me was "da holy ghost." Some divine spirit had gotten inside of him. I wondered if this was like "the hags risin'." Every now and again the round man would stop and leap into the sky, as if he were on a trampoline. Then he would start to run across the stage once more. Meanwhile the choir, so together and so orderly in the beginning, would become a colossal parade of bodies flinging themselves here and there. Some sang and shouted "Hallelujah" as they stood; some sat down crying; some were on their knees with hands stretched out to the Lawd praying. And some joined the round man as he ran around the stage.

At a certain point, Apostle Arturo Skinner would lift himself from his wooden chair and walk solemnly to the pulpit—a large Bible tucked into his right elbow. He looked at us in the pews, turned to look at the round man, the organ lady, and the choir, then looked back to us and raised his hands, and it was as if God himself had entered the room. We became quiet in anticipation of his words.

brothas and sistas, hah!

i'm here ta tell ya, hah!

that the laaawd don't like ugly, no! lawd don't like no ugliness

are y'all wid me?

i said are y'all wid me now?

time done stop lawd, hah!

i said time done stop, hah!

what we gonna do lawd?

we gonna pick some flowers, hah!

and bury our future, hah!

and we gonna build a new house lawd

and we gonna paint it blue lawd

i said we gonna paint it blue, hah!

so we can feel that old-time spirit a-goin', hah!

feeel it! thank ya jesus!

feeel it! thank ya jesus!

With each howl from Apostle Skinner the churchgoers veered and whirled with such raw and unfiltered emotions that I was utterly dizzy.

"Sickness!" Arturo Skinner shouted from the top of his lungs, "is of the devil!"

"We are here!" he screamed again, "to reach the lost at any cost with the message of the Pentecost!"

With that, we got up and stood on the long line that led to the altar where Apostle Skinner was "touchin' every last head with the prayer oil of da Lawd." I was scared of Apostle Skinner and his prayer oil, of the people speaking in a foreign language they called "talkin' in tongues," of the constant references to dying and the thin line between heaven and hell. My mother held me in front of her when we arrived in front of Apostle Skinner. He beamed at me as he bent down, and poured extra prayer oil into his web-like hands before he squeezed the front and back of my head hard between his greasy palms. I felt absolutely nothing but smiled anyway at this giant of a man before walking away, the prayer oil dripping down my face and the back of my neck.

After we returned to our seats, Apostle Skinner would ask who among us needed "a healing." People in wheelchairs and people with canes came to the front of the church. People who said they were drunks, drug addicts, or both pushed their way to the front of the church, too. One by one Apostle Skinner laid his hands on each of them, praying a mighty prayer.

"Lawd Jee-zus! 'Buke the devil from this soul! 'Buke it now, God. Heal this sinner! Hold this sinner in your arms and lift him up like you did me, Lawd. In Jesus name, A-men."

Then the miracles happened! A woman who could not walk blasted from her wheelchair and skipped in the aisles. A man with a cane stood erect, broke his cane across his left knee, and jumped for joy. These healings happened every Sunday and every Tuesday for years, because of the healing powers of Apostle Skinner. And when he died, the new preacher, Reverend Ralph Nichol, performed the same exact miracles each and every single time we went to that church.

Yet I did ask myself again and again, if God were so forgiving, so powerful, so healing, so full of miracles, why then were my mother, Aunt Cathy, Anthony, and I forever stuck in the ghetto, in poverty, with rats, roaches, and murder, madness, and mayhem everywhere?

The second church we attended, Reverend Ike's Christ United Church in New York City, was completely different from Apostle Skinner's. I was always far more excited to go to the New York church. We went through the same ritual to prepare for it, wore the best clothes that we owned, and then we obediently waited on Kennedy Boulevard for the 99S bus to take us from Jersey City to New York's Port Authority Bus Terminal on 42nd Street, where we caught the A train to 175th Street. Inevitably, another train would run right next to ours—stuffed with people like us—painted with the liveliest colors and graffiti words, just like our train.

When we arrived on Broadway at Reverend Ike's, I would stare in childlike wonder at "the miracle star of faith" that crowned the roof of the church, visible from multiple directions. Inside this dazzling building—also called the "the Palace Cathedral"—there was gold everywhere. Upon entering, we were immediately given an envelope for donations and encouraged to give generously. Much bigger than the Deliverance Evangelistic Center, this church was an old movie theater that Reverend Ike had purchased and converted into this place of worship. Reverend Ike's sermons were on television and radio, as if he were a Black Billy Graham, preaching to millions of followers around the world.

There was not a lot of shouting, hooping, and hollering at Christ United Church, but it felt like a party, a show, or a concert. There was a band with several musicians and singers—but not a choir—and occasionally women danced in the aisles, wearing the same kind of miniskirts women wore in the movies or in the 'hood in Jersey City.

The scene set perfectly, Reverend Ike would rise from a gold-fringed, velvet chair the size of a king's throne, which sat atop a red-carpeted stage. Sometimes he would stand and sometimes he would perch on a stool as he spoke. I was awestruck by this Black man with "the good, curly hair, just like White folks," the smooth brown skin, the blinged rings on his fingers, the expensively tailored suits, the ever-present rose in his lapel—always on the left. His favorite word was "prosperity," and his favorite saying was "You can't lose with the stuff I use." The church was swollen with throngs of oohing and aahing worshippers—most of them women, like my mother and Aunt Cathy, who sat with their children.

"The lack of money is the root of all evil!" Reverend Ike declared, and the women cried "A-men!" and "That's right!" and "Dang, he so pretty! Preach prea-cher!"

"Close your eyes and see green!" Reverend Ike commanded us to do, and we did. Then he added, "Money up to your armpits, a roomful of money and there you are, just tossing around in it like a swimming pool."

Reverend Ike—just like our family—was from Ridgeland, South

Carolina. Somehow he had made it out and made a fortune as a preacher. Now he was helping others to find their fortunes.

"Ladies, reach into your pocketbooks for five dollars for the donation, but get up and give me twenty," Reverend Ike instructed—to much laughter and applause—and the spellbound women did exactly what he told them to do.

The majestic, seven-story organ played as five thousand people lined up to give their donations. If we were lucky enough, Reverend Ike might look our way or even touch us. One time, he patted my nappy dome as I strolled past him. My mother and the other adults who saw it said, "Boy, you sure gonna get a blessing now!"

But we never did. We gave what little money we had to other churches and revivals, too, but none changed our lives—no matter how many times we listened to Apostle Skinner, or to Reverend Ike on the radio, or saw Reverend Ike on television, or played 45s of Reverend Ike's sermons on our cheap record player. Both preachers distributed "prayer clothes" to their followers—like free lunches or boxes of government cheese—with strict guidelines on how to use them on our bodies and in our homes. Both Apostle Skinner and Reverend Ike told us that if we just followed our Lord and Savior Jesus Christ, a better day was coming, that our lives would be safer, richer, and that we would live forever in the kingdom of God they called heaven.

In my mind I questioned their logic—albeit vaguely—but couldn't think of anything else to believe. What outlet for my misery and sadness and hunger was there other than prayer, or Apostle Skinner's prayer hotlines, or the mailings that we opened with great anticipation whenever Reverend Ike sent them? Reverend Ike amplified our optimism with game show–style tales of followers who received checks for thousands of dollars in the mail, new Cadillacs, or new homes simply because of their donations to his church and their belief in him, which led to their newfound prosperity.

Yet it was at home, as my mother sat alone in the kitchen, her battery-operated radio tuned to WNJR, the gospel station out of Newark, that I often felt more of the presence of God than I did in those churches. I felt it in the solitude of clanking pots and pans, in the sound of my mother scraping her raggedy slippers from the sink to the stove and back again, or in her dogged efforts to strike a match to light that stubborn old oven. My mother would sing, moaning and groaning, softly, the words of an old spiritual. It did not matter the song or the words. My mother just fell right into the lyrics and rode that wave—God's wave—thanking Him for another day, even if today was more difficult than yesterday.

9

My father

Ma?

    Yeah boy?

Where's my daddy?

    You ain't got no daddy, boy.

Where did I come from ma?

    You came from me.

But teacher told us that you need a mommy and a daddy to make me.

    What your teacher tellin' you that for?

She said everybody should have a mommy and a daddy.

    Well, your teacher might be right but you ain't got no daddy.

Why ain't I got no daddy ma?

    Because—

Because what?

    Because he wuzn't no good, like most of 'em.

But I want a daddy like everybody else.

    You ain't got one boy, except me—I'm your daddy.

You don't look like no daddy to me.

    Boy, don't you sassy me.

I ain't ma, but where's my daddy?

    I donno boy. Leave me alone.

But ma, where did I come from?

    Ah, you, um, you came from a deer. We went to the woods and kilt a deer and made you from it.

For real?

Uh-huh.

So the deer is my daddy, ma?

No, you ain't got no daddy.

Why not?

'Cause.

'Cause what?

'Cause I said so. Now hush up before I slap you for askin' me all
them fool questions!

I'm sorry ma but I wanna know where's my daddy?

NEVER REALLY knew my father. I never called him Father, or
Dad, or Pop, or sir. I called him what my mother and everyone else
in Jersey City called him: Cunningham. His name was Elize Cunningham; that is how my mother spelled his first name, so I spelled
it that way, too.

I cannot recall the first time that I met my father or when I first
thought that I should have one. Most of the children in my building,
in my 'hood, had single mothers, *and that was it.* I did not think anything was wrong until I saw a lot of television shows that featured fathers.

The first series that ignited my father-want was *The Courtship of
Eddie's Father.* I was five or six years old when I began to yearn for the
kind of bond Eddie and his father had. Television programs with fathers like *The Brady Bunch* and *Good Times* magnified my dream. I envisioned myself lifted from my apartment and dropped instantly into
the middle of one of these television families—their dad, my dad . . .
their family, my family.

Around this time my father, Cunningham, came around. We were
too poor to afford a telephone in our apartment, so my mother and
I walked around the corner to a drugstore on Jackson Avenue with a

phone booth so she could call and talk to him. After she hung up this time, my mother told me that my father was coming to see me, and that he had seen me before—when I was a baby. He had a sister, Ollie, and my mother had allowed Ollie to take me to South Carolina as an infant. My father came from the same state as my mother, though a different part. They had met in Jersey City, but my mother did not talk about how that happened.

On the day my father arrived at our apartment, I stared at him from a distance. He was a foreigner to me, and my mother had taught me never to talk with—or to get close to—strangers. He had a plump, round reddish-yellow face, a black derby hat with a red feather glued to the left side, a pair of round granny glasses, a pig-like nose, and a jovial laugh that came from his gut. He never removed his hat, even indoors.

He smiled at me and called me "Cel-vin" with the Southern drawl of a man raised on runny, buttered grits, crispy, fried bacon, and thumb-thick pork-sausage links. I knew that my name was Kevin, so I did not answer him. He called me to him. I looked at my mother, then at the living-room floor. My mother told me to say hello to my father.

My father asked if I would like to take a ride with him in his car. Again, I looked at the floor. My mother said that it was okay, so I went with him. We got into a brown car that he said was a Gran Torino. On the floor were rectangular plastic things he called eight-track tapes, which could play any kind of music that I wanted. I sat in silence. So rarely did I ride in cars that the experience seemed unnatural, but also cool.

My father drove us to Jersey City's Journal Square, one of the main shopping areas in Jersey City. We went to a store that sold watches and he told me to pick one out. I remembered the Timex commercials from television—"Takes a licking and keeps on ticking"—so I picked one. My father pulled out a thick wad of cash—the most money that I had ever seen in my life—and I was astonished. Was he rich? Was he what they called a millionaire?

On another day not long after that, my father came again to pick me up, this time in his "tractor-trailer truck." He worked as a truck driver and was "always on the road." He even said that he would love to take me along sometime. When I realized that my father's truck had several pictures of naked women taped here and there, I felt embarrassed and afraid. My father hooted loudly at my shame. He told me that I would be a man one day and would understand.

My father took me to buy my first bicycle, with training wheels, so that I could learn how to ride on my own. I was happy to finally have a bike like the other kids on my block. Around this time, my cousin Anthony had gotten his first watch and his first bicycle from his father, John Gamble. Perhaps the men really cared about us, or perhaps they felt a sense of competition. In any case, we loved the gifts and the attention.

My father sat sometimes with my mother in the living room when Aunt Cathy and Anthony were out. They spoke in hushed tones and whispers of "marriage" and "help raisin' this boy." My father had a Polaroid camera and took pictures of me posing by our old rickety black-and-white television set.

On a couple of occasions my father took me to his house on Bayview Avenue in Jersey City, between Ocean and Garfield. It seemed like a castle to me. He had a real pool table in the basement where I played endlessly with the colorful balls, pushing them back and forth with my pint-size hands.

My dad reintroduced me to his sister, Ollie, and her son, a boy she had adopted named Robin. My father told me that Robin was my cousin. My father smoked a lot of cigarettes, Viceroys, his favorite. And he also had a glass of alcohol whenever the mood hit him.

Abruptly, I stopped seeing my father, and my mother stopped talking about them getting married. He never came by again. Once, I asked, "Ma, is Cunningham gonna buy me something else?"

"Boy, don't ask me no questions about that goddamn Cunningham. He ain't nothin' but a no-good red nigga."

I stared at the floor, fearful that my mother would beat me if I asked her any further questions.

One rainy day when I was eight years old, my mother told me to put on my clothes; we were going around the corner to the drugstore to call my father. My heart pumped with excitement—in sharp contrast with my mother's somber and resolute demeanor. When we got to the phone booth, I hoped that she would put me on the phone with my father, but I just stood there at the open door as she fingered through her black plastic pocketbook for the coins to call him.

I heard my mother ask for my father. I heard my mother ask my father how he was doing. I heard my mother tell my father that she really needed help raising me, and that she needed money to support me. I heard my mother's voice grow angry and tremble as my father said something that she did not like. I heard my mother's voice become sorrowful as she begged my father for help, her desperation a ball of vinegary saliva wedged at the back of her throat. I heard my mother curse at my father. I heard my mother plead with my father once more, her bloodshot eyes tearing up. I heard my mother's defeated, child-like whimpers, her last gasps of defeat. Finally, my mother slammed down the phone.

She grabbed me by the arm and faced me directly as she spoke:

"That damn Cunningham ain't no good. He told me I lied to him—that you ain't his son, that he ain't your father—and here you is just as red as that no-good red nigga. He said he ain't never going to give me a 'near nickel' for you ever again. Whatever you do, Kevin, do not ever be like your father!"

I held my mother's hand tightly as we walked out of the drugstore into the rain that poured down on the ashen asphalt of Jersey City. My mother's hurt became my hurt. There was finality to the conversation my mother had had with my father. As quickly as he had come into my life he was gone . . . *forever*.

My mother and Aunt Cathy talked endlessly in the kitchen about hoping to find husbands and getting help with Anthony and me. For a couple more years, these two relatively young women allowed a man here or there to court them, even to take them out, but inevitably they were disappointed. The men were no good, they wanted to have sex or to move in with us and live off our mothers' meager incomes. They saw our mothers as nothing more than pit stops on their trail from one hot cooked meal to another.

"I can do bad by myself" became the rallying cry of my mother and Aunt Cathy, and of the legions of other single mothers in Jersey City's ghetto. My boyhood hopes of having a father were inflated, deflated—popped!

Each school year, I would lie about my father's name. One year he would be Michael—like Michael Brady from *The Brady Bunch*. The next year he would be James, like James Evans from *Good Times*. My teachers had to know that these were childhood fantasies, but they never tried to embarrass me by asking why my father's name changed from year to year.

In my eight-year-old universe, a titanic black hole opened up when my father disappeared. Why did I feel that way? My father had never really been there. Nevertheless, I felt consumed with jealousy whenever I saw other boys with their fathers on the streets of Jersey City.

Why did they have what I did not? What had I done that was so bad? Why had my father done this to me and to my mother? This feeling of emptiness, of hurt, of pain, of father-come and father-gone, of father lost, would torture me through my teens and into adulthood. I struggled and tripped over myself trying to understand what it was to be male, a boy, a man. I cried for days over my father's absence, cursed him savagely in my thoughts, and vowed that if I ever saw him again I would ignore him. Or I would beat him mercilessly for what he had done to my mother and me.

10

My mother [part 2]

But what a mother you were:
You taught me to talk
Taught me to know my name
Taught me to count to read to think
To aspire to be something.
You, my grade-school educated mother,
Gave me my swagger—
Told me I was going to be a lawyer or a doctor,
Told me I was going to do big things,
That I was going to have a better life
Than this welfare this food stamp this government cheese
Had pre-ordained for us.
And we prayed, mother, yes lawd we prayed—
To that God in the sky, to the White Jesus on our wall,
To the minister with the good hair and the tailored suits,
To the minister with the gift
To chalk on busted souls and spit game in foreign tongues—
And back then, ma, I did not understand the talking in tongues
The need to pin pieces of prayer cloth on our attire
The going to church twice a week
The desperation to phone prayer hotlines when there was trouble.
But what you were doing, ma,
Was stapling our paper lives together as best you could
Making a way out of no way

Especially after my father announced,
When I was eight,
That he would not give "a near nickel" to us again.
And he never did, mother, never—

M Y MOTHER beat me for as long as I can remember. She used her hands, one of my belts, or "a switch"—a strong, flexible type of wood yanked from bushes in our 'hood. Of all the weapons at my mother's disposal, the switches caused the most damage—inflamed welts would rise on my arms and legs where my mother struck me. The switch guaranteed pain, to ensure that I understood the severity of my errors. While my mother beat me, she repeated, as each blow landed: "You gonna be good? You gonna be good?" That refrain gave me nightmares that still haunt my sleep.

One time I got lost in a department store. When she found me, she grabbed me hard by the arm with her left hand and walloped my narrow butt with her right. I screamed and cried as other shoppers ambled by as if nothing was happening. Another time, when I was in the fourth grade, I was bringing mad ruckus to my teacher, as I had been doing for several years. My mother was summoned by the school and forced to take off work. As my mother and I stood in the hallway of P.S. 38 a Black vice-principal named Mr. St. John told her that if I did not learn to behave myself I would be suspended from school. He gave the most horrific depiction of my bad behavior, how I had dissed the teacher, Mrs. Koles, and completely and knowingly disrupted the class and the progress of other students. My mother's chestnut-colored eyes glared at me in a way I had not seen before, and her nostrils flared. In one swift and methodical motion, my mother slapped me across my face, in front of Mr. St. John, like she had never slapped me in her life.

My puny body nearly toppled backwards into the tile wall. Stunned and embarrassed, I later looked in a bathroom mirror and saw her entire handprint outlined on the side of my face. I had become accustomed to my mother whipping me in the privacy of our apartment and thought of the department store beating as an aberration—a onetime occurrence. But for my mother to do this to me in front of a school official—who could not conceal his ample amusement and delight—was beyond humiliation.

Yes, I had been a bad boy for some time in school. In fact, kindergarten, when I was five and six, was the only grade level—other than eighth grade—where I did not have serious behavioral problems. I did not know why I acted out in school. . . . I just did. I could not do anything at home because of my mother's too-many-to-count rules: *Do not touch the stove. Do not sing before 10 A.M. because you will be mad the entire day if you do. Do not put your hat on the bed—that's bad luck. Do not speak or move if there is thunder and lightning. Do not ever answer the door if someone rings the bell or knocks; just be quiet and be still. Do not ever touch or open the windows. Do not go to sleep without praying to God: "I lay my head down to sleep. I pray the Lord my soul to keep. If I shall die before I wake, I pray the Lord my soul to take. . . ."*

There were so many rules and superstitions, I could not keep up. I constantly upset my mother and hurt her feelings. Her anger seemed persistently in search of a target. I had no brother or sister to deflect her, and I feared my mother—and her rage—and considered the possibility that one day she might kill me.

Perhaps, that's why school became the one place where I could be freer. My mother's preparation served me well. I loved school and the opportunity to learn. I breezed from one grade to another at the top of my class. But my behavior always presented my greatest challenge. I took offense at any slight or dis from a fellow student or teacher. I slammed my hands on my desk when the teacher said something I did not like, and I talked back a lot. I would protest a task I did not want to do by rising slowly from my desk and moving turtle-like to the blackboard or to the supply closet.

When old Mrs. Noonan, my third-grade teacher at P.S. 34, disciplined me by making me stand in a closet with no door—as was her practice with unruly students—I entertained the other students by gyrating like a belly dancer. Infuriated, Mrs. Noonan demanded that I wash out my mouth with soap and water. I refused and responded as my mother did on occasion: "Go to hell!" Horrified, Mrs. Noonan told the principal and the principal called my mother.

It became the norm for my mother to miss work to deal with my constant misbehavior in school. My report cards, each year, would include some variation of "Kevin is an excellent student, he is super-bright, but he does not know how to get along with other people." My mother did not like the poor marks that I received for social behavior. She took great pride in the fact that I always had perfect attendance and the highest grades across my report card. At the end of each school year she would cross out the bad grades for my behavior.

The more I got in trouble in school, the more my mother beat me. At first I just took the beatings, squirming but absorbing the whacks, the slaps, and the lashes. But as I got older—around age seven or eight—I refused to just suffer peacefully. By the time Anthony and I were eight years old, my mother and Aunt Cathy had gotten separate apartments, at 232 Dwight Street. This gave me the room I needed to maneuver and run away from my mother the moment that I knew she was reaching for my belt or one of the switches she always kept in a corner.

She ain't beatin' me no more! I'm not gonna take that. I'm faster than her and I am going to run. But where? I know where! I can run under the bed. She's too big to get me there. I will run under the bed. My mother will yell and curse and kick the bed, but she will tire herself out. . . .

Of course, my mother was smarter than I was. When I changed tactics, she also changed tactics. Since I was a big little boy, my folding bed was in the living room by itself. On one particular night, after I had made my mother especially angry for some infraction or another, my mother snored away in the bedroom and I fell deeply asleep, until—

Whack!

My mother loomed above me attacking ferociously with a switch in one hand as she held me down with the other. I could not run. I could not move—I was dazed and terrified that my mother was beating me in my sleep. I cried—a long and mournful howl—praying that someone would come and stop my mother, and rescue me. But no one cared. And no one came. This was the ghetto. This was how it was. Every day was punctuated by cries and yells for help, from adults and from children, and by ambulance and police sirens. Noises were such a part of our daily existence that we felt like something was wrong—on any given night—if there was complete silence.

So I screamed, as she beat me and asked again and again, "You gonna be good? You gonna be good?"

I could never answer my mother's question, even as the beatings multiplied from month to month, then week to week. Sometimes I felt as if I were being beaten every day of my life. My mother became a monster to me, joining the ranks of the rats that I feared; the criminals we imagined would climb our fire escape and enter through our kitchen windows; the thieves on the street who might stab us and take the few crumpled dollar bills, coins, and food stamps we had; the social workers I feared would take me away; and the principals who threatened my mother with sending me to a special-education school because of my bad behavior.

I lived in absolute terror of my mother, trembled and flinched when she spoke and stared at me in anger. Her words and the names she called me became gloved fists—delivering jabs, uppercuts, and body blows to the very little confidence I already had. She called me "dummy" or "big dummy," which the comedian and actor Redd Foxx as Fred Sanford called his son Lamont on the popular television show *Sanford and Son*. She also called me a "mental case," believing me to be crazy. I heard those deeply painful words repeatedly—when I was "bad" or for no reason at all—and I came to believe that I was stupid, inferior, a mistake, a walking breathing disaster and, yes, crazy.

I cringed whenever my mother, in a fit of rage, would say that she should have given me up for adoption at birth. My mother and I never hugged, never kissed, never said "I love you" to each other. My mother just did not show affection, not with her sisters, her brother, her mother, or her father. I came to believe that it was utterly unnatural for people to show affection, and when I saw Puerto Ricans in Jersey City hugging and kissing, I thought that they were abnormal.

I resembled my father, with his reddish-brown skin, the shape of his head, and his distinctive facial features. It seemed as if my mother directed my beatings at him as much as she did at me.

"You just like your no-good father, that damn Cunningham!"

"Don't be like your father!"

I was awfully confused. Do not be like my father . . . but I am just like my father? I did not know how to relate to my mother. If I spoke too much and asked too many questions, she beat me. If I misbehaved in school, she beat me. If I brought home a bad grade from school, she beat me. My mother beat me in the daytime. My mother beat me at night. My mother beat me when I was awake. My mother beat me when I was asleep.

One day, I did escape her by darting under her bed as roaches and rats had done. She cursed me violently, shook the bed mightily for me to come out and take my punishment, but I did not budge. I waited and waited until my mother had worn herself out, vowing that I would sleep under the bed, beneath her snoozing body, if necessary. This worked that time and a second time. But the third time I dived under the bed, she ripped off the blankets, sheets, and pillows then heaved the mattress from the bed, revealing my scrawny body lying belly down on the cold, wooden floor beneath the metal frame. Then she split it apart to get to me. I shouted and squirmed, and just as I was pushing myself from beneath the frame of the bed, my mother dropped it on my right foot. Perhaps it was an accident, but it hurt nonetheless.

"Aaaaaaaaaaaaaaaa!"

I bawled in agony, the weight of the metal frame mashing the blood and the bone in my foot. My mother continued to beat me with a belt on my arms, on my back, on my legs as I writhed in pain with the bed on my foot.

As she beat me, I mentally escaped into the living room and listened to the television news. I heard unfamiliar names like "Vietnam," "Watergate," and "Patty Hearst," and so I flipped channels in my brain to something familiar and safe like *Schoolhouse Rock, Soul Train,* or *American Bandstand.* As she beat me and yelled "You gonna be good? You gonna be good?" I focused on the words in the opening of the 23rd Psalm that we heard in church, which my mother had told me to recite whenever I was in trouble: "The Lord is my shepherd; I shall not want. . . ." Then I switched to the lyrics of the one song that spoke to me more than any others as a kid—Billie Holiday's "God Bless the Child." *Maybe, Kevin, the music will save you.* The whipping carried on until my mother wore herself out. Finally, the bed beating was over.

This was not the last whooping that I received from my mother, but it is the one that has stayed with me most vividly. That beating left me shell-shocked, wary, stunted, and traumatized, scared not only of her more than ever before, but also of the world. It was then that I began to think: *I hate you, Ma. I hate you! I hope you die! I wish you would have given me away at birth!* But I loved her, too. I felt like a prisoner with a life sentence in my own home.

11

The library

ma-dukes took me to the greenville public library in jersey city, new jersey—where i was pimp-smacked into life—

ONE SATURDAY morning a naked orange sun rose outside our windows. My mother shocked me into consciousness as she always did, barking my name—"Ke-vin!" I rubbed crust from my eyes, unpeeled my blanket, and slid my feet into slippers so that I could go relieve myself in the bathroom.

But today, my desolate eight-year-old world would experience something new.

"We're going to the library to get library cards," my mother said as she removed my plate of half-eaten grits, scrambled eggs, and bacon from the kitchen table.

I was thrilled and confused.

"Ma, what is a library, what's a library card?"

"It's a place with lots of books for smart kids like you, Kevin. With the card you can take books from the library and read them, then bring the books back."

I was beyond ecstatic. I loved reading and learning new words and my mother incessantly asked me to read and pronounce words. In school I breezed through the work from grade to grade because my mother had prepared me so well.

"You gotta go further in school than I did. I only got an eighth-grade education. I ain't book smart like you is," my mother said to me more times than I could count.

In my mind, my mother was the smartest person I knew because she'd taught me everything that I knew and fought hard for me to go to "better schools" that would teach me a lot and prepare me for life.

"You gonna have a good job when you grow up because you know how to read and write and do math. A lot of people ain't smart as you. Your grandfather Pearlie had a second- or third-grade education 'fore he died. Your grandmother Lottie can't read or write nothin'. She just touches the pen tip with her finger when it time for her to sign her name to something. Mean she approve what she 'spose to be signing."

I loved my mother's stories—no matter how regularly she told them. I was enchanted by this land she had come from, South Caro-lina—Down South—with its peculiar institutions and accents and its mystical superstitions and the tales of hunger and poverty. So when my mother told me that we were going to the library, I thought of her stories and the stories I learned in school. In those stories, I left be-hind my sadness and loneliness.

My mother and I left our red-brick building at 232 Dwight Street and hiked along Bergen Avenue, past empty-eyed winos and drug ad-dicts, past burnt-out buildings and turned-over garbage cans, past tossed, empty containers of Kentucky Fried Chicken and McDon-ald's, past discarded heroin needles and sneakers hanging from the wires of telephone poles, past neck-rolling, gum-smacking Black and Puerto Rican women in slippers and hair rollers, past children run-ning after the ice-cream truck and old Black and Puerto Rican men sitting on plastic and wooden crates, some gawking and whistling at my mother in ways that made me furious.

At the intersection of Bergen Avenue and Kennedy Boulevard, my mother held my right hand hard as we waited for the light to turn so we could cross the boulevard to the Jersey City Public Library—the Greenville Branch.

Inside, the size of the library enthralled me. Books were everywhere. The library quickly became as important to me as the corner candy store. An older White lady with glasses gliding down her teeny, sharply pointed nose greeted my mother and me and smiled.

"Welcome to the Greenville Public Library. Is this your first time?"

"Yes," my mother said. "We here to get library cards for me and my son."

"That would be just fine. Always good to see a parent and a child get library cards together."

With that the librarian passed my mother papers "to fill out for you and your son." My mother jotted our names and address and birth dates on the paper. For the first time, I saw when my mother was born: 1943. I counted in my head as fast as I could and realized that my mother, in this year 1974, was thirty-one years old. That age was mad distant to mine, and I wondered if my mother was a senior citizen or even a dinosaur.

After my mother finished, the librarian went to an odd-looking contraption and stuck small pieces of periwinkle-blue cardboard inside. The machine made a cranking racket, like the coughing car engines on our block. The librarian took the cards from the machine and carefully placed them in miniature, yellow envelopes, wrote my mother's name on one and mine on another, and then said, "Now you are ready to check out books."

I practically ran myself out of my sneakers, I was that eager to get started. My mother grabbed me by the arm as I headed the wrong way—to the adult section.

"Over there, boy!" My mother pointed to an area highlighted with large, tablet-like letters: "FOR CHILDREN." I wanted to stay with my mother in the adult section. I could see her through a glass window that separated our sections, sitting down and reading *The Jersey Journal* newspaper, which is all that she would read each time we hit up the library. My mother loved newspapers.

Over the next four years, I got lost in the Greenville Public Library, my appetite for knowledge as immense as the Grand Canyon—the image of which was Scotch-taped to a wall in the Children's Room. I read about the history of baseball and football, beginning my life-long love of sports. I read about magic and inventions, and became fascinated with mystery and intrigue, building and exploring. I stud-ied books about visual artists like Salvador Dalí, whose melting, sur-real sketches revived my ambition to draw pictures, which I had been doing exceptionally well since kindergarten. I browsed books about the weather, about old-school Hollywood actors and actresses like Clark Gable and Greta Garbo, and dreamed of being both a weather-man and the star in my own movies.

I used my library card with such frequency that it became soiled and tattered. I checked out and devoured books at our school li-brary at P.S. 38, too. I could not get enough of reading, and learn-ing. I would read and analyze the signs on buses, the graffiti art on boarded-up building shells. I perused *The Jersey Journal* newspaper with my mother. I was engrossed by the pamphlets about the end of the world that the Jehovah's Witnesses would give us whenever my mother let them in for a spell. I read the endless mailings from the two churches that we attended—Reverend Ike's in New York City and Reverend Skinner's Deliverance Center in Newark, New Jersey. My nappy head was an overfull piñata—filled with words and pic-tures both real and imagined, and clobbered repeatedly by competing questions, and fears.

By age eleven I had exhausted the children's section of the library, and my mother relented and permitted me to wander the adult area. I was not looking for anything in particular, but one title leapt out at me from the shelves: *For Whom the Bell Tolls.*

I had watched a movie with that title one weekend on television starring Gary Cooper. Did the book steal that title from the movie? It was a thick book, old and dusty, the writer named Ernest Heming-way. I had never heard of him before, but something told me to check this book out.

Over the course of two or three months I read *For Whom the Bell Tolls* with dedication. I struggled through the story of war and romance in Spain and worked through the occasional Spanish words, but I grasped enough of *For Whom the Bell Tolls* that it liberated my imagination in a transcendent way.

When I finished, I wanted to keep the book forever and to sleep in my folding bed with it. Never before had I been so challenged and inspired by a book. Never before had I been so curious about an author. Never before was I in such a hurry to go back to the library, to look through the *Encyclopedia Britannica* as we had been taught to do in school, to find out more about this man "Ernest Hemingway."

I was captivated by his escapades. The bullfights in Spain. The fishing in Cuba. The house in Key West, Florida. I had not known that such a man could exist. I was envious of his wondrous life. Only ambiguously did I catch that he had died by suicide, stemming from depression, and I elbowed that away. Thus it was there, in the hush of the library in Jersey City—an urban environment that otherwise strangled and entrapped me, and which I only escaped by going Down South every few years—that I came alive unexpectedly and magically to a universe of freedom and limitless possibilities—simply because I had taken out this one book and gotten to know this one writer.

I want to be a writer. The idea took root and grew. I had never before felt anything this sure or this right. *Like Ernest Hemingway, I am going to be a writer.* I did not dare share this decision with my mother, or my Aunt Cathy, or my cousin Anthony, for fear that they—my closest relatives—would mock me or call me "crazy." Nor did I reveal this to my teachers or classmates or the boys in my 'hood. I did not want to be told that it would never happen, that boys like me could not have such dreams.

It was my secret. From that eleventh year of my life through my high-school graduation at eighteen I read writer after writer. If I could not physically leave my hometown, or escape the numbing sensation of being trapped in a concrete box, well at least my mind could be free to go wherever a book or play or poem took me. I read S. E. Hinton's *The Outsiders*, the short stories of Edgar Allan Poe, the plays and sonnets of William Shakespeare, Charles Dickens's *Great Expectations*, George Eliot's *Silas Marner*, Geoffrey Chaucer's *The Canterbury Tales*, Voltaire's *Candide*, and the poetry of Emily Dickinson. And with each sentence or paragraph or phrase read and reread, with each page flipped—one piece of literature after another completed—a budding satisfaction blossomed in my heart, an exhilaration that yelled: *I want to be a writer!* Me—a Black boy—a man-child with no father and no money; a dude who walked with his head bowed, eyes looking down at the broken-glass and dog-mess ground, hands buried in the front pockets of his pants, who kicked rocks and empty soda cans down the mean streets of Jersey City. I now carried the dream with me everywhere. I held on to it as if it were life itself. It was something for me to believe in, even as I doubted myself and wondered, over and over, if I would live to age fifteen, to eighteen, to twenty-one, to thirty. Those books, those readings, those many words gave me a faint hope that some other life and some other world were possible, if I could just hold on—

12

Work

all I want is the opportunity to have an opportunity

MY MOTHER and Aunt Cathy constantly worked, but we were poor. We were so poor, in fact, that whenever my mother and I walked from our apartment at 232 Dwight Street to the local grocer up the block on Jackson Avenue, her blues song-and-dance to the White man butcher was "Please give me a dollar's worth of baloney, and slice it uh li'l thicker—*please*." It felt like we were Black beggars—open palms pleading for extra food from this butcher with huge, meaty forearms.

My mother made sure that we never starved. We were damn near close, but we always had food. Sometimes it was merely a baloney sandwich spoon-licked with mayonnaise or mustard and a can of soda each.

In order to make ends meet, Aunt Cathy and my mother took any work that they could get, penciling in application after application, double underlining "HELP WANTED" ad after "HELP WANTED" ad in *The Jersey Journal*. Their backs, legs, and feet were knotted from forty hours per week on assembly lines as they boxed pencils or pieced together radio parts. They sat humiliated and disrespected as minimum-wage attendants on school buses filled with rowdy ghetto kids. Their lives and work options matched their education levels and skills, which were cruelly limited because of their childhood poverty, back in the day, Down South—

The first job my mother had was at the age of eight in a field picking someone else's cotton. She was a pretty little chocolate girl working side by side with neighbors and kinfolk and strangers the age of her parents, and her grandparents, and her late great-grandparents. All were engaged in a poor people's campaign to make something from nothing. They awakened each day while God's door was still painted black. My mother often recounted how grueling the work was. The sun chewed ya up and spit ya out like a stale piece of tobacco. They worked like machines, these black brown caramel red yellow children of da Lawd, a cotton sack with a strap around their shoulders. Row by row they went, bent over like they was 'bout to eat the earth, plucking blossomed cotton, as many as each hand could carry, then tossing the harvest into a sack. South Carolina Geechees by accent and birth, cotton pickers by profession, these black brown caramel red yellow children of da Lawd got paid by how much they pulled that day. The White folks never really paid them much for what they did. They could do that because they had the power, and the colored folks, as my mother called Blacks, had nothing. Nope, there was no choice. What little money these cotton pickers made would be spent at the stores owned by the same White folks who had them slogging in the fields.

That is why my mother, Aunt Birdie, and Aunt Cathy wanted to escape from that. By the time that they were teenagers, the three sisters had become "the help" just as my grandmother Lottie had been, human robots—*yes suh no suh yes ma'am no ma'am*—in the homes of the local Whites. They did not want to be stuck in that place for the rest of their lives, even though the notion of leaving South Carolina—and their families—terrified them. But they also knew cousins who had kicked fear in the groin, got on a Greyhound bus, and journeyed up north to New Jersey and New York, where there were opportunities for Black people like them. They had heard tall tales of Black people in fur coats driving elegant cars and eating the finest foods there. If they worked hard enough, if they saved enough money, they reckoned that they could do the same.

But my mother and aunts needed a multipart plan. They'd heard reports of rich White people in Miami hiring young Black women from Southern states like South Carolina to toil for them in what were called "sleep-in jobs": domestic workers who lived with their employers. It was resolved that my mother and Aunt Birdie, the two older sisters, would go to Florida, hustle mad hard, save money, then come back to South Carolina to get my Aunt Cathy, before heading north for good. Aunt Cathy could not go to Miami because she was still a minor, only seventeen.

When they arrived in Miami in 1962, my mother was half-past eighteen and my Aunt Birdie a quarter past nineteen. The two sisters found a room to rent in the Black part of Miami called "Colored Town." They worked and lived there about a year, long enough to earn money to go up north. Before heading up north, my mother returned home to South Carolina to work an additional ten months while Aunt Birdie went ahead to pave the way in New Jersey. Miami had been their test run to prove to themselves they could be away from their mother and father and from the backwoods of South Carolina and fly on their own. Then they did it.

Aunt Birdie came back in early 1964 to take my mother and Aunt Cathy to Jersey City. When they arrived, a mass hysteria was gripping the region. My mother thought there was an invasion from outer space, because she kept hearing, "The Beatles are coming! The Beatles are coming!"

An older cousin named Al Wright already lived up there. Even though they also had many cousins in New York City, Jersey City was not as big and bullying. But they did work in and around New York City, in the homes of wealthy White people. One White man wearing only a bathrobe surprised my mother one day as she scrubbed and cleaned in his Scarsdale home in Westchester County. He asked her to sit awhile in the living room, and when she did so, he opened his legs wide to reveal naked private parts. In complete shock, my mother managed to get out of there without being further sexually assaulted. She never returned to that job.

The three Powell sisters got a single room together in a rooming house. Many of the folks in the Black section of Jersey City—"The Hill"—rented out rooms to new arrivals from South Carolina, North Carolina, Georgia, and Florida. Working very hard, but far too poor to afford their own rooms or apartments, the three young women shared not only a single room but also a single bed so that they could save the few coins that they earned.

This was why my mother never stopped working. This was why she told me, every year of my life, that I must go away as she had at age eighteen, to make a life for myself, because being eighteen meant that I was grown. This was why one day, when my cousin Anthony and I were eight, my mother and Aunt Cathy took us to the local grocery store and told us matter-of-factly that we were not coming home with them; that we were going to stay for a couple of hours and bag groceries with the other little boys. We had to work. Instinctively Anthony and I knew it was time, just as our mothers had known when they were little girls.

Bagging groceries led, a couple of years later, to the job that every boy in our community wanted: delivering *The Jersey Journal* newspaper door to door. My paper route was partially in a Black 'hood and partially in a White 'hood. Every paperboy had his own pushcart, and I took care of mine with immense pride. I hand-wiped it with a cloth and soap inside and out at least twice a week. Immediately after school, I began my route. The office manager threw a bundle of newspapers at workers, and we'd have to carefully separate the papers without tearing a single one. I organized the papers in my cart neatly by the order of the blocks on my route sheet.

In my first two weeks on the job, some customers—especially the White ones—would yell and curse me for being late or for the way that I handled their newspapers. I felt that some of the White customers did not like me because I was Black, unlike their previous newspaper boys. But the majority of my customers—Black and White and a few Latinos—came to hold me in high esteem. I mastered how to work each block with speed and efficiency, literally running back and forth across the street as if I were a sprinter in the Olympics. People noticed my effort, and I began signing up new customers and winning bonuses.

I was proud of myself, and whenever I had a spare moment, I would nourish my love of knowledge by reading *The Jersey Journal*. I was dumbfounded by the articles about politicians getting busted, arrested for crimes, and going to jail, and I was mesmerized by the academic and athletic achievements of youth like me. I could not imagine that I could be in *The Jersey Journal* myself, because I felt that I was not good enough at anything.

No matter, my mother was proud of me. She bragged about how her son went to school every day, received excellent grades, had a job after school, and was not going to wind up on the corner like the other boys in our neighborhood. Through my reading and through hard work, I began to gain an identity, a sense of purpose. I had money in my pocket. I was able to help my mother buy my yearly school clothes and footwear, and like most of my male friends I blew as much of my money as possible collecting stacks of baseball cards, or in the pinball and video game machines that seemed to be in every candy store. "Save your money," my mother scolded me on multiple occasions. I was forming a work habit that would define my life, but I was also acquiring a recklessness with money that would come to nearly destroy me.

13

Aunt Birdie

what happens
when a woman
dares to split
her lips and use
the tongue
the universe
and the ancestors
gave her

MY AUNT Birdie Lou Powell was always in my life, but also mad invisible. She and my mother were the best of friends and the tightest of sisters, but they were also hostile enemies and hyper-competitive rivals, depending on the day, the month, the year, and their most recent dispute. For as long as I could remember, their convos would start pleasantly enough then turn into the twisted sister version of *Family Feud*.

"Shirley, you always got somethin' smart to say. Why you so mean, girl?"

"Hell with you, Ditty! I don't need you to tell me nothin'. You need to mind your own damn business, heffa!"

Ditty was Aunt Birdie's nickname. And the sisters threw "heffa" and other insults back and forth perfectly naturally. Both were fiercely independent and wanted to control every aspect of their lives. Both had been abandoned by the fathers of their children. My Aunt Birdie had also been violently abused. Both labored extremely hard, saved every nickel and dime they could get, and resolved not to be destroyed by poverty. But after my Aunt Cathy came north, my mother quickly became closer to her.

Perhaps this was because whatever my mother said, my Aunt Cathy did. My mother talked to my Aunt Cathy any way that she wanted to—she was the mean one, and Aunt Cathy the nice one. My mother loved being the boss, loved shouting orders. My Aunt Birdie loved being a boss, too, and she wanted far more than what my mother and Aunt Cathy settled for in Jersey City. My mother and Aunt Cathy seemed to resign themselves to being poor—to bare survival—while my Aunt Birdie decided that she wanted to win.

Whereas my mother and Aunt Cathy accepted that they would never finish their education, Aunt Birdie got her GED, went to nursing school, and used the money that she earned as a nurse to complete a four-year degree at Jersey City State College and become a schoolteacher.

In the early 1970s, where my mother and Aunt Cathy fought battles royal with their tenement-building superintendents, Aunt Birdie became one of the only women to be the super of a building in Jersey City. Where my mother and Aunt Cathy were content to rent one apartment after another, Aunt Birdie bought house after house, supremely determined to be the owner and landlady herself. Where my mother and Aunt Cathy were limited by the fears that they had brought with them in those cardboard suitcases from the backwoods of South Carolina, Aunt Birdie lived a life of daring— flying on planes here, there, and everywhere, learning how to drive, owning her own car, and unafraid of new experiences. And where my mother and Aunt Cathy sent my cousin Anthony and me to the best public schools that they could, Aunt Birdie busted barriers and sent her daughter, Monique, to private schools for much of her early education.

"Birdie crazy, you know," my mother said, filled with jealousy.

"She be doing a lot of things you ain't 'spose to be doing," my Aunt Cathy agreed.

"Humph. That heffa know planes be fallin' outta the sky, but she run to get on a plane any chance she get. Actin' like she White or somethin'. Not me. Them planes is dangerous. They be crashin', and people be hijackin' them . . . them foreigners," my mother would say.

"You know she got a gun, too, right?" my Aunt Cathy weighed in.

"Yeah, she sick in the head. What a woman having a gun for, actin' like she a man?" A volcanic laugh erupted from my mother, hot and full of fire. "Aba-goddamn. Yeah, Ditty ain't in her right mind."

"She sure ain't," said Aunt Cathy.

"And I bet she's been on birth control pills after she done had Monique. I ain't messing with no birth control pills. Ditty need to be like us and leave them no-good men alone, like Monique's father," my mother said, in a tone of self-righteous indignation.

At that point, my mother and Aunt Cathy would sit silent at the kitchen table for a spell, having exhausted this particular conversation about Aunt Birdie, which they had repeated for years.

Yet I was riveted by Aunt Birdie's magnetic personality. I never got to know her as well as I knew my Aunt Cathy—my mother made sure of that. But, whenever she was around, I stared at her and when she caught me looking, she'd smile and wink slyly, as if she knew that her grand escapades excited me. She liberated my imagination in the same way that reading did, and made me wonder, as I watched airplanes glide above our ghetto clouds as a child, if Aunt Birdie was on one of them. Aunt Birdie's life offered me a small opening into the larger world.

14

John Travolta

heck, I wanted to be a big man
I wanted to be a star—
and I loved the way them stars' hair
looked in them magazines and in them movies
and what not

AS A CHILD I was unapologetically addicted to television shows and movies and I could never get enough. They showed me lives of people who were very different from me, and they transformed my humdrum existence. Our undersized black-and-white television set, with its big circular knobs and two bent and broken antennas, got only about half the channels with any frequency. And because it was so small, it was right there in childhood that my eyes were damaged, making me permanently near-sighted.

My Saturday lineup featured *Schoolhouse Rock*, *Soul Train*, and *American Bandstand*. On Sundays when we did not go to church I watched *Davey and Goliath*, *The Little Rascals*, *Laurel and Hardy*, *The Bowery Boys*—and probably every Abbott and Costello flick ever produced. I inhaled every episode of my favorite sitcoms, *Happy Days*, *Laverne & Shirley*, and *Three's Company*, the triple threat of blockbuster hits on Tuesday nights. I wanted to be like the Fonz—able to snap my fingers and to make girls dive from the sky into my bony arms. But my spirit was more in tune with that of Charlie Brown: insecure and misunderstood, occupying space but never fitting in anywhere. My mind filled with wicked sexual daydreams and night dreams about Laverne and Shirley, about Chrissy and Janet on *Three's Company.* To me these were the most beautiful women on earth and I desired them. I stared at the TV screen any time they came on, imagining myself, at age eleven, twelve, thirteen, fourteen, kissing, cuddling, and making sweet and endless love to them.

I felt similarly about the women I watched in movies—Marilyn Monroe, or Ginger Rogers, or Ingrid Bergman, or Katharine Hepburn, or Natalie Wood, or Barbra Streisand. I thought that these women represented God's bright and shining examples of infinite beauty and class. I wanted these women—or someone like them—and I was mesmerized by their talent, their grace, and their self-assurance. In my child's mind I imagined that they saw me, too, and would come through the screen to press their mouths against mine just as they did with their screen partners like Fred Astaire, Humphrey Bogart, Clark Gable, James Stewart, James Dean, or Kris Kristofferson.

I wanted to be those men: fearless, heroic, resolute, dangerous, unpredictable—epitomes of manhood. I wanted their might, their minds, and their hair, flawlessly combed back like a majestic and royal crown. Yes, I wanted that kind of hair very badly. I fretted daily about why mine was mad nappy, not curly or wavy. I secretly hated on Kiki at P.S. 38 because he had good hair: untamed, enormous loops of shimmering curls that he appeared to shake on purpose, knowing that the girls got weak-kneed at the sight of the pretty boy with the good hair bobbing and weaving down the hall.

One day in late 1977, when I was eleven, a phenomenon called John Travolta, in a movie called *Saturday Night Fever,* shook America and rocked my world. Because of my mother I had already developed a love of music: Motown and Stax Records, James Brown, Diana Ross, Sam Cooke, Linda Ronstadt, Stevie Wonder, Elton John,

Donna Summer, Earth, Wind & Fire, the locked and loaded harmonies of 1950s doo-wop, and the unfiltered, soul-busting spirituals of the church. The money that I earned from my six-day-a-week newspaper route permitted me to go to Sound Machine on Journal Square and purchase my own 45 records. And boy did I. Chic, the Jacksons, GQ, KC and the Sunshine Band—anything that I could play on our Green Stamp record player.

But Travolta Fever was something new. Disco made me feel as if we were one nation under a funky groove. Travolta had captivated me as Vinnie Barbarino on the TV show *Welcome Back, Kotter*, and was now at the epicenter of this music and dance trend.

I wanted to be John Travolta! I pored over every magazine article about him, studied any interview that he gave, bought dollar books that alleged to be his "official biography" or "authorized story." I was delirious when I discovered that he was from New Jersey like me.

I went to an Asian jewelry store on Journal Square and acquired as many fake gold necklaces as I could, and at home slowly threaded them around my neck as Travolta did in *Saturday Night Fever*. I stood in front of the bathroom mirror and tried with all my might to squeeze and fold my chin into a cleft like Travolta's—until my lower face throbbed in agony. I wore my shirts open like his to reveal my chains and my embarrassingly scrawny chest. I got five pairs of polyester, multicolored, Swedish knit pants to match my five shirts. I crooned and danced to the banging vocals and beats of the *Fever* soundtrack, doing my best to emulate Travolta's choreography in the movie. Finally, I went and copped a few tools that I was convinced would transform my nappy hair into the good hair of John Travolta: a jar of Dax Wave and Groom, a tough-as-nails brush, and a black doo rag or "wave cap."

Once I'd scrubbed my hair thoroughly, I lowered my paws into the Dax waving cream and generously applied it into my naps. Then I took the brush—the kind that a horse trainer might use—and pressed the bristles deep into my scalp—back and forth. Lastly, I donned the doo rag every night, securing it snugly on my head. I awoke most mornings dizzy, my head pounding and a sharp line knifed into

my forehead from the tightly wound doo rag. My hair did get a little curly, a little wavy. But the grease smelled funny, and anytime I
touched or scratched my head, my fingernails were left with black debris beneath them.

A few months after *Saturday Night Fever*, John Travolta's second
major motion picture, *Grease*, premiered. Unfortunately, the only theater playing the movie in Hudson County was in neighboring Bayonne, New Jersey, a city that a lot of Black people avoided, unless they
lived or worked there. But I was determined.

"Ma, can we PLEASE go see *Grease*, please?"

"Bubba, we ain't going all the way to Bayonne for no daggone
movie!"

"But Ma, it ain't just any movie. It's a John Travolta movie. I gotta
see it, Ma, you don't understand."

"Boy, you act like them buses run all night out there. We can't get
stuck in Bayonne for some dang movie."

But I was unyielding, nudging my mother from sunup to sun-
down as the release date for *Grease* approached. Ultimately I broke
her down and we rode the Bergen Avenue bus to its last stop—right
at the city line between Jersey City and Bayonne. Then we took another bus along Bayonne's Broadway to the old DeWitt Theater, an
antique fortress of a building. There, we stood in line with other
moviegoers—many of them children with their parents like me—but
we were the only Black people. I did not care. Inside we grabbed a
box of popcorn and shared a bottle of soda, and when the lights went
down, there he was—

He had the slicked-back, ducktail hairstyle, the gangsta strut,
the black leather jacket, the high-water black jeans, the penny loafer
shoes, the cigarette hanging like a lollipop from his mouth. I fell in
love with Sandy Olsson, Olivia Newton-John's character, who now
replaced the female stars I'd previously sweated. I drooled over her
voice, her stringy blond hair, her Ivory-soap skin, and her aqua-blue
eyes. When Danny and Sandy reunited in the movie's climax, I un-
derwent a sort of ecstasy.

When the movie let out, I wanted to run out into the streets, but my mother immediately returned me to reality and informed me we were stuck, because of that "damn John Travolta." There were no buses at that hour running to or from Bayonne. We lingered and prayed for a long time for a taxi, hoping that no one would bother or attack us for being in a White community after dark. Finally, we did get a cabdriver, a bearded, cranky White man who was not pleased that we were going to the ghetto hub of Jersey City. I did not care. I was the luckiest boy on the planet. I had seen my hero John Travolta as I had never seen him before.

15

White people and my new White neighborhood

and when we finally moved out of the ghetto
around white folks
you felt good
we was movin' up
and flying like birds released from their mother's grip for the first time

WHEN ANTHONY and I were nearly thirteen, my mother and Aunt Cathy had had enough of 232 Dwight Street, but where could we afford to go? It was not like our financial circumstances changed much year to year. We were poor people with measly wages, welfare checks, food stamps, and free government cheese. Our mothers scoured *The Jersey Journal* for apartments, circling and double-underlining anything that looked promising. Yes, wherever my mother was going Aunt Cathy was going, too. That was how we rolled, together, a small but tight family.

They finally discovered something on a corner of Bergen Avenue right in the heart of "The Hill," a decent enough red-brick structure. But my mother and my Aunt Cathy did not like one particular thing about the area: a gang of Black boys, about the same age as Anthony and I—roughly twelve, thirteen, fourteen years old—were fixtures on that corner. My mother and Aunt Cathy were afraid of what would happen to Anthony and me if we found our way into that gang of boys.

Another option—dangerous in a different way—that my mother and Aunt Cathy felt they had to test was moving to an apartment building and a street, 56 Linden Avenue, in the White Greenville section of Jersey City. Anthony and I would have to transfer from Public School Number 38 to Public School Number 20, since that would be our new district. This would be the fourth grammar school that Anthony and I attended.

But why were we going to move around White people if they did not like us and my mother did not really like them? My mind flashed back to P.S. 38, a school on the other side of Kennedy Boulevard—the unofficial dividing line between the Black and White communities—which Anthony and I had entered at the age of nine. We had been trying to get into that school for a few years, but were put on a long waiting list. This is why we attended P.S. 34 for one year, in the third grade, after leaving P.S. 41. When we finally got into P.S. 38 we had classmates of many different backgrounds—Black, White, Latino, Asian, and Middle Eastern. As most children did, I made friends fast—not thinking about race, culture, or skin color.

My friend Ralphie was Italian; George was Irish; the Noriega sisters were Puerto Rican; Manny was Filipino; and Cleetus Jenkins was "mixed"—his father was Black and his mother was White. It didn't matter; these were my friends.

But almost as soon as the academic year began that September, we children were told not to go outside during the lunch hour, because "the BONES" were coming to protest our school. We ignored the warnings to stay inside and went out into the fenced courtyard area anyway.

On the other side of the fence, a gang of White boys—much older and bigger than any of us—ran toward us, throwing rocks, sticks, and empty glass soda bottles at us. We screamed and ran, even though some of us wanted to fight them back. The White gang targeted those of us who were Black, yelling abuse like "nigger," which was painful to hear.

Cleetus Jenkins was standing a few feet away from me when he was struck dead in the face with part of a brick tossed through a huge opening in the fence. He fell backwards to the ground, crying hysterically, blood spurting from the area right above his left eye socket. Some of the angry White boys jeered and applauded: "We got that nigger good!" Was Cleetus Black like me, if his momma was White? Soon the police arrived and the White boys fled fast. After that, police were always at the school.

I learned that BONES meant "Beat On Niggers Every Second." There were rumors of other clashes between older Black boys from Jersey City and these White boys who terrorized Black children. I had nightmares about Cleetus getting smashed with that brick, of his White mother coming to school and saying, "They're so dumb they don't realize they hit one of their own with that brick." The episode also made me think of Martin Luther King, Jr., how he was killed by a White man, for fighting for Black people. I was suddenly afraid of White people.

Race consciousness had not really been a part of my mentality until the BONES gang attacked us. After that, I paid closer attention to the conversations between my mother and my Aunt Cathy. I noticed how they referred to Whites in public as "W people," or whispered "White people," never saying the word "White" aloud. Behind closed doors my mother referred to White folks as "crackers." We never had White people in our apartment except for a repairman, a social worker from the welfare agency, or a police officer called in because we thought someone had broken into our home. I never went into the residences of White people, was never invited, in fact. My school friend Ralphie, the Italian-American, would bring me to his side door sometimes after school, and that was as far as I ever got. His mother or father never invited me in, and there was an unspoken agreement between Ralphie and me that the matter should never be broached.

My mother and I watched two television programs together during these years that affected us profoundly. First was *The Jeffersons*, the sitcom. Whenever George Jefferson called a White person a "honky," my mother erupted in laughter. She laughed so hard she cried, tears filling her eyes. I thought about how my mother said White people in South Carolina labeled Blacks every kind of horrible name imaginable, and how Blacks had to accept it. So maybe this was my mother's revenge, to hear George Jefferson say for her what she could not say herself.

The second TV show was the eight-part miniseries *Roots*, which blew me away in its depiction of the scope of what had happened to Blacks. I knew that Black people had been slaves, because it was casually and quickly mentioned in our history schoolbooks—a random paragraph here or there. But until *Roots*, I'd had no idea how we got to America and how we were treated on those plantations. Yet I was still too young to fully grasp the magnitude of the effects of slavery on Black people, on White people, on America.

Nonetheless, two scenes from *Roots* would stay with me for years to come: Kunta Kinte's hands and body suspended from a rope as he was lashed savagely with a whip and told to say his new name of "Toby," and later, when his daughter Kizzy, as a bent, elderly woman, hawked a wad of spit into the water cup of a White woman she had grown up with as a child who acted like she did not know her.

My mother and I did not say much about watching *Roots* together, nor did we ever discuss the series (or, for that matter, *The Jeffersons*). We went on with our lives. But we felt a mistrust of Whites from our lives in the South and the North. Whites seemed to own and control everything; Blacks seemed to have nothing and were dependent on Whites, or the government, or both, merely to survive. And in most stories I heard about Black experiences with White people, Whites were extremely cruel. In the safety of our own company:

"Them crackers ain't nothin', man. Always tellin' a nigga what to do."

"Yeah, they run the world and they sure want to run us into the ground, too. White man talk about I can't get no raise unless I put in my work *and* work more hours. He already paying me peanuts while he ain't doing nothin' all day 'cept acting like he the big man and I am just his nigga."

"Boy, don't you ever mess with no White girls, ya hear. Ain't no reason for that. They don't want you and you should not want them."

"White folks sure different than us colored folks. Humph. They food taste different, they smell different, and they act like they know everything. They sure wanna be the boss all the time. Act like niggas ain't got no sense at all."

This emerging awareness of race—of the inability to erase or obscure my Black flesh—and my fear of Whites made me dread the April day in 1979 when we were to move from the Black ghetto of Jersey City to the White neighborhood near the border with Bayonne, New Jersey. The movers lugged our furniture and few meager belongings into 56 Linden Avenue, a light sandy-brown building with four floors. The street was sandwiched between Ocean Avenue and Garfield Avenue and, as far as I could see, was the cleanest block we'd ever lived on. I was also instantly struck by how much prettier and larger the houses were, how much more alive and greener the trees and bushes seemed.

Aunt Cathy and Anthony had an apartment on the first floor, and my mother and I settled into apartment 303 on the third floor. Soon after we had moved in, I went out into the street to play baseball.

I loved baseball, especially my New York Yankees. In 1977 and 1978 I was euphoric over them winning back-to-back World Series. I would often rush home from school to watch afternoon games on Channel 11. The Yankee announcers Phil Rizzuto, Bill White, and Frank Messer became like family members to me: I knew their personalities and voices and banter so well. I had dreams of playing Little League baseball like other boys in Jersey City but could not afford the uniform, baseball glove, or spikes needed to participate. I did eventually play—not very well—in the Babe Ruth League and later in high school for a brief time, but much of my ball playing was in games of stickball or punch ball.

I had noticed some White dudes playing stickball on a wall in front of the brown house two doors up from my building on Linden Avenue and figured I could do what I had been doing for years in other parts of Jersey City: just walk up and introduce myself and join the game. So I did.

There was a boy name Goldie, with a blond buzz cut. There were twin brothers—one skinny and one chubby—named Donny and Joey. Goldie, Donny, and Joey were playing around with a rubber ball and stick, deciding when to start up a game. When I introduced myself, the White guys were cool, although I could detect Goldie was uncomfortable with me. He was about my age and we were both older than Donny and Joey. Goldie had this aura of superiority about him, of being the boss, and he quickly determined it was time to play.

"Joey, you and me, and, Donny, you and the nigger."

My Dumbo-like ears were set afire with rage and shock. Hearing that word coming from Goldie's mouth, the mouth of a White boy my age and my size, was infuriating. I was primed to explode.

Goldie took stock of my facial reaction and of my body language, so for good measure, he said it again.

"Donny, you and the nigger on the same side."

"What did you call me?" I asked, incredulous.

"You are a nigger, right?"

I grabbed the stick we were going to use from Donny and chased Goldie down the street to his house, threatening to kill him. Goldie made it safely into his front door and hid, a laughing coward, behind his mother. She stood between us staring at me and the stick with blue, unsympathetic eyes.

"He called me a 'nigger.' I did not do anything to him," I said, through tears.

His mother said, matter-of-factly, "Oh, he did not mean anything by that. You boys need to just go on and play."

I had no response. I did not know what to do with that so I let it go, and we did go on to play stickball. And soccer. And football— my cousin Anthony and I and our new White friends sometimes using parked cars as the sidelines in the street, sometimes playing in the dead of winter in the snow in the cemetery around the corner on Garfield Avenue. I just wanted to fit in with these White boys, and to not cause any trouble.

Thus I decided to be like the White boys. To walk like them and to talk like them. I had never heard Black people refer to themselves or each other as "cocksuckers" or "douche bags" and other foul insults, but this is what the White boys on the block said to each other. I had never seen Black people spit at each other, curse at their mothers and fathers—in public no less—and say such things as how much they hated their parents and wished them dead. But this is what some of these White boys on the block said to their parents.

No matter—I coveted their big, plush homes, and was embarrassed to live in our apartment building. I envied the way my White friends' hair could do all kinds of things that mine could not. I secretly lusted after their sisters, their female cousins, even some of their mothers, if they were relatively young. My heart mushroomed with pride the more the White dudes on the block began to trust and to accept me—whenever one of them said to me "You are not like the rest of *them*." No, I was not. I was not a "nigger." Although I had chased Goldie when he called me a "nigger," it had been both because I hated that word and because I did not consider myself like other Black folks. I never believed I fit into the ghetto, or that I belonged there. But did I truly belong in this White world either?

Because most of us on Linden Avenue were New York Yankees fans, we had extraordinary moments of bonding across racial lines. When Yankee catcher Thurman Munson crashed a plane that he was flying in between games in August of 1979, the boys on the block— White and Black—came together to grieve, to cry, and to express our shock that one of our heroes could be gone so young.

One day, my cousin Anthony and I were sitting on the steps of a Black church—one of the few in the area—at the end of Linden Avenue, at the corner of Ocean Avenue, talking about baseball. We heard a truck's wheels screeching down Ocean and turned to see it collide with a smaller truck crossing the intersection. The crash was so deafening that Anthony and I were immobilized with horror. When we could finally stand, we saw an older White man we knew in the smaller truck. He lived on Linden, and we jokingly referred to him as "Popeye" because he had so many tattoos and chunky biceps. We saw Popeye gasp his final breath of life and collapse backwards in his driver's seat.

The driver of the bigger truck stared into space, speechless, terror on his face. Soon Popeye's mixed-race family rushed into the street. Popeye's wife was Black and his children every shade of yellow, red, and brown. The police, fire engines, and ambulance soon arrived. There was no traffic light at this intersection of Ocean and Linden, and it was perilous. And now this White man was dead.

Anthony and I were so traumatized at the sight of seeing a man get killed in front of our thirteen-year-old eyes that we never discussed it again. Never. Nor did we come forward when Popeye's family asked residents in the area if they had witnessed the crash, even offering a reward. We did not say a word. My guilt at staying silent gave me nightmares where bags of blood hung above me and collapsed onto my face. I would awaken, covered with sweat and goose bumps on my arms and legs. But I was afraid, afraid to speak for a White man, and against another White man: afraid that Anthony and I would be hauled off to jail for saying we saw something.

16

Man-child

like billie you are
a field hand picking strange fruits
from those dead tree limbs

WORK WAS still very much a part of my life as I entered my teenage years. CETA summer jobs had been created, we heard through the grapevine, for "disadvantaged" kids like Anthony and me. CETA stood for Comprehensive Employment and Training Act. Anthony and I showed up for work in the early summer of 1979. We were among about thirty boys—thirteen, fourteen, fifteen years old—all Black like us. The job meet-up site was on Route 440 in Jersey City, near the weather-worn Roosevelt Stadium where Jackie Robinson had played his first professional game as a minor leaguer.

A potbellied, middle-aged White dude with a stern gaze and rugged manner welcomed us—sort of—to "man's work." He lipped and sucked hard on a cigarette, his rapidly blinking eyes examining the row of us lined up against a wall. We were nervous and happy to be there, but also terrified.

"You boys got lucky. Lot of kids like you wanted this here job this summer. Not that many jobs to go around, especially for people like you. But our mayor and the city and state trying to make sure every-one has an opportunity, ya understand?"

Some of us nodded timidly; others peered straight through the man, too shook to make direct eye contact; others looked at the ground or their sneakers. For some reason I was not afraid of this particular White man and looked him up and down and right in the eyes as he ambled back and forth—like a cop on his beat—in front of us.

"Now, this ain't easy work. This work ain't for any of you boys who like to act la-zy. We going out into the fields, to some of the nicest parts of Jersey City, to help beautify our city."

We boys were loaded like cargo into minivans and transported to "The Heights," or Jersey City Heights. The moment I recognized that we were in a majority White neighborhood, I got scared. There were ornery-acting teenage White boys, the kind who would belong to the BONES, heckling us.

We unloaded from the minivans and walked to an undeveloped vacant lot where grass and weeds grew neck-high. We were given "tools" with which to cut the high grass and weeds, but those tools were virtually ineffective. Most of us used only our hands. It was mis-erably hot and humid under the sun, but we boys chopped, cut, and pulled grass for hours, swept, shoveled, and picked up debris from the lot and the sidewalks. We were not happy. We said as much whenever the White boss man was nowhere to be found.

"These White people crazy! They take us ghetto niggas and bring us all the way out to their neighborhood to clean their streets but our streets look like a gutter."

"Yeah, you would never see them out here cleaning up dog mess the way we is doin' right now."

"Hell, nah, I ain't pickin' up no dog mess, nigga. That's yo' mom-ma's job. She and the boss man be doin' it in the minivan when you ain't lookin'!"

"Man, screw you! Yo' momma got a wooden leg and walk like she got a kickstand attached to her butt!"

"Yo momma so Black people think she the night sky with stars when she show her teeth."

As always when our playing of the dozens was getting good, the White boss man would show up to make sure we were working hard. For some reason he took a keen interest in me.

"Kevin Powell!"

"Yes, sir."

"I wanna see you right now!"

The other boys bowed their heads in unison as if in a church prayer and looked at their feet. Anxious that I was going to be the first to be fired, I followed the White man to one of the minivans and then he turned to speak with me.

"You ain't like the rest of these boys, Powell. I've been watching you, the way you work, and the way you speak. You are different and don't belong out here. We want you to work in the office back at the headquarters."

I did not know what to say. So I said what I thought I was supposed to say.

"I like working out here with the fellas, sir. I am fine right with them—"

The man studied me with a puzzled expression, poked the top of his head with his left index and middle fingers, rotated his neck to remove his cigarette, and then dribbled a string of corn-yellow saliva to the ground, right near my sneakered feet.

"Boy, what is wrong with you? We are trying to give you a promotion, an opportunity, and you telling me you don't want it. What kind of—"

He caught himself mid-sentence.

I now had a dilemma. If I took the promotion, the other boys, including my cousin Anthony, would regard me as being given special favors and treated better than them by these White people. But if I turned down the opportunity, these White people might view me as a problem, like I had a chip on my shoulder, as one mean White male teacher had said to me a lot at P.S. 38. Like I thought I was better than White people or something—or too dumb a "nigger" to see a great opportunity there in front of me. I decided to do it.

"Smart boy you are. When you report in tomorrow you will stay in the office when the others ship out. Won't it be great to spend part of your summer in an air-conditioned office?"

My mother was overjoyed about my promotion.

"Good! See, them White people like smart colored folks. I raised you right."

The next morning at the office a different White man greeted me and said I would be working with him directly. He was lanky, a bit younger than the dude who bossed us around in the field. He wore a shirt and tie, but said it was fine for me to continue to wear the yellow CETA T-shirt that they'd given us kid workers to wear. When it was time for the other boys to ship out, I avoided making eye contact with them, including my cousin Anthony, but I could hear what they were saying as they marched to the minivans.

"How this nigga get to stay in the office?"

"White man told him to stay. Gave him a new job. We kill ourselves in the hot sun and this kid gets to cool out in the AC."

With the boys gone, my new boss handed me paperwork, which I knocked out with ease. He praised me; his secretary did, too, and they both made it a point to show me off to every single White person who visited the office that day, and for the rest of that week. Meanwhile, the other boys were openly jealous of my new gig.

"Man, how much them White people paying you up in there?"

"Do they buy you lunch and everything?"

"You think you can get me a job in the office, too? I can sweep or mop or clean or whatever. Just help me get out of that hot sun."

It was a no-win situation. But the guilt of being in that air-conditioned office with these White people while the other Black boys labored and struggled in the scorching sun finally got to me.

"Sir, I don't want to work in this office anymore," I said, looking down at the floor tiles.

"I do not understand. Why not?" the White man asked, disbelief creasing the edges of his mouth.

"I don't know," I lied, still looking down, my back hunched, my skinny legs wobbly as Jell-O.

"Are you sure?" the man asked. His secretary was listening, too, and seemed disappointed.

"Yes, sir," I mumbled, barely audible.

After a long moment of quiet the White man said that I could return to the field with the other boys.

"You can finish today here then go back out tomorrow."

That was not good enough for me. I wanted to get away from these White people as fast as possible.

"Can I go out today, please, sir?"

He was silent again.

Then: "Yes," but he was no longer looking at me.

In a split I was in a minivan with another White man driving back to Jersey City Heights, to the field. The man never said a word to me, so I said nothing to him. In short order I was in the field with the other boys. They were surprised to see me.

"Man, why you back out here? They fired you from the office?"

"Nah, I asked to leave."

"Man, you crazy. Ain't this nigga crazy? Got a chance to work with the big White folks and he quit. Ain't that somethin'?"

I grimaced and cursed these Black boys on the inside, and started chopping at the high grass with my tool. I desperately wanted to flee from these Black boys and from the White people who bossed us around every single day.

◆

Near the end of my eighth-grade year at Public School Number 20, I had the second-highest grade average in my class—right behind a genius of a Black girl named Vivian. I had fought tooth and nail to get better grades than Vivian throughout the school year, but she was smarter than me. Vivian would give the valedictorian speech and I would give the salutatorian speech.

It was one of the best years I'd had in school since kindergarten. Except for jumping into that fight that belonged to my cousin Anthony, I did not have a single behavioral problem. My mother was shocked. Hell, I was shocked. No three-day suspensions. No principals telling my mother they would send to me a special school for "bad boys." No more physical beatings from my mother. Finally, I had outgrown her.

But when I realized I would have to be on stage to give my speech, I was frightened. The only other time that I had ever been on a stage was in the fourth grade at P.S. 38 when our school did an adaptation of the Broadway show *1776*. I had played Thomas Jefferson and had to speak and sing my lines. My mother and the audience could barely hear me. When the curtains opened and I saw the full auditorium, I became paralyzed. My embarrassment was made worse by the fact that the Black boy who played George Washington—named Anthony Washington—was beyond excellent, a natural-born stage performer. After that disaster I vowed never to set foot on a stage again, turned down every request for me to join school groups of any kind, and focused only on sports.

Yet I was excited, too, about giving my speech. Painstakingly, I wrote each word by hand—thinking long and hard about what I wanted to say. I had been told that I was not only speaking for myself but also for my classmates as we prepared for high school. So I talked about our future as teenagers, and about us as future leaders, as the future of America. I thanked our teachers and principal and vice principal, and our parents and our families.

On graduation day, my mother and Aunt Cathy could not have been prouder of my cousin Anthony and me. They'd never gotten high-school diplomas themselves, but we were now a step closer, and this was a big deal. As we paraded in our caps and gowns into the broiling and cramped auditorium on a sweltering June day in 1980,

I thought about how I, now age fourteen, was just four years away from being able to leave Jersey City. My mother had been telling me I would one day go to college since I was three or four years old.

When it was time for me to speak, I was mad nervous behind the wooden podium and my kneecaps clapped together repeatedly. I read my speech, scarcely peeping at the audience. I was shook, oh yes I was. But I was also determined not to botch it, and I did not. When I was done, there was thunderous applause. I was vindicated. Little did I know on that day in Jersey City that I would one day give speeches across America and even overseas; that public speaking would become as natural to me as breathing; that people would tell me that a speech I had given had touched their lives. I just knew that I was at long last heading to high school.

17

High school. And the police.

Will those dreams
I had as a child come
to pass Will I fall
through the sky
landing in a pit
of purple rats as
the apocalypse
loosens its belt
and beats the
pavement until
welts the size of
africa's left nostril
quake my puny
bones

I HATED HIGH school right from the beginning. When I set foot inside Academic High in September 1980, I was immediately turned off by the dullness of the grubby, bare-knuckled Ukrainian building that served as the makeshift home for the school. But my mother and Aunt Cathy—two single Black mothers raising Black boys alone—were determined that my cousin Anthony and I would go to the best public high school in Jersey City, and Academic—a magnet institution—was as good as it got.

Academic had only been around a few years, and applicants had to navigate a vigorous process in order to be accepted. Our mothers considered our admission to be a major triumph. I did not. I wasn't feeling the requirement to wear a "uniform" of a shirt, tie, slacks, suit jacket, and dress shoes each day. Also, Academic had no lockers, so we had to tow around our bulky textbooks all day. And I did not like that we were called "the smart kids" in Jersey City. Being called smart as a teenager was like being called corny—or, worst of all, a sucker. Suckers got beat up, or jumped, or robbed.

But I had no alternative—this was what my mother wanted. Throughout my life, she had emphasized the importance of getting a better education than the one she had gotten in the dusty, dirt-road town of her native South Carolina. My moms drilled into my head that I could do something with my life if I went to college.

At Academic I did enjoy being challenged by the best students and best teachers in Jersey City—at least that is what we were told—and we were pushed and expected to seek a higher education. So, during my ninth-grade year, I sent away for glossy brochures from colleges and universities across the United States. My universe was Jersey City, yet I was excited when I received information from schools like Pepperdine University in California, or the University of Puget Sound in Washington State. I had no clue how a poor person like me could pay for college. But I dreamed anyway. And it was during my ninth-grade year and the first part of tenth grade at Academic that I finally gathered the courage to write. I loved the fiction that we read in school, so it was only natural that I tried my hand at it, and I modeled my early writing after the works of Edgar Allan Poe. One English instructor told us to write from our own experiences, so I dutifully did as I was told. I identified with Poe's gruesome tales of murder and mayhem, but my short stories included lots of references to gargantuan black rats with electrified extension-cord tails and winged flying cockroaches with spiky fangs. Rats and roaches had played a major role in my formative years and troubled my brain and my dreams for years to come.

I also continued to love sports, and signed up for the freshman baseball team. We had to sell one hundred boxes of M&M peanuts to cover the costs for our uniforms and our equipment, but I was too socially clumsy and uncool to ask people on the street or door-to-door to buy boxes of candy from me. Instead, I wolfed down the one hundred boxes myself over the course of one week. Those M&Ms finished rotting and uprooting chunks of bad teeth long punished by soda, candy, cupcakes, and other sugary foods. My mouth pounded with pain by the time that I told my mother what I had done.

"Boy, is you crazy! I ain't got no damn money to be paying for that candy!"

"I know, Ma, I—"

"Hush your mouth, boy! That's one hundred dollars for one hundred boxes of candy! I ain't buying you nothin' for Christmas for that, and you gonna have to pay for your own school clothes for winter because I can't afford this. A-ba-god-damnit! Jeee-sus, this boy—"

My mother did eventually pay for the candy, and I did play baseball. I was now fifteen years old, and I don't think I'd been to an eye doctor, to a dentist, or to a general physician more than once each in my life. I had been to the emergency room to treat broken fingers, and once to get stitches in my forehead after running, head-first, into a flagpole while playing football in the fourth grade. Our poverty combined with my multilayered anxiety about doctors—particularly dentists—limited my medical visits. I suffered through my preteen and teen years with toothache after toothache, and fear kept me from going to the dentist again until I was in my early twenties.

I did not want to return to Academic for tenth grade. I was doubly antsy and felt inferior to most of the other students—I did not fit in with the popular or hip kids, and my attempts to make it with girls were weak at best, except for a school party or two, which my mother grudgingly allowed me to attend, where I slow dragged and "felt up" girls as I had seen boys do in the movie *Cooley High*.

◆

One day in the tenth grade I was on the Bergen Avenue bus playing the back going from Academic to Linden Avenue, where I lived. A group of boys sat with me, including a Puerto Rican fella named Richie. Richie and I had graduated from P.S. 20 together and were friends. Richie came from a large and widely admired family—his dad a remarkable local baseball coach and Richie and his brothers all-star athletes right through their high-school years in Jersey City. So it was cool to know him.

But for some reason on this frosty winter day, I was in a foul and sinister mood as I sat on that Bergen Avenue bus. When Richie lobbed a wisecrack at me and the other boys roared with amusement, my dynamite temper detonated and Richie and I cursed and threatened each other.

Before I knew it Richie and I were rolling on the floor of that Bergen Avenue bus as our schoolmates screamed and cajoled each of us to beat the other down. Punching, biting, clawing, kicking, I faintly heard older passengers shrieking in horror. The bus driver yelled for us to stop, but we did not, so he pulled the bus over. Richie and I kept scrapping.

Soon, two White police officers climbed onto the bus through the now-open back door, wrenched Richie and me apart, and removed us from the bus. For some reason my arms were pressed behind my back and I was placed in handcuffs, but Richie, a light-complexioned Puerto Rican, was not. Richie and I were walked to a police car. One officer gently put Richie into the front seat while the other—a redheaded man with a shaggy red mustache—rammed me into the backseat. His name was Officer O'Connor. Enraged, I ran my mouth as only I knew how:

"Hell with you Richie! I'ma finish kickin' yo' butt!"

Richie peered at me through the fence-like metal divider, scanned my arms cuffed behind me, and laughed. That infuriated me further. Officer O'Connor roared at me to shut up.

In my rage, I yelled back at Officer O'Connor, "Hell with you!"

In an instant, Officer O'Connor balled up his large right fist and punched me dead in the nose. Stunned, my hundred-pound body crumpled and I fell sideways in the police car. For a moment I saw nothing but the heads of Officer O'Connor, Richie, and the other policeman hanging from nooses, and then they were gone. . . .

. . . My ears felt as if someone had fired a rifle bullet through one and out the other. My life passed before my eyes. I saw my dead grandfather when I was six or seven, lying in his coffin. I saw my mother crying and collapsing at my funeral. Tears surged from my eyes. I was terrified, imprisoned by this police officer. My beige ski jacket was now painted with my own blood. I thought I was dead—or swaying somewhere between the life that I knew and that toxic enemy we called death.

"Now shut up!" Officer O'Connor snarled at me. Richie unscrewed his neck cautiously to peer at me; the revulsion in his eyes at the sight of my blood-drenched jacket frightened me even further.

Once we arrived at the precinct in Downtown Jersey City, I was placed inside a holding cell and handcuffed to its black bars while Richie was allowed to sit in a chair near the front desk. Eventually he was released, and I was told that I was being charged with resisting arrest and with disorderly conduct. At fifteen I did not know the meaning of those words. But I did know I was in trouble—big trouble.

I was offered nothing to drink, no food, and no medical attention for the couple of hours I was there. Every time a White police officer strolled in, he would look at me as though I were a caged bird or animal in a zoo or circus; or he'd giggle derisively, or make a lame joke about my condition. I was so afraid because I thought the police were going to attack me again, so I said nothing and kept my eyes trained on the floor. I was gasping for tiny sips of air as I could not breathe through my nostrils. I stood there for what seemed like an eternity, handcuffed to the cell bars as fresh urine trickled down my left leg.

When my mother arrived, she squealed at the sight of me. The White police officers behind the big high desk and the others milling about gazed at her impassively. My mother screamed: "What happened to my son? Who did this to him?" Still no response until the officer behind the big high desk finally said: "He got into a fight on a bus and got arrested, ma'am. You can sign for him and we will release him. He will get a court date."

My mother scribbled her name on some documents, and I was freed. She told me to go to the bathroom to wash my face, and for the first time I saw the damage. Officer O'Connor's punch had swollen my entire face. The front of my beige ski jacket was covered with blood, and my lips were inflamed and appeared to go in opposite directions. Mucus, dried saliva, and blood blotched my cheeks, nose, chin, and neck.

My mother and I took a bus from the police precinct to Jersey City's Medical Center. I was treated and told that my nose was not, in fact, broken. A Black nurse urged my mother to file a report and to contact an organization I had never heard of, the NAACP.

A few days later someone from the NAACP called, but I was terrified—I never wanted to see Officer O'Connor again—so I lied and said that I was fine and that I did not want to file a report or press charges. I only wanted to go to court and get it over with.

When my court date arrived, I stood before a judge, who, much to my astonishment, was a Black woman named Shirley Tolentino. She told me that I would have a record until I turned eighteen, and that if I stayed out of trouble it would then be erased. The judge was stern, but she looked on my mother and me with pity. My mother looked worn out, as if she had been beaten up, too.

That day in court I could see that there was nothing but teenage Black and Latino boys like me there. Many of them were being sent off to a place called "juvenile detention," or "juvy." Imagining myself behind bars for life scared me. This was the closest that I had ever been to the criminal justice system, and I thought it a place where you go and never come back. Once out, in the oppressive polluted air of Jersey City, I walked next to my mother and kicked a can down the street as if I were kicking my life away. My mother kept her small body taut, her face filled with worry that I had not seen before.

"I don't think you gonna make it, boy. You been givin' me trouble your whole life," she said.

My mother's matter-of-fact, jarring assertion hit me hard. I vowed never to get in trouble again, but it seemed as if I could not help myself. I was expelled from Academic High School for the fight on the bus and the subsequent arrest. Honestly, I felt relieved to get away from that school filled with cornballs and squares.

My mother took me back to a distinguished Black man at the Board of Education—Dr. Franklin Williams. When the principal of P.S. 38 had tried to boot me out years before and send me to a school for troubled boys, my mother had pleaded with Dr. Williams to intercede, and he had done so. Now, here we were again, the single mother and her problem man-child.

I was supposed to go to Snyder High School, which was located in our district. My mother was dead set against that idea. Snyder "boasted" a reputation as the worst and most violent high school in Jersey City, where students fought, did and sold drugs, cut school, and where female students often became pregnant. Dr. Williams understood my mother's concerns, took into account my excellent grades in spite of my destructive behavior and trigger-happy temper, and sent me to Dickinson High School instead.

Dickinson sat on the border of Downtown Jersey City and Jersey City Heights, and I felt a great sense of relief when I got there. The student body of DHS—a mammoth structure that had served as a bomb shelter during World War I—consisted of many poor Black and Latino kids like me, but also included White and Asian students.

Unfortunately, I did not stay out of trouble for long.

About a year later, when I was sixteen, on a sizzling summer day on our Linden Avenue block, I was bored and got the idea to place a stray black cat into the fenced-off yard that was the home of the most vicious mongrel in our 'hood, a jet-black dog named King. Once inside the fence, the two animals went at it, and the other kids laughed at what I'd done, all except one of the newer kids in the neighborhood who went and told his father—a Black man—who had recently moved into a house on the block. What began as a dumb boyhood prank turned into a verbal altercation between the Black man and me, during which I cursed him out and flung a brick at him.

The Black man retreated angrily into his home, and I smugly assumed a posture of victory, clutching my crotch with my right paw and bragging to the other boys, both Black and White, how I had told him. Shortly thereafter, however, the police showed up—turns out this Black man was also a police officer. White police officers came directly to me and asked me what happened. I made up a lie about how the black cat jumped itself over the gate. The Black cop told them that I was a liar, that I had thrown a brick at him, threatened him, and that I was a menace to society. He finished by saying, "Take him away." Once again I was handcuffed and put into a police car and brought to the precinct. Once again I was charged with resisting arrest, with disorderly conduct, and with a whole bunch of other stuff that I did not understand. Once again my mother had to come down to get me. Once again she had to scribble her name on pieces of paper before I was released, and once again she said to me, in a woeful tone, "Boy, I don't think you gonna make it."

And once again I found myself in court before Judge Shirley Tolentino, who was not pleased that I was back. Once again my mother pleaded my case to the judge. Because we could not afford a lawyer, the court assigned one to me, and while I do not remember what he said, I do know that both my mother and this lawyer emphasized my excellent grades in school. Judge Tolentino said that she had every right to send me away to juvenile detention, but once more she did not, instead telling me to stay out of trouble or I would be sent to a juvenile detention center for sure the next time.

The year was 1982 and hip-hop had exploded on the scene as the music of my generation. Grandmaster Flash & the Furious Five had released a very bleak and eerie song called "The Message." It spoke in the rawest conceivable terms about life in the ghetto . . . about making bad choices . . . about what happened to boys like me who wound up in jail. I could hear those lyrics in my head as Judge Tolentino gave me her warning.

I did not know why I was spared. It did not mean that I calmed down or changed dramatically; I did not. But I did think of the choice between college and jail more than ever. I still had no clue how my mother and I would pay for college, but I just knew I had to get there.

◆

I sank into a kind of debilitating depression. I felt a paralyzing gloom and crushing loneliness. Part of the reason was the fractured bond between my cousin Anthony and me.

After I was kicked out of Academic High School, we floated even further apart. By the beginning of our junior year, I was at Dickinson and Anthony had transferred to Snyder because he did not want to attend the same high school as me. Though we had once been as connected as blood brothers, Anthony and I no longer spoke as we once did, except when we got together on the block to play one sport or another. I felt as abandoned as I had when I was eight years old and my father told my mother he would never give her "a near nickel" for me ever again.

During this period, I delivered groceries for Randy's, the local market at the corner of my block. I was the first Black boy this White Italian family had ever trusted enough to hire to transport groceries to their mostly White customers. Beside myself with pride, I had my shopping cart and I had my system, which I had honed during my years as a newspaper delivery boy for *The Jersey Journal*. Randy and his family and their White clientele marveled at my speed and my manners.

But one thing that bothered me greatly was that no matter how much Randy complimented me or showed me off to his White patrons who came into the store, he never allowed me to graduate to working the cash register as he had the White and Puerto Rican delivery boys. I seethed privately at this slight, but I got my revenge on him when I realized that most of these old White customers—humpedback women who could hardly walk or stand—trusted me so much that they did not even bother to conceal where they kept their money to pay me. They also moved so slowly that they did not notice when I began to go into their open purses or wallets or cabinet drawers and deftly slide $10, $20, or more into my pockets. I cleaned up and I felt no culpability whatsoever. My adolescent mind rationalized that I, too, was being robbed by not being paid well, and by never being given the opportunity to work the cash register. For sure I was a thief in every sense of the word: I even stole from my mother's purse in her bedroom closet.

I had made a new friend at Dickinson almost as soon as I got there: a wild boy named Vincent from the Greenville section, where I lived. We broke into students' lockers together. We wrote on walls with Magic Markers—his graffiti tag was "Vinnie Vin" and mine was "kepo1." We marveled at the tags of a Jersey City graffiti writer known as "Never" whose name was everywhere yet no one seemed to know who he was. We engaged in petty crimes, stealing from random shops and stores, or robbing "sucker ducks" as we called helpless prey, at knifepoint.

In those ratchet flashes of high school—when I was clocked by that cop, kicked out of Academic, and became a petty criminal while maintaining outstanding grades—the days, the weeks, the months of my teenage years accelerated between life and whatever, yo. I sprouted from five feet to five foot ten in a matter of months, my high-pitched voice miraculously deepened, and my sandy-brown hair flowered into a reddish afro.

The memories of my teenage years stay with me to this day: my tickled bewilderment as Jimmy Carter, "the peanut president," lost to Ronald Reagan amid the Iran hostage crisis. I remember the sour flavor of death in my mouth when I heard that former Beatle John Lennon had been killed outside his apartment building near Central Park in New York City. I remember the sorrowful feeling of doom when only a few months later President Reagan and Pope John Paul II were shot and wounded. I remember the fury that I could not control when my moms said something cruel to me and I chucked my record player into our living room wall; or the day I chased Reggie, a Haitian boy from the block, with a baseball bat, and broke a window in his house.

I remember feeling a sense of belonging and acceptance when a White boy from the block drank from the same bottle or can of soda as me; I remember the unexpected epidemic of stabbings and gun violence, and the growth of an addictive new drug called "crack," a drug that converted one innocent, clean-cut girl from my high school into a nasty-mouthed hooker trolling and begging along Martin Luther King Jr. Boulevard, the former Jackson Avenue.

I remember the beginnings of my blooming and limitless love affair with hip-hop; how our street uniforms were painstakingly creased Lee jeans, sporty Le Tigre shirts, baseball caps jammed with plastic or newspapers, and suede Puma sneakers with untied "fat shoelaces"; how I popped, locked, break-danced, and recorded songs off the radio with my cassette player, especially the New York shows of Kool DJ Red Alert and Mr. Magic. I remember how real rude boys would roll up on unsuspecting victims in the dead of winter, flip their male peers upside down, and casually steal their Puma or Adidas sneakers from their feet, leaving them barefoot in the snow.

I remember the racial pride I felt the night of the *Motown 25* anniversary special, when Michael Jackson performed "Billie Jean" and strutted, twirled, and moonwalked into global superstardom. I remember the electric boogaloo that whooshed through my frail frame as my homie Vinnie Vin built a "coffin" for his DJ turntables and retooled enormous speakers in his bedroom so they sounded like the ones at Jersey City block parties.

I remember the Sony Walkman I played obsessively, especially the provocative music of Marvin Gaye's "Sexual Healing." But I also remember the terrible fickleness of my teenage years when I decided one day to trash my 45 records and my extensive baseball card collection because I was now too big for such childish activities.

I remember how we produced our own vocabulary, where things that we dug were "fresh" or "def," something we did not like was "wack," a good friend was your "homeboy" or "homeslice," Jersey City became "Chilltown J.C.," and if you said something that we agreed with, we said one word: "Word."

I can still remember my resentment as my cousin Anthony became a track star at Snyder while I floundered in baseball and track at Dickinson, reduced to being a surly bench warmer and an undisciplined and mediocre runner; the humiliation I felt when I went to West 14th Street in New York City to go shopping after getting paid from work on a Saturday, only to get bamboozled into a street game of three-card monte and lose $200 to a grungy, gap-toothed hustler.

I remember experimenting with "99 cent malt liquor," cigarettes, and weed—anything to get the high to delete the insanity from our young lives. One afternoon, an older Black male from around the way even told me to try mescaline, but my mother's words not to do drugs won out. And yet one day I did allow my friend Vinnie Vin to convince me to put a pinch of cocaine powder on my tongue, and I can still feel how it numbed and maimed my lips, my gums, my mouth, my head, for several hours, to the point that I thought I was going to croak.

And I can still recall the sheer terror whenever my mother chided me not to get a girl pregnant, saying it would ruin my life. I loved girls, but had to bury my craving to have sex. Instead, like so many other teenage boys, I frequented the "peep shows" on 42nd Street in New York. But at the same time, I was also reading George Orwell's novel *1984*, and marveling at a book that was set in the year I was to graduate high school.

◆

I returned to Dickinson in September 1983, ready to get my high school years over with and behind me. I had spent the summer working at Randy's and training for cross-country track—not with Dickinson but with my cousin Anthony's Snyder High runners at Jersey City's Liberty State Park. I was determined to be a good long-distance runner. My wiry, lengthy legs, my giraffe's stride, and my ample speed enabled me to run the middle distances. Cross-country track would prepare me for indoor and outdoor seasons, and I'd heard that colleges would give "scholarships" to athletes able to compete at that level. I thought that this was one of my only shots to get a free college education; I had no clue there was any other way to do so.

But a few weeks after the school year began, I had a run-in with my guidance counselor, a White man named Mr. Rossi. He said something to me that I did not like when I was walking in the hallway between classes, and I responded with a wise-guy retort. He summoned me to his office, where he searched my folder, but he seemed unhappy that he could not find anything on me—plus my grades were at the top of my class. Believing Mr. Rossi could not do anything to me, I anticipated a meaningless reprimand, until his eyes widened.

"You don't live in the correct district for this school," he said.

"No, I, uh, got special permission to—" I muttered, not sure what to say.

"You live in the district for Henry Snyder High School, young man, and that is where I am sending you. You are outta here. We do not need your kind at Dickinson."

I was devastated. My mother received a call and was told that I was being removed from Dickinson and sent to Snyder. I did not want to go to Snyder, but there I was, a few days later, walking up to its front door. Everything that I'd heard about Snyder was true: students were hanging out front, no books in hands, smoking cigarettes, slinging curse words and objects at each other. Just inside the main entrance was a metal detector to prevent the flow of guns and knives into the school. In the hallways, students openly "dissed" and bullied each other—behaviors that they directed toward teachers and staff, too.

Quite a few students clowned the principal, who looked like a Black version of Frank Perdue, the chicken man, to his face. I found myself living my worst nightmare.

After I got kicked out of Dickinson, college looked more unattainable than ever. It embarrassed me that I was now attending my seventh Jersey City school—four grammar schools and three high schools. That fact, coupled with the number of times that my mother and I had moved during my life, meant that I barely had maintained any legit friendships, either, so on top of everything I was lonely. "BE ALL YOU CAN BE" military recruitment posters were all over Snyder, including the guidance counselor office, but there was very little information or ads about college. I resigned myself to the idea that maybe, just maybe, my only escape from the concrete box would be enlisting in the army.

I retreated into myself and decided never to take the Bergen Avenue bus to school; it was packed with supremely unruly Snyder students. I discovered a rear entrance to the school on the Kennedy Boulevard side, which I used for my entire year at Snyder. Day after day, I walked alone with my book bag—head bowed—my eyes forever lowered, minding my business, conversing to no one along the way to and from school.

But I did join the track team and ran with the other Black and Latino boys, and much to my surprise and delight we swept the Jersey City championships in cross-country, with our freshman, junior varsity, and varsity teams winning their respective brackets. It was a righteous feeling and—for the first time in my life—my name appeared in *The Jersey Journal* newspaper. I stared at my name and race time daily, in a state of total disbelief. Our star athlete—a Dominican kid named Leonardo—dominated the cross-country, indoor, and outdoor seasons in Hudson County during our senior year. Guys on the track team hipped me to something on 42nd Street that I had never considered: I could pay a small fee to have sex with a prostitute as other boys had done, and that's how I lost my virginity, in less than ten minutes in a back room of an X-rated theater.

◆

I had no guidance in how to pick colleges, so my first two choices were schools whose sports programs I admired: Syracuse and Penn State. Next I applied to Pace University in New York, because I loved math and I thought that I could be a good accountant. Pace was the only college or university that I visited, but as soon as I got to downtown Manhattan, I felt completely out of place. I did not see any Black faces, except for one Black girl who would not even look my way just to say hello.

Finally, I applied to Rutgers, The State University of New Jersey. I was advised to apply to at least one school in my home state. Tuition would be much cheaper because I was "disadvantaged," and I could apply for the Educational Opportunity Fund (EOF).

I filled out my college applications and financial-aid forms as my Snyder High guidance counselor, Ms. Francesca, instructed. Because my mother and I were poor, the application fees were waived. My mother did not understand the forms, but because she had raised me to go to college, she proudly signed every paper I asked her to right by the X. I was so grateful to my mother for this.

As I waited for answers from colleges, in the meantime one teacher in particular, Mrs. Lillian Williams, took a special interest in me. She encouraged me to enter a citywide writing contest for public-school students, sponsored by the New Jersey Education Association, on the theme "A Strong Nation Needs Strong Public Schools." I had not written anything on this level since I'd given the commencement speech for my eighth-grade graduating class four years before, but unbelievably I won. While I still loved reading, I had abandoned the notion that I could be a writer. No one in my world was a writer, and I did not know how I could make such a career happen. But there I was with the $100 savings bonds prize, an accompanying certificate, and my picture in *The Jersey Journal*. My mother was proud of me—and I was proud of myself. I had done something that made my mother happy, and I had won money doing it, too. Noting my potential as a writer, Mrs. Williams urged me to enter another contest, this one for Snyder students, and I wrote an essay about Jackie Robinson and won that one, too. *Could I actually be a writer?*

But not every experience at Snyder was as pleasant. First there was my Physics teacher, Mr. Stiller, an old White man who made no effort to hide his hatred for Black and Latino students: "I like shooting cans. Puerto Ric-cans. Me-xi-cans. Domini-cans. Ja-mai-cans . . ."

And on he went. The Black and Latino students would laugh hysterically—except me. I never budged from my screw face. Mr. Stiller would eyeball me quizzically. I knew enough at that point that if I laughed at his racist jokes I would also be laughing at myself.

About a month or more after I submitted my college applications something told me to stop by my guidance counselor's office. To my horror, all four apps were sitting there right where I had left them. Ms. Francesca had never mailed them.

"Oh, my, I forgot, Kevin. But if you do not get into any schools, you can always join the army. That is a great option, to serve your country."

Pissed, I politely retrieved my applications and mailed them myself that day. Ms. Francesca was a nice enough White woman, but she had no idea how much her actions had hurt me. Motivated by Ms. Francesca's ignorance and reckless disregard for my future, at the urging of Mrs. Williams I decided to take the SATs a second time to raise my scores. I even got a voucher to pay the test fee. But then I twisted my ankle badly while running in the state cross-country championship and could not walk without excruciating pain. Unwilling to accept any excuse for my not going to college, Mrs. Williams arrived at my home and drove me to and from the SATs. She was that unwavering in her support of me. I never told Mrs. Williams—or anyone else—what Ms. Francesca had done. And I never mentioned to Mrs. Williams that I knew her husband, Dr. Franklin Williams—the Black man who worked at the Board of Education in Jersey City—who had helped my mother on countless occasions throughout the years.

◆

The next few months of my senior year went by in a blur. As I had done at Dickinson during my junior year, I passed on going to the prom. I did not have the courage to ask any girl to go with me; I was afraid of being rejected. I also did not have the money for it, and I watched in disbelief as other students bought fancy outfits, rented stretch limos, and discussed what liquor they'd drink and which hotel rooms they would be coppin' for the night. I was too focused on getting the heck out of Jersey City and did not want anything or anyone to block me from my great escape. I had come too far and survived too much to screw it all up now.

The sacrifice paid off: I was accepted to each of the four colleges to which I had applied. I could not believe that I had a choice; but really, I didn't, because the out-of-state prices for Penn State, Syracuse, and Pace gave me only one option: Rutgers, which offered me admission, free tuition, and even regular "refund checks" to purchase books through its Educational Opportunity Fund. The best part was that I could start in late June, a week or so after graduation, in a special summer program for kids like me.

◆

When our June 1984 graduation rolled around, my friend Leonardo was our valedictorian. I was happy for him and helped him write his speech. On graduation day it was boiling and muggy in our auditorium. Antique fans recycled the heavy, hot air, and a crowd full of loud and hyperactive relatives roared the name of their loved one as each received his or her diploma. Cousin Anthony and I had the same last name so we went up right after each other. I won a special English award and an award given to the student with the highest overall average in mathematics. Our mothers sat there stoically in the audience as their boys' names were called, as emotionless as they had been those several years in our holy-roller church in Newark.

When I shook the principal's hand, I glanced at my mother and

Aunt Cathy and thought about the fact that Anthony and I had done something that they had never done: we had completed high school. And with that, God willing, the promise of a new life much better than anything they could have imagined loomed before us. They had survived absent fathers, vicious poverty, slumlord apartment building owners, minimum-wage job after minimum-wage job, welfare, food stamps. In the face of all that, their sons had made it through. I choked up as I left the auditorium stage, both happy and terrified of what awaited me now. The future was finally here for me. My mother had raised me to do something with my life, always reminding me that when I was eighteen I had to leave home, as she and her sisters had done, because eighteen meant that I was an adult. I was going to college.

A few days later my mother and I loaded my meager belongings into our older cousin Al Wright's car and we all drove down to New Brunswick, New Jersey, to the main campus of Rutgers University. I had rarely been in a car or on the New Jersey Turnpike. In Jersey City my life essentially encompassed the apartment that we lived in, the block that we lived on, maybe five or six blocks north, south, east, and west, and the journey each weekday via foot or bus to whatever school that I attended.

As we reached Rutgers, my heart soared. I had never seen anywhere as abundantly green and as expansive as the campus. I had never seen such stately architecture, such ancient and broad-shouldered trees. There was also the soothing cascade of the Raritan River, which carved through and separated New Brunswick from Piscataway—such was the immensity of Rutgers that it occupied two cities.

We were on a strip called College Avenue on the New Brunswick side, and I was taken to a dorm building called Clothier Hall. There, I met students who were from "North Jersey" and "Central Jersey" and "South Jersey." We went to a reception for new students, and then I was alone. I had never been away from my mother for a single night in my first eighteen years of life, and at long last we were separated. I cried; and I cried even more a couple of days later when I learned that my cousin Anthony had signed up for the U.S. Navy and was on his way to boot camp. I sobbed because I understood that the life I once knew was over for good; that whatever I was going to be was what I would make of myself. I had no other choice. I had come too far to turn back or fall down now—

PART II

---

living on the other

side of midnight

18

Rutgers University

You, my grade-school educated mother,
Gave me my swagger—
Told me I was going to be a lawyer or a doctor,
Told me I was going to do big things,
That I was going to have a better life. . . .

ONCE THE summer of 1984 was over—Prince's *Purple Rain*, and Carl Lewis's Olympic gold medals, and a summer of classes, workshops, and a field trip here or there to expose us to "culture"—I moved out of Clothier Hall and into the secluded and suburban Busch Campus. I was the only Black person in my entire dormitory, and as I waited for my roommate to show up, I could hear White male students talking in the hall:

"I wonder who is getting stuck with the *Black* guy."

"Glad it is not *me*."

"Me, *too*."

"Yeah, they got problems, real serious problems, those *nig-gers*."

They were talking about me as if I was not quite human, not even there, and I was intensely angry. Soon enough my roommate showed up—a bespectacled, White, nerdish dude from Kenilworth, New Jersey. He was nice enough, but my feelings of isolation, of invisibility, and of loneliness were too much to overcome. Matters were made worse when I tried to interact with the White kids in my dorm. They would ask me ignorant questions such as: "So, how do you comb your hair?" "Can you break-dance?" and "What is it like growing up in the ghetto?"

I felt as if I had no safe place in those first few weeks of that fall semester, other than when I was with two Black guys: Peter Channer and Sidney Tatem.

Peter had also gone to Dickinson High School, but I hadn't really known him; I met Sidney at Rutgers. Peter's family was from Jamaica and Sidney's from Bermuda. It was the first time in my life I became close to Black folks who were not American Black folks. They were brilliant, opinionated, critical thinkers, and passionate about learning. Peter dubbed everyone "Captain," so we dubbed him "Captain," too. We were inseparable and began calling ourselves "three the hard way."

One day Sidney and I were waiting for a campus bus right near my Busch dorm. We did not even think about our being the only two Black students chillin' at an otherwise crowded bus stop. A slow-moving campus police car crept up and stopped right in front of us. The officer pushed down his window and pointed to Sidney and me and asked us for our ID cards. Taken aback, Sidney and I looked at each other and protested. "Why are you asking us and not the other students?" The officer—apparently accustomed to doing this regularly—was angered by our response, and stammered something about "campus safety policy." Sidney and I looked at him like "Whatever" and remained adamant in not cooperating. The officer called for backup, and three or four other campus police cars appeared out of nowhere. The officers surrounded us, asked if we were students, and demanded to see our student ID cards. Outnumbered, we relented, and the officers gave us an ambiguous warning about "disobeying the law." Right there we decided to write an article about our experience, and to file a complaint with the campus police.

Composing that article—the first time I had ever written about racism publicly in my life—proved to be emancipating. Many Black students applauded us for our courage, especially because we were eighteen-year-old first-year students, but I could tell that White students in my Busch Campus dorm disliked me more after our article appeared.

That friction came to a head one late September evening when my roommate and I got into a heated argument about our dorm area. I had noticed that he kept his things separate from mine, like the room was segregated into "Whites only" and "Coloreds only." I resented him for it, hated him for it, in fact, and hated the White students in the building who never spoke to me, who seemed to be afraid of me, or who otherwise rarely made an effort to acknowledge my existence. My blood was boiling, and as the argument escalated, I picked up a nearby extension cord and began swinging it wildly in my roommate's direction. But as I made one of my untamed swings, my right shoulder popped out of its socket—I had dislocated my shoulder. A screech of pain and terror whizzed from my slipped joint over to the base of my throat, shot from my mouth and nose along with big gooey balls of saliva and boogers. My roommate just looked at me blankly. I screamed as I rolled and kicked on the dorm room floor. A white female residence hall adviser rushed in. An ambulance was called. I was carted, in humiliating fashion, from the room, past a phalanx of White students looking at me with the same blank stares as my roommate.

At the hospital my shoulder was un-popped and shoved back into place, but now the anger and hatred I had felt toward my roommate was replaced by a blistering sorrow about ever coming to college in the first place. The joy I had felt in that summer program was gone forever; instead there was a numbing sense of alienation—and dread.

A few days after the fight with my roommate I had to go to a disciplinary hearing with my right arm in a sling, as a grievance had been filed against me. I was not suspended from school, but I was given a stern warning about my violent behavior, and I was told that

I was being transferred to "The Towers," a dwelling on the Livingston Campus.

The Towers was where I would live for the remainder of my time at Rutgers University. I preferred it because the Livingston Campus— jokingly called "da projects" by Black and White students alike—had more Black students than anywhere else in the Rutgers–New Brunswick community. As detached as I had been from Black people for much of my life, Rutgers made me realize how much I needed to see those Black faces, somewhere, anywhere.

◆

A force was unleashed on Rutgers' New Brunswick campus that fall semester of 1984. In the preceding summer months we incoming freshmen had sat in front of a television set enthralled by the Democratic National Convention speeches of the Reverend Jesse Jackson and New York governor Mario Cuomo. Up until that point I had never thought about changing the world, about being involved in any student organization or activity. In my mostly sad and lonely high-school years I'd merely existed class-to-class, year-to-year. The only nonacademic activities that had interested me were baseball and track. Students who worked on the school newspaper, or in student government, or in the many clubs that existed, seemed strange to me, as distant from my reality as it was to not be poor.

But then I met *her* one sunny day on a College Avenue bus at Rutgers.

Her name was Lisa Williamson; she was a junior, two years ahead of me, and she immediately took a liking to me. She had a round baby face, a dynamic smile that extended from border to border of her cheeks, cherubic eyes, and a womanly plumpness that reminded me of my mother. Lisa's voice was commanding yet soothing, persuasive yet gentle. She took to me like the big sister I never had, and hell, I even called her "Mother" for a spell given how much she embraced, pushed, and supported me.

But the first time Lisa attempted to hug me, I froze and then recoiled in horror. Lisa was perplexed. In my eighteen years of life my mother and I had never hugged, had never kissed, had never said to each other, "I love you." Thus I had no foundation for accepting the sisterly affection that Lisa was trying to give me.

"What is *wrong* with you?" Lisa said, hurt.

"I, uh . . ." I could not even look at her.

"Kev, you have never been hugged in your life, have you?"

I was ashamed. I shook my head no as I averted my eyes.

"Well, you are going to learn how to love and accept love if you are going to be around me," Lisa said.

Lisa was determined to school me about life, and about what she and other Black students called "the struggle." She educated me on "the Anti-Apartheid Movement," told me about Nelson Mandela, Winnie Mandela, and Steve Biko, as well as the African National Congress and the Pan Africanist Congress. Lisa said what Black people were going through in South Africa was no different from what Black folks and Native Americans had suffered through here in America: apartheid meant segregation. Blacks had to carry "passes" to identify themselves as they moved around in South Africa; there was a color caste system; Blacks, Coloreds, Indians were all treated terribly, though Blacks remained at the bottom. There was violence, torture, imprisonment, murder, and a kind of White racism and terrorism that quickly brought to mind the Jim Crow America my mother had often described when I was a child. *Do White people hate Black people everywhere on the planet?* I wondered. It was mind-blowing to learn about South Africa.

Lisa also introduced Sidney, Peter, and me to other older, upper-class Black students: Glenn Arnold, Guiffre Hollingsworth, and Marian Pitts. We learned from these campus leaders that during World War I there had been a heroic Black figure who attended Rutgers named Paul Robeson. He had earned a scholarship to what was then Rutgers College—only the third African American to do so, and he was the lone Black on campus when he enrolled in 1915. Robeson became one of Rutgers' most acclaimed students ever, and

received top honors for his debate and oratory skills; he earned fifteen letters in four different sports; he was elected Phi Beta Kappa;
and he was his class valedictorian when he graduated in 1919. Paul
Robeson would go on to be a lawyer (graduating from Columbia
University while playing professional football and teaching Latin
on weekends to pay his law school tuition); an acclaimed stage and
film actor; a world-renowned concert singer who could sing in multiple languages; and an "activist," a word that I had never heard before. That a man like Paul Robeson existed, was Black like me, was
a native of New Jersey like me, had walked the same Rutgers yard as
me, was mind-boggling to say the least. *Why had I never heard of him
until now?* These older Black students said it was because of his "politics," his outspokenness on behalf of the less fortunate in America
and the world. Robeson had been pretty much erased from history,
even though Black Rutgers students had fought to have a cultural
center named for him.

To be an activist was to be a threat to those in power. The older
Black students told us they were activists, too, that they belonged to
an organization called the African Student Congress (ASC), which
represented the entire Black student body at Rutgers. On one particular day, in the meeting room of the Paul Robeson Cultural Center,
they locked the door with Peter, Sidney, and me in there and began
to interrogate us—with an intensifying urgency—on every aspect of
Black history. Glenn—tall, dark brown–skinned, built like a football
linebacker, always in his uniform of blue jeans and a T-shirt, with an
immaculate afro—held up a weathered black album cover, which had
the white text "Malcolm X: Message to the Grassroots" written on it.
I had never heard of him, but they told me that the "X" meant he had
decided to abandon his surname because it was a slave name given to
his Black ancestors by their White slave master. I had never heard anything like this and it jolted me to think a White man named Powell
had once owned my family. I realized then that I might never know
my true African name because, like much of the history and culture
of Black people, it had been deleted by White people with power. It

was liberating to know there were African Americans who had the audacity to change their names, as a path to freeing themselves from the bondage of their past.

But because I had never heard of any of the Black women and men the older students questioned us about, I felt ignorant and inferior. Reduced to tears, I wanted to bolt from the room as the grilling went on for several hours. "Bull sessions," as such interrogations were known, were rites-of-passage that older Black RU students engaged younger Black students in, to see if they had potential to be campus leaders one day. Up to that point we had been so full of ourselves—Sidney and I, in particular, were proud of the fact that we had given the school the middle finger with our editorial about the campus police. But this bull session served to prove that we were not at Rutgers merely for ourselves or to obtain a degree. We were part of a grand and monumental tradition of Black students at the university that extended back to Paul Robeson.

When the bull session was over, I felt like I had gone a hundred rounds in a ring with Muhammad Ali or Sugar Ray Leonard. But I also felt empowered, if terrified. My mind ran to every single instance of when I had been dissed in some way by White people in my life, how I had scarcely learned anything about Black history, in spite of going mostly to the best public schools in Jersey City. How Black history had been reduced, in my entire schooling up to this point, to a few paragraphs about slavery; vague references to Rosa Parks on that Montgomery, Alabama, bus; selected parts of Dr. King's "I Have a Dream" speech; George Washington Carver and his experiments with peanuts; and Jackie Robinson breaking the color line in baseball. I was disconcerted that I knew so little about myself and my history.

I was determined to correct that.

First I made my way to the Rutgers Student Center on College Avenue and immediately joined our school's anti-apartheid movement. Black, White, Latino, and Asian students were in the midst of a sit-in, protesting Rutgers doing business with corporations that supported, either directly or indirectly, the racist and vicious apartheid regime in South Africa. I had never really thought of Africa before, certainly not as a place that should matter to me. Suddenly, not only was I learning about Africa by way of South Africa, but I also was learning about other parts of Africa, and Black people in the West Indies, too, thanks to my connection to Sidney and Peter. I joined several Black student organizations, including the African Student Congress, the West Indian Student Organization, and the Paul Robeson Pre-Law Association. The Paul Robeson Cultural Center became my second home; and I began to read everything there I could, beginning with *The Autobiography of Malcolm X.*

That book changed my life. I was shaken when I read that Malcolm's father, a preacher and follower of legendary Black nationalist Marcus Garvey, was beaten and killed and his body thrown across a railroad track and split in half by a train. I cried as Malcolm's mother fell into extreme poverty and insanity while she attempted to parent more than half a dozen children as a widow. I understood Malcolm when he said that they were so hungry that he would "eat the hole out of a donut." I followed Malcolm as his family was ripped apart, he and the other children sent to the Depression-era version of foster care, to new families. I related to Malcolm saying he felt like the "mascot" of well-meaning Whites in his eighth-grade class, because he was the only Black student there. I understood his loneliness, his isolation, his attraction to the streets once he made his way to Boston to live with his sister Ella; and then also to New York City, working on the railroad as a Pullman porter. I hit rock bottom with Malcolm as he descended into drug dealing and drug use, and I went to prison with him for seven years. "Satan" they called him his first year or two in jail because of his atomic-bomb temper.

And I was rescued just as Malcolm himself became rescued. The self-education he gave himself through reading books was a revelation to me, as his insatiable thirst for knowledge became my insatiable thirst, too.

When I got to the end of *The Autobiography of Malcolm X,* nothing in my narrow worldview had prepared me for Alex Haley's epilogue about Malcolm's final days. I felt Malcolm's survival blowing in the wind, the threats to his life, the bombing of his home where he lived with his wife and small children, his desperation to find his way after he had been kicked out of the Nation of Islam. And my God did I feel like I was there with Malcolm X on that arctic Sunday afternoon, February 21, 1965, at the Audubon Ballroom in New York City, when bullet after bullet devoured his flesh, killing this giant of a man just about fourteen months before I was born.

I howled after setting the book down. Nothing I had ever read in my life had had that kind of impact on my mind, on my soul, on my body. I cried tears of depression, of grief, of loss for someone I had never known. I wept because it was Black men who had cocked the guns and squeezed the triggers that murdered Malcolm.

But I also walked away from the book determined to know Malcolm X. I borrowed and copied his speeches, "Message to the Grassroots" and "The Ballot or the Bullet." Malcolm became my first real father figure—at age eighteen. In Malcolm, I had discovered the perfect Black man. I rejected almost everything associated with Dr. King, stopped paying attention to anything said about him, except for the fight to make his birthday a national holiday. Because of the way Dr. King had been presented to me during my years in school, I felt that he was soft, corny, a sucker, a butt kisser of White people. Malcolm was strength, coolness, power, unapologetic anger, an imposing and uncompromising figure. I wanted to be Malcolm X so badly that I began to talk and walk like him, I wore a watch (he always did), and I even found some horn-rimmed glasses to wear, just like his.

I also imagined myself giving speeches to large street crowds as Malcolm had done. But I was downright afraid of confronting and chastising White people as Malcolm did, at least at first. I was likewise anxious about the new ideas whirling around in my head. I shared some of them with Sidney and Peter, and I asked questions of Lisa Williamson and the other Black student leaders. But I mostly kept these ideas to myself.

Because at first I was spooked that someone was inside my head, reading and hearing my feelings, recording them. And when I went home for my first Thanksgiving break from school, my mother wholly rejected my ramblings about Blackness, about fighting the system and "the White man," about Africa, with an unpretentious response after listening to me go on for what must have been half an hour:

"Boy, we don't know nothin' about no Africa, you talkin' that fool talk like you ain't in your right mind. We from South Carolina, that's where we from. We American, we ain't African! And you better leave them White people alone! You know what they did to Dr. King!"

◆

Around that time, two other Black men affected my mind and spirit greatly.

In 1984, Reverend Jesse Jackson made his first historic run for President of the United States. I had never heard or seen a Black man speak the way he did. Though I had grown up in the Black church and listened to many preachers talk, Jesse Jackson represented what he spoke about: hope. When he said things like "Hands that once picked cotton will now pick the president," my heart swelled with pride. When he said "We are going from the outhouse to the White House," that South Carolina–born Civil Rights icon spoke for Black folks like me only a generation or two removed from the permanent poverty of rural America. When he talked about bringing all kinds of people together via his Rainbow Coalition, it made me think of what I was witnessing with the anti-apartheid movement at Rutgers, young people of different races and creeds united for a common cause.

I was also struck by the fact that while Jackson had been involved in the Civil Rights Movement in the 1960s and had even worked with and for Dr. King, he was still a young and hip man in his early forties: towering and handsome, with what my mother called a good grade of curly hair. Man how I envied his children—especially his sons—for having a father as great as he was!

In April 1985, anti-apartheid student leaders brought Reverend Jackson to Rutgers to support our movement. I was assigned the task of being one of the several student "security" members for the event. I was so nervous that I could not breathe. When he arrived, he was even taller than I had imagined. I forgot about my security post and shoved myself forward to get as close as I could, to see and touch the man. I followed every word he said, and when Reverend Jackson was done, I lunged forward to shake his hand.

The second man to affect greatly me was Louis Farrakhan. Because of my interest in every aspect of Malcolm X's life, I also found myself curious about Islam, and what it meant to be a Muslim. I knew that Minister Farrakhan had gotten himself into some sort of trouble for his confrontational language in defense of Jesse Jackson when, in early 1984, the reverend had offended Jewish people by referring to Jews as "Hymies," and New York City as "Hymietown."

I did not know there was a history of any kind between Blacks and Jews. White people were White people to me, no matter what other identity they claimed. A few Black male students and I—including Peter and Sidney—went to Madison Square Garden to see Farrakhan speak in October 1984.

I was not prepared for what I found there: thousands of well-dressed Black men, with suits and bowties, neat, close-cropped haircuts, squared backs, a firm politeness, and a seriousness that I had never witnessed before. I was mesmerized. In the arena, there were Black people everywhere, including Muslim women dressed in white from head to toe, as straight-backed and as solemn as the men. This was so different from the Black church experience of my youth. There seemed to be a sense of purpose, of a common direction and of common goals. We had no seats, but we stood among a sea of twenty thousand people. The Felt Forum, next door, had another three to five thousand people watching on closed-circuit television. When Minister Farrakhan took the stage, surrounded by Muslim women dressed in sharp, white, military-like uniforms, his voice filled the Garden:

"And let me say this, those who condemn me, who call me a bigot; who call me a racist; who call me a hater; who call me an anti-Semite; I want you to listen to me real carefully tonight. And if anything like that comes out of my mouth raise your hand and stop me, hear. But you'd only be raising your hand no matter what your color is and cheering me on. Because that is what they say I am; but tonight you judge for yourself."

For the next couple of hours I hung on every word. I felt something that I had never felt before: I wanted to join this thing, this crusade, especially when it was said that God was Black. *What?* How could God possibly be Black when every image I had ever seen of God—well, of Jesus, God's son—had been White? What did Louis Farrakhan mean, and why did these thousands of Black folks in attendance, Muslims and non-Muslims alike, agree with him with such great enthusiasm? And if God were truly Black and we were made in God's image—as I had been told since I was a child—then did that mean that we Black folks were close to God, closer than I had ever imagined?

Minister Farrakhan's discussion of Black history reminded me of the bull session those Rutgers Black student leaders had put us through: I was once again embarrassed by how little I knew about myself, about Black history, about Black people. So when the event was over, I once again turned to books. I had a work-study job at Rutgers' Alexander Library, and I turned an otherwise boring gig into my own personal empowerment center. I discovered where the Black interest books were—the E185 section of the library. And I spent hours poring through Lerone Bennett's *Before the Mayflower*; Claude Brown's *Manchild in the Promised Land*; books about ancient Africa, slavery, segregation, and lynchings; meditations on the colonization of Africa and the West Indies; the writings of literary and intellectual giants like W. E. B. DuBois, E. Franklin Frazier, Frantz Fanon, Harold Cruse, James Baldwin, and Amiri Baraka. It was jarring to read that Christopher Columbus and other "explorers" had committed mass genocide and terror against those they called Indians. Equally jarring to learn that American "founding fathers" like George Washington and Thomas Jefferson were slave owners, even as they were fighting for their freedom from the British.

I made discoveries in Black literature as well. I took a class on the Harlem Renaissance, discovering celebrated writers like Langston Hughes and Zora Neale Hurston and Claude McKay and Countee Cullen, and for the first time in my life I came to firmly believe that I, too, could be a writer.

As I learned about these Harlem Renaissance writers' lives, their contributions to American and world literature, something opened up in me that I had never before sensed so profoundly: I began to believe in myself in a different way, I began to see myself as part of something that was bigger than I was. Yes, I was still the only child of a single mother, born and raised in the ghetto. But the poems, essays, fiction, plays, and autobiographies of these Black writers, these Black thinkers, these Black leaders, gave me a sense of hope, of possibility, of history, of connection to a tradition.

I read works by Richard Wright, Ralph Ellison, Haki Madhubuti, Henry Dumas, and anything to do with being Black and male in America. And I studied diligently the Civil Rights Movement. I was flabbergasted to learn that Dr. King was only twenty-six when he led the Montgomery Bus Boycott, or that both he and Malcolm X were only thirty-nine when killed, neither man making it to forty. I was blown away that nonviolent young American soldiers were so instrumental in the victories of the Civil Rights Movement, from the activists of the Student Nonviolent Coordinating Committee—called SNCC ("snick") for short—to the Freedom Riders who challenged segregation on interstate bus trips, to the preteens and teens who confronted attack dogs and water hoses in the famous campaign in Birmingham, Alabama. And I watched videotapes and listened to cassette tapes, too, by folks like the comedian Dick Gregory, and the revolutionary musicians the Last Poets, Bob Marley, and Steel Pulse. I attended every single Black event on campus, often sitting right up front. I was transfixed by *Black Power* by Stokely Carmichael, *Die Nigger Die!* by H. Rap Brown, and George Jackson's *Soledad Brother*. Those books—and the manner in which two visionary young Black men, Huey Newton and Bobby Seale, came together to create the Black Panther Party—showed me that freedom, justice, and equality would be the fight of my life, for the rest of my life.

Identity was not something I had considered very deeply before this. The more I learned the more I thought of the diverse groups I had grown up with in Jersey City who took pride in who they were. Proud to be Italian, proud to be Irish, proud to be Polish, each laying claim to a land base where her or his people had sprung from the earth like a new plant baptized by the sun. If they were who they were, then I was an African. I was no longer merely Black, or Negro, or colored, or a nigga. I was an African, and the revelation felt like centuries of oppression and self-hate were miraculously being scrubbed from my mind, from my soul—

I was in my late teens, and I had stumbled into my calling—to be a writer, an activist, a servant for the people. Even if it meant I would not live a long life, even if it meant I would have to make the kind of sacrifices that those before me had made. There was no turning back now. I had learned too much and felt too much and had to do something.

But I remained conflicted. I had gone to school with White people for many years in Jersey City, and had spent the last five years in my hometown living with my mother in that White 'hood. I was angry at what I was learning and feeling about the entire White race, but still I found White women attractive.

The first one I liked and pursued was named Laura. I met her when we both worked for Rutgers Housing the summer after our first year in school. She had orange-brown hair, a Coca-Cola bottle shape, tranquil blue eyes, and a dashing smile. Laura's appetite and fascination were equal to mine, and before I knew it not only were we having intercourse regularly, but I was also passing her Black historical books to read, including Malcolm X's autobiography. My racial and sexual self-reproach convinced me that I could somehow recruit this White woman to be down for the cause of African Americans. And she seemed quite eager to learn from me.

Laura came from a working-class family and was one of the only White students working for Rutgers Housing; the rest of us were Black or Latino. Although there were a couple poor White families in Jersey City, I never really thought of White folks as poor, at least not as poor as Black people. One day, Laura and I got into a vicious quarrel about race and racism, and I summarily called her a racist. She cursed me out, and later put all the Black books that I had given her into a clear plastic shopping bag and left them with a note on my dorm-room doorknob.

I was terrified that Laura might say something publicly to get me in trouble, although I had no idea what she could or would say, and when I told Peter what had happened, he told me not to worry about it, and to leave her, and all other White women, alone.

But I could not. During my sophomore year in college I dated a stunning Scottish woman named Una who reminded me of Madonna. She had a short pixie haircut, a dancer's body, and her magnetic green eyes formed the base of an inverted triangle with a pointed button nose as its tip. Like me Una loved to dance, so we traveled to New York City to Danceteria, the popular club. Racial guilt gripped me when Una and I took a breather and sat next to a group of Black women with no dates. They did not say a word, but their eyes, facial expressions, and body language slapped me upside my head. I quickly grabbed Una's hand and returned to the dance floor. But as with Laura, an exchange about race abruptly ended our relationship. Una casually mentioned that there had been a crime in her area, and that a Black man had committed it. She went on to make negative remarks about the ghetto, and clearly the connection was over.

I had one final sexual encounter with a White female student at Rutgers, who lived on the same floor of my coed dorm during my sophomore year. Her name was Angelica and she was

Italian-American, with a mane of jet-black hair and chocolate-brown eyes. One day I stopped to have a chat with her and one thing led to another. But then right in the middle of our lovemaking Angelica started talking about the color of my skin, and the size of my lips, and I realized that I was nothing more than Angelica's racial sexual fantasy, the mythological Black male sex monster—capable of pleasing or conquering a White woman.

On the other hand, I had also been using Angelica and Una and Laura. They not only allowed me to fulfill my lifelong dreams about White women, but I also felt that I was paying back the entire White race for slavery, for segregation and the lynchings of Black males, for every act of terrorism that White America had ever committed against Black America. Angelica's words so deflated me that I was done with White women right in that moment. I hated her, I hated the White people at Rutgers, I was mortified that I had had sex with these White women, and I considered myself a pitiful hypocrite.

I submerged myself into an unapologetic Blackness. I stopped drinking white milk, I stopped eating white bread, and I covered every inch of the white walls during my second through fourth years at Rutgers with the Blackest posters I could find. I only sat in the "Black section" of the various campus cafeterias as we self-segregated for a sense of unity and peace of mind in an environment we felt often unwelcoming to Black students; and I routinely walked the campus, along with Sidney and Peter, decked out in dark black sunglasses the way Stokely Carmichael or H. Rap Brown or the Black Panthers had done in the 1960s. For the remainder of my time at Rutgers University I barely had anything to do with White people—students or faculty—unless it was in the form of protest, challenge, or confrontation. I deemed myself to be the angriest Black person on the planet. I often would deliberately angle my shoulders or hips to bump into White students—male or female, did not matter. I realized that Whites seemed to be innately terrified of Black people, so I used that to my psychological advantage. As soon as a White student said "I'm sorry," when I trespassed on his/her space, I launched into attack mode:

"You should be sorry for what you and your people have done to the Black race for four hundred long years here in the wilderness of North America. You owe us!" Dumbfounded and clueless, the student would either rush off, horrified, or stand there in a daze.

Two of our leaders, Lisa Williamson and Glenn Arnold, helped organize a reenactment of the famous "Freedom Rides" of the 1960s, to heighten awareness of the violations of basic voting rights happening in our time (President Ronald Reagan's 1980s). The trip was being partially coordinated by the Reverend Dr. Ben Chavis of the United Church of Christ Commission for Racial Justice. Dr. Chavis spent a decade as a political prisoner in North Carolina as part of the famous "Wilmington 10" case (he had been charged with arson and conspiracy). Just a few years removed from prison, Dr. Chavis was as brilliant and articulate as Jesse Jackson or Louis Farrakhan, and he had also made the heroic sacrifice of spending significant parts of his life in jail.

We drove Down South from the New York City headquarters of the commission, and stopped along the way in Washington, DC, and Atlanta, Georgia. In both places, we met legendary Civil Rights pioneers like Julian Bond and John Lewis, and they made sure we knew about the Civil Rights Movement. Now it was our time to take up the charge, since the Reagan administration was knocking African Americans off the voting rolls in the South based on technicalities, just as had happened in the Jim Crow era.

At every stop, Ben Chavis mesmerized the crowds at events that were equal parts church revivals and community rallies, packed with Black folks of every generation. I was struck by the number of elders we met, whose curved spines and awkward limps betrayed bodies running on the fumes of faint hopes and fatigue, and whose crooked, arthritic fingers had picked cotton, chopped wood, washed someone else's clothes, and cooked and cleaned in someone else's home. They had such humble pleas: Can we vote without interruption or interference after all we've been through? Can we be treated like full citizens, *please*? Can we be free, *finally*?

When we returned to the North, I was doubly determined to fight racism and to change the world. I always carried a small notepad and pen and was writing for our weekly Black and Latino student newspaper. I wrote essays; I reported on campus events; and I learned how to do layout, graphic design, and headlines. I spent my time at the Paul Robeson Cultural Center almost daily—writing and attending organization meetings and strategy sessions on solutions for Black student empowerment at Rutgers. What helped greatly was a new computer called an Apple Macintosh—a rectangular box much smaller and more compact than any computer I'd used before. Our center had a few of them, and that machine and its floppy disks became my best friends.

Lisa Williamson had left Rutgers without graduating and was now the youth director for Ben Chavis and his Commission for Racial Justice. I began spending a lot of time with my "big sister" in New York City. I stuck to her, attending rallies and marches with other youth leaders, enthralled by her oratorical gifts as a speaker, her ability, whether she was there in person or on the radio or television, to make it plain for the masses of our people. She was becoming famous, and I was extremely proud of her, and profoundly grateful for the impact that she had made on my life. I would do anything she asked of me; that is how much I believed in her, and how much I believed in our youth movement.

In December 1986, when I was twenty years old, I got an opportunity to write for the *Black American* newspaper. They could only pay me $25 per article, but since I had never been paid for writing before, it felt like a lot of money. The owner and publisher of the newspaper was an old West Indian man name Carl Offord. He and his family ran the tabloid, one of many Black weeklies in New York City in the 1980s, including the *Amsterdam News*, the *Big Red News*, and the *City Sun*. I wrote my first story about the murder of Michael Griffith, a young Black man who—along with other Black males—had been brutally attacked in a section of Queens called Howard Beach. They had traveled to this mostly White, working-class community to buy a used car. A mob of White men savagely beat Michael Griffith and his two Black friends. Running for his life and chased onto a highway, Griffith was struck by a car and killed. It was one of the vilest racial attacks in New York history.

The death of Michael Griffith came on the heels of the police murders of Michael Stewart and Eleanor Bumpurs. Stewart—a graffiti writer—was arrested for spray-painting a subway wall. After his apprehension, Stewart wound up in a coma for thirteen days—with facial bruises and abrasions on his wrists—and died of cardiac arrest at the age of twenty-five. A physician who witnessed the autopsy on behalf of Michael Stewart's family said that Stewart died of "strangulation." Eleven police officers were involved in the incident; all were White.

Eleanor Bumpurs, a sixty-six-year-old African-American woman, was shot and killed on October 29, 1984, by members of the NYPD. The police were present to enforce a city-ordered eviction of Ms. Bumpurs from her apartment in the Bronx (she was four months behind on her monthly rent of $98.65). In requesting NYPD assistance, the New York City Housing Authority (NYCHA) workers told police that Ms. Bumpurs was emotionally disturbed, had threatened to throw boiling lye, and was using a knife to resist eviction. When Bumpurs refused to open the door, police broke in. During the struggle to subdue her, one officer shot Bumpurs twice with a twelve-gauge shotgun, claiming that Ms. Bumpurs was charging officers with the alleged knife. (Much of the controversy centered around the fact that Eleanor Bumpurs was shot twice, though the first shot blew off one of her hands.)

Lisa was also working on the issue of children having to live in New York City's infamous welfare hotels. Providing alternative housing for poor single mothers and their children, these buildings stood in the heart of midtown Manhattan. While walking past the Martinique Hotel at Broadway and 32nd Street one day, Lisa noticed Black and Latino children just hanging out, begging for money or sometimes robbing people. She inquired who they were and so began a partnership that would last for several years. Lisa and I, and other youth and student activists like Ras Baraka, Haqq Islam, Steve X, Eric Muhammad, and Nicole Lind, would engage these young people in everything from reading and writing classes, to basic hygiene, to building and creating an "African Youth Summer Survival Camp" for them in Enfield, North Carolina, one of the main hubs for the United Church of Christ in the South.

Despite this personal progress, I knew old ways of thinking were hard to shake. One spring break, when I was back home in Jersey City, I decided to call my high-school friend Vinnie Vin. He was a DJ, still building his sound system and the coffin to hold his turntables. He casually mentioned that he needed some wood and other items for his latest setup, and he phoned his friend "Big Feet," a guy I had previously met in passing. In short order, Vinnie Vin and Big Feet and I were walking down Danforth Avenue, one of the main arteries in Jersey City, toward Route 440, where there were a ton of stores. At Rickel, a home-improvement outlet, just as we were about to cross Route 440, Vinnie Vin announced the plan. Big Feet and I would serve as decoys, pretending to shop while Vinnie Vin threw the items that he needed over a fence at the back of the store. And that's what we did.

Big Feet had disappeared somewhere in Rickel, so Vinnie Vin and I met outside the store and began walking back up Danforth Avenue, planning to return later to retrieve the stolen items. At some point Vinnie Vin glanced over his shoulder and hollered "Five-O!"—street code for the police. I made the mistake of turning around fully to look, then back at Vinnie Vin, who had miraculously disappeared in those few seconds. Before I could get away, an unmarked police car leapt the sidewalk and pinned me against the wall of a gas station. The officers apprehended me, placed me inside their car, and drove back to Rickel. There, in the security office, was Big Feet, looking as crushed and broken as I felt. The head of security, a relatively young Black man with a drippy Jheri curl, interrogated us, one at a time, asking why we were stealing from the store. When he saw our ID cards, and realized that we were both in college, he could not disguise his frustration and outrage.

"You two are in school and you are doing this? What is wrong with you? You have something to live for and you are stealing things, trying to ruin your lives?"

We were ashamed and terrified, and I really thought that we were going to be arrested and sent to jail. I had become what my mother warned me not to be: a common criminal. But to our great surprise, the man said that because we were in school, he was going to let us go.

That was the last time I saw Vinnie Vin and Big Feet, and once back at Rutgers, I vowed never to do such a dumb thing again. I wanted to be a writer, a leader, a dope blend of Malcolm X and Langston Hughes.

But I still had not overcome my debilitating fear of speaking in public. Lisa often tried to get me to talk in front of people on campus and in New York City, but I steadfastly refused. I honestly did not think that I had anything important to say, and I also knew that years and years of my mother telling me to "shut the hell up," and calling me "stupid" or "dummy," had taken their toll. Except for writing, I did not feel that my voice mattered.

As a result of my preoccupation with being a writer, and my on- and off-campus activism, my grades suffered in a way that they never had in my life, which became a serious issue. College held no interest for me, except as a place where I could debate, read books and watch documentaries, organize, strategize, rally, mobilize, yell, scream, curse, and shout. I regretted declaring Political Science as my major, since I was often the only Black student in class. I felt that the professors were often liars defending White racism in America and across the globe. Part of my "true" college education came via the many speakers we brought to the school, people like Kwame Ture (formerly Stokely Carmichael), Dr. Abdul Alim Muhammad, and others. We produced panel discussions, poetry readings, and a national youth-and-student conference that led to the formation of the Na-

tional African Youth Student Alliance (NAYSA). We protested anything and everything that President Ronald Reagan stood for, as well
as his second in command and eventual successor, George H. W.
Bush. And we certainly admonished the Rutgers University administration loudly and consistently for what we perceived to be its racism when it came to funding for Black organizations, for trying to get
rid of Black professors and our Africana Studies Department, Black-
themed dorms or dorm floors, and even the Paul Robeson Cultural
Center. When we felt that the school was not doing enough to retain
Black students—especially Black male students—we created our own
high-school recruitment weekend and made various RU departments
pay for it. Many of those high-school students wound up coming to
Rutgers, through the same Educational Opportunity Fund that enabled me to go to school.

Utterly obsessed with leadership and activism, I often took and
dropped courses freely, doing just enough each semester to stay in
school for the next term, and I was perpetually on academic proba-
tion. I believed that my experiences as a student leader at Rutgers and
what I learned by going back and forth between New Brunswick and
New York City during my third year in college provided me with a
priceless education.

I was also regularly attending Mosque Number 80 in Plainfield,
New Jersey, one of the many chapters of the Nation of Islam. Although I never officially applied for my "X"—signifying that I was
willing and ready to give up my "slave name" of Powell—I held fast
to the beliefs of the Nation. We did military-style training and fit-
ness exercises with the Fruits of Islam, our men's division, as we
recited and trooped to the chant, "E-LI-JAH MU-HAM-MAD!
M-U-H-A-M-M-A-D!"

The Honorable Elijah Muhammad had been the decades-long
spiritual head of the Nation of Islam (NOI) until his death in 1975.
Born Elijah Poole in Sandersville, Georgia, Muhammad had been
jailed a couple of times, once for resisting the draft for World War II.
Though he never stopped moving from city to city in the 1930s and

1940s, he continued to build the NOI, which he had inherited from a man named Wallace D. Fard. In the 1950s, the extraordinary Malcolm X accelerated that work. Fresh out of prison, Malcolm almost singlehandedly transformed the NOI mosque by mosque and started the NOI's weekly newspaper, *Muhammad Speaks*.

We brothers and sisters at Mosque Number 80 were hopelessly devoted to the cause. We stopped eating pork, ate fish and brown whole wheat bread, and refused to even say "Hello" because, as we were told, "Hell is a low state, and the Black man and the Black woman do not need to get any lower than where we've been." Instead we greeted each other in Arabic, "*As-salaam alaikum*" ("Peace be unto you"). The response was "*Wa-alaikum salaam*" ("And unto you peace").

I started wearing starched white shirts with bow ties, and after reading one of Mr. Muhammad's books, *How to Eat to Live*, I thought long and hard about what I put into my body. I certainly was not going to drink alcohol again, nor would I smoke cigarettes. We learned basic life skills, including hygiene and self-maintenance, and also what to do when stopped by the police: "Brothers, always keep your hands on the steering wheel where they can be seen, and always say 'Yes sir' and 'No sir' to police officers." The NOI gave us hope, provided us with social services, and veteran members like Brother Kareem—who had known Malcolm X personally—connected us with the glory days of the NOI.

At the same time, we resuscitated a student organization called 100 Black Men of Rutgers University. Unaffiliated with the national organization of the same name, we set the goal of graduating one hundred Black men from Rutgers every academic year. When David McKnight, Darwin Beauvais, and I took control of 100 Black Men during our third year in college, along with Moses Montgomery, we transformed it into an on-campus version of the NOI—absent the religious component. There was now security for our programs; every member dressed in a suit and tie for our events; we took road trips to attend student leadership conferences; we connected with students doing similar work, like Ras Baraka and April Silver and the Black Nia

Force organization at Howard University in Washington, DC; Danisa Baloyi at Columbia University in New York; Zaneta Williams at the University of Texas; and Nicole Lind at UCLA in Southern California (who spent much time on the East Coast with us). And we even started throwing campus parties in my third and fourth year, all in an effort to reach the student population, as Malcolm X famously said, "by any means necessary."

And it was working. With older student leaders like Lisa Williamson and Glenn Arnold now gone, Rutgers belonged to us. Black students—even those who refused to support us publicly—respected us. White students feared us, which we loved. And I was beginning to find my voice as a speaker, at least in meetings for 100 Black Men, and also at our campus umbrella organization for all Black groups, the African Student Congress. We plotted and planned throughout the summer of 1987, readying ourselves to provide a new vision for Black student and youth leadership to Rutgers—vision and leadership we hoped would resonate across the nation.

Yet I was still a poor Black person living hand-to-mouth. I had no savings, and the only extra money I had was from my library work-study job on campus, freelance writing here and there in New York City, and the times my mother would mail me $5 or $10. As a financial aid student, I received my refund check each semester, but that money disappeared as fast as it came. But it did not matter. Freedom, justice, equality, and the energy that I felt fighting for those things as a young person mattered most to me. Twenty-one years old, and with three years of college under my belt but not the credits to match, I already knew that I would need at least five years to graduate.

◆

In spite of that, the loneliness and low self-esteem and self-hatred that had been my life in Jersey City were gone—I had found my voice and my purpose at Rutgers University. I began college wanting to get a degree and a good job so that I did not have to be poor any longer, just as my mother had instructed. But I had found something much greater. All the rebelliousness in my bones—dating back to my childhood—was being channeled into being an agent for change. I did not know where I was going, but it felt good to be going somewhere—anywhere—and doing things I loved and was passionate about for once in my life—

19

Kicked out of college

i ache until it is wet, naked,
full of bounce: a gushing wind
corners a heart; puffy cotton veins
snap the way grandma lottie
broke string beans in the front yard.

B Y THE fall of 1987, I knew in my bones that it was my time to
be a leader at Rutgers. We had transformed 100 Black Men into
the dominant Black student organization on campus, and my
college mates had even assumed control over both the African Student
Congress and the Paul Robeson Cultural Center. But my first test of
the new semester came when Black female students on the Douglass
College Campus complained to us about the racism that they experienced in their dealings with White female students, including efforts
to eliminate the Black student living space for women.

Although Felix Jackson was the chairperson of the African Student Congress, I quickly became the spokesperson for this protest. I
knew how to write, how to organize people around a cause, and suddenly I was speaking in public, too. When the university rebuffed our
efforts to address the students' grievances fairly, we decided to plot a

takeover and a sit-in of the entire dorm space on Douglass Campus. We held on as long as we could. We brought sleeping bags; soda and food were strewn everywhere; we held meetings at all times of the day and night; and there were petty arguments and petty divisions. But we made our point, and the university was deeply embarrassed by the media attention that we drew to our cause. Rutgers even enlisted moderate Black faculty and staff members to reason with us, but we refused. We tied the disrespect shown these Black female students in their dorm to the state of Black students campus-wide, to the dwindling number of Black faculty and staff, to the terrible racism of the curriculum in most of the majors, and to what we felt was an incredibly hostile and disrespectful environment for Black people at Rutgers University. And even though we were righteously angry, we managed to present our concerns with grace and eloquence.

We halted the sit-in at the end of the semester in December, right before the winter break, and only because we felt that we had made our point, and the university was responding to our demands. After that success, I ran for, and won, the position of chairperson of the African Student Congress. While I had previously held important positions in other student organizations, I had never before served as the actual leader of a student group. Being out front terrified me, but I had earned this new role. I decided to create a bold agenda by purging the organization of men I thought were weak leaders, and of Black female students who too often brought up how we men treated the women in the organization. In closed-door meetings, I and some of the other male leaders went so far as to tell these women that they must be "lesbians" or have "deep emotional issues" given how much they complained. Slowly, but surely, quite a few drifted away from the organization.

Meanwhile, other Black male student leaders and I decided that we needed to do something big to make our mark on campus. By 1988, Minister Louis Farrakhan of the Nation of Islam was popular on college campuses across America. White students, particularly Jewish students, regularly protested his presence, whereas Black students applauded him. We were keen to invite him, and picked the date of April 6, 1988, for the minister to speak at Rutgers University. The RU administration attempted to block us at every turn, and the major Jewish student group on campus, Rutgers Hillel, asked us not to bring Minister Farrakhan to Rutgers. The RU administrators advised other groups not to cosponsor the event, thinking that they could stop us by eliminating our funding sources (his fee was $10,000). But we found a loophole in the standard RU contract for speakers—much to the chagrin of the school—that allowed us to get outside groups to help finance our programming. We packed ourselves in cars and rallied student groups from other Jersey schools like Princeton and Kean to help pay Minister Farrakhan's honorarium. No one had done this before.

As the winter of 1988 fed into the spring of 1988, my stress levels rose dramatically as I sought to balance being a full-time college student with being a full-time student leader. One Black professor, whom I had previously admired, actually told my peers that I was "an academic failure." I seriously began to wonder if I would ever graduate. As the date drew near for Minister Farrakhan's visit, I started receiving repeated death threats from anonymous callers and opted to purchase and carry a knife for protection.

When Minister Farrakhan arrived, I was the only student from Rutgers allowed to have dinner with him, at the home of Brother Kareem. A small man in person—much more so than I'd expected—Farrakhan was awfully soft-spoken away from a microphone. The minister expressed his great sense of pride in our efforts as young people, and told me that we represented the future not just of the Nation of Islam, but also of America.

As the de facto Black student leader at Rutgers, it fell on my shoulders to introduce Minister Farrakhan at the event, held at the Rutgers Athletic Center (RAC), the largest space on campus. Facing a standing-room-only audience, I stood there in my suit and crisp white shirt and bow tie and did my best to prepare the audience for our distinguished guest. I heard Minister Farrakhan's talk through a fog, because I could not believe that in the face of determined opposition to his presence we had pulled it off. But I did find it troubling that Minister Farrakhan only met with me, ate dinner, gave a speech without a question-and-answer session, and was gone immediately after he spoke with that $10,000 check in hand. All that work on his behalf and he had offered no interaction with the students. This, coupled with rumors swirling that year that Reverend Jesse Jackson, my other hero, was having extramarital affairs during his second run for president, left me disillusioned about Black leadership in general, and about these two men in particular.

A couple of days after the minister's visit I was inside our African Student Congress office at the Paul Robeson Cultural Center, talking to Felix Jackson. As we talked, a woman called Shelley Rodgers stopped by, one of the handful of Black female leaders who had either left the African Student Congress, or whom I encouraged to leave when I took over. Doing my best to ignore her, I told Felix to ask Shelley not to come back again. As I turned my back to the two of them, Shelley charged toward me as if she were going to hit me, rage in her eyes. Quickly I reached in my jeans pocket and pulled and flicked my knife open in my right hand. Shocked, Felix knocked the knife from my hand, even though I never made a motion to use it. Shelley left the office in a huff and I thought the matter over, but Felix turned to me, shaking with fear.

"I can't believe you just pulled a knife on Shelley."

"Man, I was not going to use it," I said. "Just wanted to scare her off, to leave me alone. I won't bother her if she doesn't bother me. Listen man," I went on, edging my chair closer to Felix's, "in case Shelley tries to make a big deal out of this, promise me you will say I did not have a knife, cool."

Felix agreed to not say anything, and I thought I was in the clear. But then I got word that Shelley had not only filed a complaint with Rutgers University, but she had also filed a report with the local police in New Brunswick. I was in double trouble. Looming before me was the possibility of suspension from college and jail time.

Behind the scenes, Glenn Arnold and other old-school Rutgers Black student leaders tried to talk to both Shelley and me, to squash any beef and to make the matter go away. They presented me with a proposed letter, to be written in my name, that they thought I should make public. I refused, and wrote my own letter instead, discussing Black self-hatred, divisions in the Black community, and the sorry state of Black people at Rutgers and in America.

And just when I thought things could not get any worse in my life, my mother phoned me one day in May 1988 to tell me that her mother, my grandmother Lottie, had died.

The next few days went by in a blur. My mother and I and my Aunt Cathy boarded a Greyhound bus for South Carolina. We met my cousin Anthony, now a four-year veteran of the United States Navy, there Down South. We learned the details of my grandmother's last moments: She was in the same gray-washed wooden house in the Wagon Branch section of Ridgeland, where the vast majority of residents in those backwoods were our kinfolk. My grandmother had battled diabetes and high blood pressure for years. She was there, as always, with my Aunt Pearlie Mae, the oldest of my grandparents' children, and the one who never left home because she was "slow" and had been that way since she was a child. My Uncle Lloyd lived just a ways up the road in his trailer, the same trailer in which he had resided since the 1970s, when he was there with his wife and daughter and two sons. His wife and children were gone now, and Uncle Lloyd, or Jabba as we called him, had fallen on hard times . . . so much so that he did not have a phone.

So when my grandmother Lottie screamed in horrific pain as her heart exploded inside her chest, my Aunt Pearlie Mae could not call Uncle Lloyd. Grandma Lottie died right there in the South Carolina clay dirt that had given birth to her seventy-six years before. My grandmother had only left the South once in her life—back in the 1970s—when my Aunt Birdie and mother and Aunt Cathy decided to put her and Aunt Pearlie Mae on a Greyhound Bus up the road a piece, to the North, to visit us. I remember the culture shock Grandma Lottie experienced, how she could not handle the fast pace of us "city slickers"; how her "sugar" acted up because her eating habits and the rhythms of her life had been thrown off so much; how her ankles had swollen on the bus ride up; how she vowed she would never leave the South again. And she never did. Until the day she died.

My grandmother's funeral took place on an exceptionally hot May day. Cousins I did not know came, one by one, to the front pews to pay their last respects to my mother and her sisters and brother and to us, the grandchildren. Unlike when my grandfather Pearlie had died in the early 1970s, the full weight of this death rocked me. I cried uncontrollably, guilt beating me upside the head as I had not seen my grandmother alive since the early 1980s, just before I had gone to college. During my college years my mother told me on several occasions that my grandmother wanted to see me. To my deep regret, I had ignored her, foolishly believing that my work for the people was more important than a random trip to the backwoods of South Carolina.

When the somber old men had lowered my grandmother's casket into the dirt in the "Black cemetery" next to the church, with each shovel scoop of coarse gravel atop her casket I thought of how little I knew my grandmother. I had never sat at my grandma Lottie's feet to learn the traditions of our families, of our people, of the American South. And now it was too late—

Back up north, my mother made it clear that I was no longer welcome in her home. This had been a long time coming. I was no longer the timid little boy afraid of my mother, and I had increasingly found myself yelling back at her when she yelled at me. I returned to New Brunswick dejected, and moved in temporarily with a fellow student leader, Moses Montgomery.

I was debilitated and couldn't sleep. Whenever I did manage to fall asleep—usually only for a couple of hours at a time—I would wake violently, sweating, panting, shaking furiously, as if something were trying to kill me. I barely managed to get myself together for the New Brunswick court hearing. Norman Epting—a member of the first large wave of Black students to enter Rutgers University in the late

1960s and early 1970s—and one of the many old-school, legendary student leaders—was my lawyer. I had never thought that I would need someone like him in this way. Fortunately, the judge merely gave me a stern warning to stay out of trouble, though he said that if I had any further violent episodes, I would definitely go to jail.

But I had one other hurdle: the Rutgers disciplinary hearing on Monday, June 6, 1988. I was especially nervous about this proceeding since the star witness, Felix Jackson, stopped returning my phone calls—in fact, no one knew where he was.

To my dismay, when Mr. Epting and I arrived at the hearing, we saw that Shelley Rodgers and Felix Jackson were sitting together, along with a Black female student named Dakota, with whom I'd once had a relationship. The Rutgers team presented evidence of my dangerous and violent behavior: my freshman-year encounter with my roommate, as well as the time I hit a female student, Piper, in the head with a stapler when she said something I did not like in our EOF office. I was stunned that these incidents were brought up. Though they never mentioned my political activism, it was clear to me that I had given the Rutgers administration a few ropes to hang me with, and they were determined to use them. And then the testimonies: Dakota stated that after one sexual encounter with me I brandished my knife proudly. When asked how long the knife was, Dakota spread her arms so wide it seemed to encompass the entire conference room.

Then Shelley related that I had "charged" toward her with the knife in hand, which was not true. Finally, it was Felix's turn. He could not even look at me. He told the truth—that he and I were in the office talking when Shelley came in, and that I pulled a knife on Shelley.

I was completely defeated; my college career was over. When I finally got the chance to tell my story, I pleaded for mercy and understanding. I talked about how I was the first in my immediate family to go to college, that not finishing college would mean that I had failed not only myself, but also my mother and my entire family. The Rutgers team looked at me unsympathetically. And just like that the hearing was over.

Outside, Mr. Epting said, "The system has no mercy whatsoever. Whatever happens to you in life from here, please get yourself a family. That is the one thing you will be able to hold on to when all else fails you."

A few days later the judgment came down officially: I was suspended from Rutgers University for one year. The conditions for my return included my having to go to therapy. I bristled at the notion that I was "crazy," that I had "emotional problems," but I had been having violent outbursts all my life—in grade school, in high school, and now here at Rutgers. Miraculously, I had managed to escape prison and getting shot or stabbed in retaliation.

That day, I took the knife and threw it into the Raritan River. I vowed that I would never again own a weapon. Next, I begged Moses Montgomery to let me stay in his room the entire summer, and I asked him and other RU close friends not to tell anyone that I had been booted from college. I managed to get part-time jobs here and there: at a local Sears (until they caught me on camera grabbing some French fries in the cafeteria and not paying for them) and at local telemarketing gigs where the pay was minimum wage but at least came weekly. I didn't tell my mother about what had happened.

Reluctantly, I started going to the therapist Rutgers assigned to me, an older Black doctor named Owen Isaacs. Never in my life had I engaged in an extended conversation with a Black man old enough to be my father. I was defensive and suspicious of him at first, until in the third session he said, "You are a prince. I do not know if you realize it, but that is what you are."

At this, the dam broke and I cried long and hard. And from there I began to tell him my entire life story, about my mother, my grandmother who'd just died, my father who had abandoned my mother and me, and about the poverty and roaches and rats. I told him about the violence and anger that had always been a part of my life and my dreams to be a writer, to change the world for the better—

In November of 1988, when my appeals had been exhausted, Rutgers University held firm with my one-year suspension. The jig was up. To add salt to the wounds the letter announcing the decision had been mailed to my permanent home address. As she always did, my mother opened all mail to the apartment, including the mail with my name on it. Surprisingly, she wasn't upset. She said, "Well, you went further in school than I ever did. You just gotta get you a job now. That's what you gotta do. You can't come back here. I done did everything I can for you. I raised you. You on your own now." I exhaled. But I was now abruptly forced, at age twenty-two, to be an adult and to figure out what to do with my life in a real way.

I had to find out if I could make a living as a writer or not. I had to leave Rutgers and the New Brunswick area. I did not want to be that old Black dude, even in my early twenties, just lingering around the campus. A fresh start was the only path. But a part of me still held a thread of hope about getting my college degree, so I moved to Newark, New Jersey, since there was a Rutgers-Newark campus there. I was sad to leave New Brunswick after four long years that had changed my life forever. But if I had learned anything in my short life it was that I had to keep moving no matter what, else I would be stuck forever.

20

Newark, New Jersey

Where do we go after
we
die
is it
to hell
to smell
the devil's fish fry
or
is it
to heaven
to catch
the lord
in
a
lie
?

S O NEWARK it was. I got whatever I had from a Harlem Y where I had briefly stayed in 1988. I also grabbed my ish from my friends' dorm rooms in New Brunswick and stuffed everything into a shoe-box space at the Newark YMCA downtown at 600 Broad Street. Just like the Harlem Y, its Newark counterpart was filled with individuals as disoriented as I: dysfunctional couples bickering and brawling with each other morning and night; alcoholic men and drug-addicted women, all looking for the next get high; bodies being used, abused, sold, to the first bidder . . .

"Say, man, let me get five dollas so I can get me somethin' to smoke."

"Hey, daddy, you so young and good-lookin'. I'll taste you for fitty cents. Wassup?"

And children with dirty faces and dingy eyes bounding off the hallway walls with sugar-induced tantrums. I knew I could not stay there for too long. But I kept hearing my mother's words to get a job and her declaration, spoken since I was a child: "I don't know if you gonna make it, boy."

Because I had met and interviewed the legendary Black Arts Movement writer Amiri Baraka, and knew his son Ras—a Howard University student leader—from my work with Lisa Williamson, I thought I should search for a room to rent in the South Ward of Newark, somewhere near where they lived. I copped a room on South 12th Street, mere blocks not only from the Baraka house at 808 South 10th, but also the Newark church I'd attended as a child. The irony of the Baraka house and the church being on the same block was not lost on me.

Settled, I figured that I could work as a substitute teacher since in New Jersey you only needed sixty credits to sub at schools. I had subbed a few times in New Brunswick, to make some quick cash, and by the time of my suspension from Rutgers I had 81.5 credits. Since I didn't have a room telephone, I had to get up early each morning to walk to the nearest schools to inquire about subbing for the day.

Newark had a reputation for being violent, and this was borne out by the folks I saw as I pounded the pavement every day: the scores of Newarkers with scabbed knife wounds to their faces, hands, and arms, even the backs of their heads. There was the real possibility that a fight could break out at any time anywhere, because folks always seemed to be fussing at each other. The Jersey City ghetto I grew up in was bad, but Newark was bad on a whole other level. It dawned on me that my years in that Jersey City White neighborhood, and four years on the pristine campus of Rutgers in New Brunswick, had dulled my sensibilities about ghetto life.

This was the American ghetto in living color. Black churches were on every corner. There were greasy soul-food and Chinese restaurants, liquor stores with bright neon lights, check-cashing places, pawnshops, funeral parlors with ghastly "Welcome" signs, home furniture rental spots, and all-purpose stores with the normal stock of soda, twenty-five-cent juices we called "quarter water," candy, potato chips, cupcakes, gum, malt liquor and beer and brandy, packs of cigarettes and loose cigarettes if you could not afford the whole pack, lottery tickets, and rolling paper for your marijuana.

I had spent four years at Rutgers reading everything that I could get my hands on about Black history, about Black culture, about Black people, but for the first time I would be residing, full-time, as a socially aware adult, amid the very people I said I wanted to help. This was different than running in and out of New York City with Lisa Williamson. I was back in the environment in which I was born, and I was terrified.

I fumbled my way around my new 'hood, where drug dealers and junkies carved out their kingdoms on every corner. Crack had hit ghettos almost around the time when I left for college in 1984, and throughout the 1980s it had annihilated people, families, communities. Newark was no different. On the one hand you saw late-model, "kitted-up" Cadillacs and Jeeps with shiny fat rims, driven by hustlers with gold rope dookie chains, gold finger rings, gold fronts on their teeth, and an air of invincibility. Their vehicles were tricked out like mobile nightclubs with massive speakers blaring Eric B. and Rakim, Slick Rick, Salt-N-Pepa, LL Cool J, and other hip-hop stars—a slow procession of ego-tripping bravado meant to smudge in the faces of the rest of what us what they had, what we did not have. But we worshipped these ghetto celebrities anyway, just by the silent and methodical ways that we looked at their moving tributes to themselves, then diverted our eyes quickly, for fear of offending. Meanwhile, crack was worse than even the heroin I recalled from my childhood in the 1970s: once full-bodied and baby-faced human beings had been reduced to skeletons, searching for fellow fiends to pass their days with.

Still crushed by the double weight of the death of my grandmother and my school suspension, I was nevertheless able to get a job with The Leaguers, Inc. A woman with whom I shared a surname, Ms. Powell, was the executive director, and she hired me to be a social worker for the agency. The Leaguers ran an early-childhood program, and they also provided resources and services for Newark residents in need of basic life necessities, like food stamps or getting drug treatment.

I was by far the youngest employee at The Leaguers, and it soon became apparent that my job had as much to do with paperwork as it did with helping people in need (if not more). We had to document everything—supplies, work hours, services provided—but I was not complaining because I had a gig.

Unfortunately I did not get paid right away, and the rent on the room I'd taken was late, so I was evicted. All the friendliness that the landlord, a middle-aged Black man, showed me on our first meeting went out the window as soon as he learned that I would be about two weeks late with my payments. I tried to reason with the man, but he closed his door in my face. I had one day to leave.

I wanted to break his door in and bash him in the head for being so cruel. But instead I decided to walk out into the cold night air, toward the drug dealers, crackheads, and gunshots I had been doing my best to avoid. Why I was going in that direction I did not know. I just walked. And then I heard a voice.

"Ke-vin."

I thought I was hallucinating, because I was also ridiculously hungry. I had been living on cupcakes, potato chips, and soda to get by day to day.

"Ke-vin!"

Again, that voice. I thought, first, that someone had found out my name and was trying to set me up to jump me and rob me of the chump change I had in my pocket. I braced myself for the inevitable.

"Kevin, it's Gerald, from Rutgers. What are you doing out here?"

I turned and saw Gerald, a student and poet I remembered from Rutgers, but whom I did not know well. He had been a couple of years ahead of me, and was one of the first people I ever saw read poetry live, which at the time I thought was so odd. I could not give Gerald a simple response. So I told him about the past year of my life. Gerald in turn told me about his life, that his teenage brother Sharif was living with him, and he was Sharif's caretaker. I learned that Gerald was gay and I shoved any homophobia I had from my brain. Gerald was offering me a place to stay and I needed it. I moved in, on Union Street in nearby Irvington, and shared a mattress on the living room floor with Sharif, living there for half a year.

It was during this time, as 1988 became 1989, that I met "Mook." Mook hadn't been to college, but he was worldly in a different way. A former boxer, he drove trucks for a living and loved to dance as much as I did. Mook had an aqua-blue Jeep, with a portable phone in it, and a booming system just like the drug dealers'. Except Mook did not sell drugs at all—shunned that, in fact, since it was all around him, including in his family. He worked hard and liked nice things. Mook and I bonded and became best friends because of our mutual love of women and dancing.

House music was all the rage in America at the time, and underground singers like Doug Lazy and Colonel Abrams dominated clubs such as Zanzibar in Downtown Newark, the Cheetah Club in Paterson, and New York City spots like 1018 and the Red Zone. British bands invaded house music, too, by way of Soul II Soul and their massive hits "Keep on Movin'" and "Back to Life (However Do You Want Me)." Mook and I often dressed alike, in thick black shoes with silver metal on the toes, polka-dot shirts, and the increasingly baggy pants that made it possible for us to move as freely as jitterbug dancers had in the 1940s. We danced so hard my knees would swell or bleed—or both—and I began wearing knee pads to protect myself. Our ritual was simple: Mook and I worked hard, and we partied three or four times a week, often getting home at five in the morning, enough time to shower and head to work. Neither one of us ever drank alcohol or smoked anything. House music was our drug, our addiction.

In the midst of this reckless living I was messing around with different women in Newark. I got badly beaten up by the friends of one woman I'd dated, and with the violence swirling around me I knew I had worn out my welcome at Gerald's place, so I moved out to a studio apartment in a forty-story building. The building had once been the cream of the crop in Newark, but now it was a place where residents threw their garbage bags onto the roof of the smaller, abandoned building next door. I had no furniture, so Mook loaned me a sleeping bag until I could afford a used sofa bed.

On my first night I could hear something stirring in the kitchen area. It had been so long since I had seen a rat anywhere I lived that I tried to push the image from my head, but there they were! Three, four rats, racing around the studio floor where I was sleeping. I screamed in horror, and became that little boy again, certain that they were going to sink their fangs into my face and arms and legs and kill me for their meal. From that night on I slept in the bathtub, until I could afford that used sofa bed. In the daylight hours, I took window screens and created a blockade so the rats could not get past the kitchen. And I only went into that kitchen when I had to cook something to eat, which was usually a frozen burger and some frozen French fries.

Then I met her, through Mook's cousin Jermaine. Her name was Bunny. Bunny had thick legs, a big ol' butt, a waist that must have been a size 20, and ballooned lips painted red by Dollar Stop lipstick. I did not even think about wearing a condom with Bunny. She wanted me and I wanted her. And we did it and we did it and we did it some more. Right on my new used sofa bed. I did not think once about anything else happening to me, even as AIDS was stalking and prowling the community. Like most people I thought of AIDS as a disease mostly gay people or drug addicts got. And I was neither. But then I got an itching sensation in and around my pubic hairs. And an odd-shaped growth on my penis. I was mortified. I had a job and benefits, so I could've gone to see a doctor, but I was too embarrassed to do so. I had heard about people "getting burned" with a venereal disease, but that could not be me, right?

I told Mook and Jermaine, and Jermaine said, "Man, Bunny is a nasty chick! I can't believe she burned you, homeboy! You better go to the clinic quick and let them check you before your joint falls off!"

Mook and Jermaine cracked up and I pretended to laugh along, like it was no big deal. But I was scared. At the clinic were Black and Latino males, all young like me at twenty-three, all there because they had been burned. Dudes were like specialists in sexually transmitted diseases, offering advice before doctors came out to see each one of us.

"Nah, nigga, you ain't got herpes, yo. If you had herpes you would be on fire, my man."

"Word is bond, you right, homeboy. I just itch a little. Last time it happened I came in here and they stuck a long Q-tip in my joint, gave me some horse pills, and I was good to go."

"Say, bruh, what you got?" someone asked me. I could not believe the conversation was that loose, that open, that invasive.

"I—"

"Spit it out, nigga. We know you got somethin', otherwise why the hell is you here?"

The circle around this one dude erupted in laughter.

"I think I got a wart or something."

"That's it, nigga! You spooked for a effin' wart! Man, you will be out in no time. Here is what the doctor is going to tell you. . . ."

And they were right. But what the doctor did not tell me was that I should not have condom-less sex again anytime soon. In the next few months or so, I passed that STD to a girlfriend back at Rutgers and to a female activist I dug from the Midwest who I encouraged to fly in to visit me. Only because the female activist had the humanity to write me a letter to inform me what I had done to her did I even know that I had not really been cured at all. I felt bad, very very bad. Eventually I went to a legit doctor to be treated. But not until I realized that my sex education growing up had been zero in school and otherwise only my moms stressing not to get a girl pregnant.

◆

It was now early 1990 and I was just a couple months shy of twenty-four years old. I had been living in my studio apartment less than a year and had squandered my money on partying and women and fancy clothes, and I had neglected to pay the rent with any consistency. I even ignored the court order to appear about back rent. One day, I came home from work to find that my door was padlocked—I had been evicted. I begged the building's super to allow me to get as much of my belongings as possible, and he did, but I still lost a lot of stuff. I called Mook and asked him for help. He said that I could stay with him but could not bring much, as he lived in the attic of his grandmother's house, and we had to make sure she didn't know I was there. Whenever Mook left, I had to leave—and whenever he came home, I had to mime his footsteps to get into his spot. This lasted for all of a month, until his grandma got wind of our scheme. Homeless and with no money—I'd quit the Leaguers, foolishly—my last resort was my friend Jermaine's apartment down the street from where I had been evicted.

But Jermaine's apartment was a place where anyone who needed to pass through could do so, so I barely ever slept. I befriended one passerby named Akbar. Akbar was a master thief, able to "boost" anything from clothing stores, selling them in the 'hood to have dollars in his pocket. He also slept in parked cars overnight, knowing exactly when to wake each morning to avoid the owners. One day he and I were just kicking it in front of the building, talking about nothing, the nothingness of our lives, shooting a deflated basketball into a garbage can. I had to go to the bathroom and went upstairs for a minute. When I came back down I saw that Akbar had been beaten with a baseball bat by some dudes from another building up the block who had declared war on anyone in our building. In that moment, it hit me that I might not even make it to my twenty-fourth birthday, that I would more than likely die there on the streets of Newark, New Jersey.

I panicked. How had I gone from a college student leader to this, from a job with benefits to nothing, so swiftly?

I had to do something. I sought out the Nation of Islam and some orthodox Muslim leaders in Newark, but they suddenly reminded me of the Black church I had fled as a teenager: much talk and dogma but very little action or support for people like me. I was essentially done with organized religion at this point in my life. I still believed, faintly, in God, but I was not sure if God believed in people like me. So I called my old Dominican friend Leonardo from Jersey City. We had hung out through our college years—he had studied at the New Jersey Institute of Technology. He had taken me, several times, up to Washington Heights in Manhattan, where there was a large Dominican community. I met some of the big ballers up there, the big-time drug dealers, including a dude named Papi who always gave us money to put in our pockets, and had once given me a "loan" of a couple hundred dollars like it was few single dollar bills. He never asked for the money back, and probably had forgotten about it. It was mad violent up there, and things seemed to be divided into camps: Dominicans, Colombians, African Americans, West Indians. But I was so desperate that, left with no other choice, I wanted in on the drug game. It had always been suggested that I could get in. But Leo was adamant I should avoid it. In desperation I asked him if I could live with his family in Jersey City. His mother, the most important person in his household, said that I could come stay with them. I had never lived with any family other than my mother, aunt, and cousin, but I did not care. They were offering me a rope to keep from drowning. And even if it meant going back to Jersey City, I was going to take it.

21

Aunt Cathy. And a new life.

i see you: dancing like a revelation
from an ancestor: chains swing wildly
from your kneecaps; your arms, guideposts
to the yesteryear when you traveled in search of a
beat, hold firm against the hurricanes of time:

WAS STILL living in Newark when I got the news from my
mother that my Aunt Cathy was not well. Must've started when
Grandma Lottie died. My cousin Anthony had gone to that funeral, stayed around Jersey City for a while, even bought a car, and
made it seem as if he would be close to his mother again. But then
he could not take it. Somewhere in the creases of my grandmother's
death and Anthony's departure and the many years of working and
walking and cooking and scrubbing and having nothing to show
for any of it, my Aunt Cathy began to crack. My mother and Aunt
Birdie immediately labeled her "crazy," a diagnosis that I could not
accept. While in Newark and still employed by The Leaguers, Inc.,
I took Aunt Cathy to a Black female therapist and paid the bill. I

thought about Owen Isaacs, the male therapist who'd helped me through my breakdown in 1988, and was praying that this woman could help my aunt.

"You ain't gotta do all that, Kevin," she said. "Don't spend your money on me. Ain't nothin' wrong with me. Shirley and Birdie the ones who crazy!"

But then Aunt Cathy went quiet—radio silent—and her eyes looked far past me . . . into spaces and places long ago from her life of pain and trauma. I had read about "Black psychology" and how the pressures of a lifetime of poverty and instability and a lack of real and consistent love could break down even the strongest person. Aunt Cathy had endured hunger as a child in a two-room shack, cotton fields where the sun fried skin and soul, a few years in a school she had to quit so she and her sisters could make some money so they could eat something some of the time—

When Aunt Cathy walked out of the therapist's office, I asked her to wait for me while I spoke with the therapist. She told me my Aunt Cathy was in need of real help immediately, else her condition would worsen. I swallowed hard, and went out to take my Aunt Cathy home. I had it all planned, what I could do to assist Aunt Cathy, but before I could even get started my mother called me one day and told me that she and my Aunt Birdie had sent their sister away, to a mental institution. There was no more apartment, no more furniture, no more nothing. I screamed at my mother in horror for doing such a thing, threatened her and Aunt Birdie. My mother would not even tell me where Aunt Cathy was. She was gone. Feeling completely powerless, I wrote a poem in tribute to my aunt.

Eventually, Aunt Cathy would be discharged from that mental institution. Somewhere in there she lost a tooth, some hair, and, at least temporarily, some additional pieces of her mind. The first time that I saw her after that she was living in a welfare hotel in the Journal Square section of Jersey City. I could not face my Aunt Cathy as she spoke to me about that mental institution, about what my mother and Aunt Birdie had done to her. I listened, then told her I would come see her as often as I could, though I was destitute and desperate myself. It would be many years before she recovered and returned to the Aunt Cathy I knew.

◆

Leonardo's mother had welcomed me into their home like a long-lost son. I had been there several times through the years. The place was full of various kinds of religious objects—Leo's mom was deeply spiritual. She spoke no English, and I spoke only a bit of Spanish, so we communicated as best we could. Leo's father was a veteran of the Dominican Republic's guerilla wars against its former dictator Rafael Trujillo, and still harbored anger about what La Era de Trujillo had done to his beloved DR. Dad's rage extended to random curses, in Spanish, aimed at his wife; to drinking binges; and to telling me how America had ruined his life. Leonardo's two brothers were there, too: Delio, a debonair guy with an uncanny ability to lasso any woman he wanted, and Manuel, the ultra-shy younger brother with a passion for anything to do with math, science, or electronics.

Leo became like the big brother I never had. Daily we ate rice and beans, watched Spanish telenovelas, listened to merengue music, and discussed women. He constantly was on me about how I treated my mother, how I spent my money, what I was going to do with my life. And ever so slowly, things started to turn around. I found work in New York City, at a telemarketing company where I called people to get them to take surveys. An old girlfriend, Nicole Lind—now known as Nicole Muhammad—got me a gig teaching English and SAT prep to high-school students through a program at New York University. And finally, I landed another part-time job, as an assistant to Sam Anderson at the New School, its Eugene Lang college division. A Black man in his mid-forties, Sam had just been appointed to run the institution's diversity program. He asked me a few questions and hired me.

Sam was a veteran of the Civil Rights Movement, and his poetry had appeared in Black anthologies in the 1960s and 1970s. He was a part of a lot of "radical" Black and multicultural political and artistic circles in New York City, and I could not have asked for a better mentor at that time in my life. Sam and I would talk about his generation, about my generation, about manhood, about life. I got to assist Sam with a major conference on the great Brazilian educator Paulo Freire; with the literary publication for his group the Network of Black Organizers (NOBO); and we collaborated on gathering information about the life and legacy of Malcolm X as Spike Lee was preparing to release his biopic of Malcolm's life. Sam was also able to finally turn me on to jazz, though it took a lot of effort.

◆

In the years 1984 through 1990, I changed and grew, much of which I owed to my relationship with Lisa Williamson, my surrogate big sister, during my first couple of years at Rutgers. I do not know if I would have become the leader, activist, or even the writer I became if she had not believed in me, pushed me, and connected me with the many people she had in her ever-growing network. I was—quite literally—Lisa's loyal servant. My mother would often say to me, "You better stop following Lisa around so much." Never had I met someone so powerful, so intelligent, so well spoken, and so open to my being a part of her life. If Lisa had told me to catch a bullet for her, I would have. I defended Lisa from attackers, accusers, haters, death threats, which only grew as her fame grew as a leader and as a spokeswoman for our generation, for our communities.

With all my travel back and forth between New York City and Jersey, I often stayed wherever Lisa stayed, shared a bed with her as a little brother would, ate food with her, made sure that she ate, carried her speeches for her, and agreed with every single thing that ever came from her mouth. It was in her kitchen at her apartment on 141st Street and Convent in Harlem that Lisa first told me that Chuck D of Public Enemy—the biggest rap group on the planet—had asked her to become the first female member. She ran a name by me that she was thinking of calling herself: "Sister Souljah." I loved it, because that was who she was, especially when, in her many speeches, Lisa would proclaim, loudly, that "We are at war!"

But there were some cracks in her armor. Souljah was terrible with money: she made it but never kept a good accounting of it, and was always giving it away. Souljah had shaky social skills: a close friend today could be her enemy tomorrow. I saw this firsthand with Danisa Baloyi, a South African Columbia University student, and one of the most dynamic leaders of America's anti-apartheid movement—Souljah seemed to cast her aside over some small infraction. I saw other close friends similarly discarded. She seemed to have constant tensions with many Black women, and I saw how despite her messages about Black unity, she didn't seem to think it a big deal when one of her boyfriends, an ill-tempered underground rapper from Brooklyn, pulled a gun on RU student Moses Montgomery at our annual Black student unity cookout one year over a contract dispute. I turned a blind eye to it all because I did not dare challenge her. Like my mother before her, Lisa was the one constant in my life—a source of strength and stability—no matter how haphazard those strengths and that stability were at times. She rewarded my loyalty by inviting me into the studio with the Bomb Squad, Public Enemy's famous production team, while they produced parts of Ice Cube's first solo album (made after his notorious split from N.W.A).

◆

By early 1990, Sister Souljah was not paying me as she had said she would, in spite of the work that I was putting into organizing rallies, marches, and protests, and the building of our network with other youth and student leaders across America. I steamed when I saw her hand money—again and again—to others, without paying me or ever giving me the job that she had promised me I would get. The final straw came after one of our many hugely successful "State of Black Youth" town hall meetings in Brooklyn. I dug up the courage to ask Souljah for payment for the work that I had put in—and she handed me twenty dollars and walked away.

I called Souljah later to have it out with her.

"I know you got a lot going on, but I really don't have any money, and I've been doing all this work for you."

"Kev, why are you stepping to me like this? You know I got you."

"Yes, but you have been saying that for a long time and—"

"Are you calling me a liar? What are you saying, Kevin? What is up with this attitude? After all I have done for you, you coming at me like this is disrespectful!"

I attempted to back down, but Souljah landed a body blow with her next words:

"I don't want you to ever call me again. Never contact me again. If you do, I am going to call the police on you!"

I was devastated. We had protested police brutality together for years, and this woman—my big sister and mentor—was telling me that she would call the cops on me if I ever contacted her again?

It was like a death to me, as heartbreaking as when my grandmother died suddenly just two years before. Six long years of working for her and following her because I thought she was one of the best leaders in America—gone.

I became severely disillusioned with activism, with community work, with politics in all forms for many years after that break from Sister Souljah. Sam Anderson and I would talk about "the struggle" as we activists called it, sure, but I only did so during the hours I worked for him, and rarely ever went to any of the community events that he and others in his circle invited me to. I had become a freelance journalist, and was writing for publications like the *Amsterdam News*, but the enthusiasm to be both an activist and writer had been killed in that one call with Sister Souljah, a call that reflected how tired I was after six long years of sacrificing my life, my college education, my family, and even my own sanity, all on behalf of others. I needed to find another way, my own way, away from my mother, away from Sister Souljah, away from the past six years of my life.

◆

By the summer of 1990 I had saved enough money to move across the Hudson River, finally, to New York City. I had survived Jersey City, and Rutgers University, and Newark, and my mother kicking me out, and Sister Souljah kicking me to the curb. I had survived the death of my grandmother. At long last, I was going to do something for myself. I was moving to New York City to be a writer.

22

Hip-hop, poetry, and New York City

rhyth mic   american   po e try
    you hear it
      and you think of me
trapped in a concrete box
      begging to be released

I **WAS READY** for New York City.

New York had been a part of my life for as long as I could remember. I had fallen madly in love with the New York Yankees in 1976, when they made it to the World Series for the first time in a dozen years and got crushed by Johnny Bench, Pete Rose, and their Cincinnati Reds. And later I loved its music scene. Back in October of 1979, the big hip-hop hit was "Rapper's Delight" by the crew Sugar Hill Gang—the group rapped over Chic's massive disco hit "Good Times." By the time "Rapper's Delight" shook up the music landscape, the basic elements of hip-hop were already there for us Jersey City kids, thanks to what was happening in the NY. In fact, several rap crews called Jersey City home, the most famous being Sweet, Slick, and Sly, local dudes who were ghetto celebrities.

Like our New York cousins, Jersey City—or Chilltown J.C., as we kids nicknamed our community—had block parties with gigantic speakers. And with those dance parties we slowly began to break away from our parents, from their hairstyles and dress, from their talk, and from their music. Motown, Stax, jazz, soul, rock, and funk were their thing. Rap was our thing (even though we were building that culture on the recycled beats of our elders' music). A TV show called *Video Music Box*, also out of New York City, hosted by Ralph McDaniels, starting in the early 1980s, captivated us. I watched Uncle Ralph, as he was called—inside clubs, at parties, on the streets—interviewing every kind of rap artist you could name.

The critical elements of hip-hop culture were taking shape: the graffiti, the deejaying, the emceeing or rapping, the dancing. By the 1980s, we also had our own vocabulary: "beef" was an argument or conflict; "my word is *bond*"; we were members of a "crew"; "def" meant something was cool; "fresh" meant something was new or good. If you were a sucker you were a "duck"; "Five-O" was the police; 42nd Street in New York City was, in fact, the "forty-deuce"; a "homeboy" was your good friend. If you were "housin' things," that meant you were taking over; "juice" meant you had power and influence. "Raise up" meant be careful, or look out; and if you agreed with something or someone, you said, "Word."

These expressions and things like our toothbrush-cleaned footwear or name belts with either our real names or our street names was part of our hip-hop declaration of independence. When Michael Jackson's *Thriller* hit big internationally, you saw dudes with Jheri curls, high-water pants with white socks, one glove, and penny loafer shoes. Some of us did that, too, but for us boys and girls from the 'hood, hip-hop provided a harder and realer image, because it was not an act or some costume we donned for a stage. In America's ghettos, we knew that we were always on stage, always being watched, so we always had to be fly. Every crew—no matter the size—stood in B-boy or B-girl poses on street corners. Every crew popped and locked and break-danced on those same concrete corners, sometimes on pieces of cardboard or linoleum, sometimes without. Every crew carried Magic Markers or spray paint to tag our names.

And then came Run-DMC, the first hip-hop superstars. They changed the game forever. Run-DMC mattered as much to us as Michael Jackson ever would. When I first heard their song "Sucker MCs," and saw what they looked like—barely older than I was, dressed in the same clothes that I wore—they became my first hip-hop heroes. Yes, I loved artists like Kurtis Blow, Grandmaster Flash and the Furious Five, the Treacherous Three, and the Fearless Four, but in Run-DMC I found my own voice, my own longings, my own vocab as a young Black male. I studied and memorized the lyrics to every single Run-DMC song, and studied and absorbed their mannerisms, the way they walked, the way they threw their hands around when rhyming.

Over time I would learn that the term "hip-hop" was believed to have been created by Cowboy of Grandmaster Flash and the Furious Five. And that Kool Herc, Afrika Bambaataa, and Grandfather Flash—each a pioneering deejay and innovator—are widely considered the founding fathers of hip-hop.

Any chance I got I was at a hip-hop club, in the Latin Quarter, or Union Square in Lower Manhattan, or the Rooftop in Harlem. Our dances had names like "the Pee-wee Herman" and "the wop," and pretty much every rap artist was sampling one James Brown groove or another as the foundation for new songs. I rarely saw anyone other than Black and Latino young people at these hip-hop jams. The Black kids wanted to rap and DJ, while the Latino kids performed daredevil break-dances and wrote more experimental graffiti.

Although I had spent the mid to late 1980s with Sister Souljah organizing youth in New York, hip-hop was always there, especially as the scene shifted from the braggadocious style of Run-DMC, Doug E. Fresh, and Slick Rick to the Black nationalist firepower of Public Enemy and KRS-One and his squad, Boogie Down Productions. Public Enemy, and especially its front man, Chuck D, were like God and the court of mighty prophets to me. Where the previous generation had had Bob Dylan, Joan Baez, Nina Simone, Bob Marley, and John Lennon to speak truth to power, to document their times, we had Chuck D. The first time I saw Spike Lee's landmark film *Do the Right Thing*, with the opening credit music "Fight the Power" by P.E., I almost fell out my theater seat when Chuck hawk-spit a massive dis of American icon Elvis Presley backed by his sidekick Flavor Flav ripping John Wayne a new one, too.

That kind of fearlessness and boldness reinforced for us hip-hop heads that our voices and lives mattered. And because of Sister Souljah's vision, we youth activists forged relationships with major rap stars, like Chuck D. Souljah created something called the "GET BUSY TOUR" that brought us all together (GET BUSY stood for General Education and Training of Blacks United to Save Youth). We were creating what became known as "hip-hop activism" without even realizing it. We also produced massive outdoor rap concerts and rallies in Harlem, at 125th Street and Adam Clayton Powell Boulevard, right in front of the State Office Building. It was there that Heavy D entered the stage through the crowd, because he wanted to be able to feel and to give back the love of the community.

Like others of my generation, I grew my original Carl Lewis flattop high, too, into a tubular 'fro that required a blow dryer with teeth on it—all the better to reach out to God's sky. These Cameo haircuts, as they were called, mimicked African royal crowns. Many, in an effort to reflect the racial and cultural pride suddenly manifested in rap music, began wearing red, black, and green African medallions or African beads around our necks (red for the blood, black for the people, green for the land). And our pants got baggier and baggier as the 1980s became the 1990s, with an emphasis on them sagging below our waists, like in the jail culture that spawned the trend. Indeed it was in prison where the same Black and Latino young males who created hip-hop culture were not allowed to have belts for fear they would hang themselves or use them as weapons. So as they left jail and returned back to the 'hoods that birthed hip-hop they effortlessly integrated prison styles into the fashions of our community and culture. I felt, also, that our pants sagging was our response, we were clear, to a world we felt did not care about us.

With this bursting Black pride, Michael Jackson quickly became a has-been to me, especially because of the chemicals in his hair, his bleached white skin, and surgery that chopped off his big, natural nose. I wanted Black self-love and MJ represented Black self-hatred.

This was "the golden era" of hip-hop and our culture was everywhere, and everyone was saying words like "Peace" and "Yo" incorporated with elements of the Five Percent Nation of Gods and Earths, a group that broke away from the Nation of Islam in the late 1960s. More and more of us talked about "doing the math," rapping or talking or building in "cyphers," and about the necessity to "drop science (knowledge)" on our communities. Hip-hop culture educated us about ourselves, about our collective history, and gave us a new way to view the world that was different from the one that we had learned about in school. And it was all to a dope beat.

◆

Around this time I found myself captivated by the writings of Nelson George and Greg Tate in the *Village Voice*. George wrote a column called "Native Son," after the classic Richard Wright novel, and he routinely wrote about his home community of Brooklyn, New York. Nelson George's writings, the films of Spike Lee, and Brooklyn rap superstar Big Daddy Kane—my favorite solo hip-hop artist ever—placed Brooklyn solidly at the center of my universe. When I finally made the move to NYC, I assumed that it would be to Harlem, drenched as it was in the history of Malcolm X, of Langston Hughes, of James Baldwin, and the Harlem Renaissance. But Brooklyn captured my imagination like no other place. Whenever I went to an event, be it a party or community gathering, Brooklyn folks always traveled in large packs, and they always represented Brooklyn loud and proud. I had felt that way about Jersey City while I attended Rutgers. We Jersey City homies even had our own official handshake, which involved slapping palms like we were about to do a traditional shake, then rotating our hands so fingers met and hands and arms went up, until our fingers gripped and clasped at the top and then dropped back down.

During my college years, digesting the speeches of Malcolm X, Stokely Carmichael, Louis Farrakhan, and other Black activists, and inhaling the music and wordplay of artists like the Last Poets, Gil Scott-Heron, Bob Marley, and Steel Pulse, freed me up as a writer to explore beyond what had been shoved into my brain as "standard English," as "classical literature." My desire to write poetry indefinitely replaced my teenage dream of being a novelist. Poetry represented the kind of short bursts of ideas and of energy that I carried with me every single day, demanding to be released. It began while I was still a student at Rutgers, when I wrote a poem that saluted Black women—borrowing heavily from the Nation of Islam and Black nationalist ideology, and constructed it in a way that I thought would make sense. The poem caused quite a stir on campus and gave me many female admirers, although it was initially "published" as a poem by our male group, 100 Black Men. I followed that piece up with a Black pledge of allegiance strictly for students. This time I made sure to put my name on the poem. It got copied and shared regularly, even in different parts of America. I knew that I was on to something, some new form of writing for me. During the same period, I shifted my emphasis from studying the writers of the Harlem Renaissance of the 1920s to the Black Arts Movement of the 1960s. If the Renaissance's Langston Hughes and Zora Neale Hurston, in particular, taught me anything, it was that the language that my people spoke, including my mother and my Southern kinfolk, was beautiful poetry, as fine as anything that I ever studied by Shakespeare, Chaucer, or Keats. But the Black Arts poets, with names like Sonia Sanchez, Nikki Giovanni, Amiri Baraka, Larry Neal, Haki Madhubuti, Henry Dumas, Mari Evans, Maya Angelou, and countless others, showed me how to blend poetic devices and techniques unapologetically with political expression.

Soon I started reading my poetry in public, first when I was living in Newark, and then when I crossed over to the East Village in the Big Apple, to places like ABC No Rio, a social center and art space. In early 1990, I read an article in the *Village Voice* about a spot called the Nuyorican Poets Cafe on East 3rd, about a young Black male poet named Paul Beatty, who had been declared the first "poetry slam champion." Paul's background, his poems, and the fact that his prize included getting his first poetry collection published, inspired me. I soon made my way to the Nuyorican and was blown away by its history.

Founded in 1973 in the living room of poet Miguel Algarín, the Nuyorican was propelled by writers of color, many of whom were Puerto Ricans born or raised in New York City. Like the Black Arts Movement of the 1960s, the Nuyorican movement provided an outlet for voices previously forgotten or ignored, folks such as Sandra Maria Esteves, Mikey Piñero, and Pedro Pietri. Their stories echoed those of the Puerto Ricans with whom I'd grown up in Jersey City: tales of love gotten and lost, of salsa music, of split identities, of rice and beans, and of congas and cockroaches.

Walking into the Nuyorican that first night I felt that I had found my literary home. There stood Miguel Algarín—the legendary figure himself—at the bar, hooting and hollering, while a White man named Bob Holman, with granny glasses and energy that felt like part circus ringmaster and part talk-show host, ran the festivities. Scared by the size of the crowd, the likes of which I had never faced before—there were probably two hundred people there that night—I signed up for the slam. When my turn came, I got up and read the poem I'd written for my aunt, "for aunt cathy," and later a hip-hop inspired poem called "Mental Terrorism." By the end of the night, much to my surprise, I had won the slam. After those essay contests in my senior year, here I was again a winner at writing, which more than made up for the many rejection letters that are, sadly, the life of a freelance writer.

I was told to return the next week to compete again. Though I was terrified—I didn't write that quickly!—the following week I stood on stage at the Nuyorican, performing a poem filled with bad metaphors and terrible hip-hop allusions. It made little to no sense, and the judges did me a big favor by giving me a low score. In one week, I had become a has-been.

My Village experience provided me with something else besides a budding relationship with the Nuyorican: I discovered the Beat Generation writers—Allen Ginsberg, Jack Kerouac, and William S. Burroughs. From there I discovered Bob Dylan's music and Welsh poet Dylan Thomas, who inspired the folksinger's name.

In the summer of 1990, Harry Allen, self-proclaimed "hip-hop activist and media assassin," closely associated with Chuck D and Public Enemy, and the father of hip-hop journalism, phoned me one day to ask if I ever wrote music articles. My first four years of professional journalism, dating back to age twenty during my Rutgers years, had been spent as a news reporter. For sure I fancied myself on the path to becoming like the *Washington Post*'s Woodward and Bernstein as an investigative journalist. But then Harry said that Danyel Smith, the music editor of the *San Francisco Weekly*, needed someone to write about a new rapper from Queens named Intelligent Hoodlum. I lied to Harry and said, "Yes, I write about music." I spoke with Danyel Smith and wrote my first music piece, which led to others, for *San Francisco Weekly*, for *L.A. Weekly*, for *Interview* magazine, for hip-hop's first publication, *The Source*, for the skateboard 'zine *Thrasher*, and, eventually, for the bible of music journalism, *Rolling Stone*. I grinded hard as both a news reporter and a music journalist, writing for every publication that I could, adding those freelance journalism checks to my pay from a part-time teaching and tutoring gig at New York University and a part-time assistant gig at the New School. Still only twenty-four, I was now writing regular reviews for *Rolling Stone*. And I was meeting a new wave of twenty-something writers like myself, penning articles and essays about pop culture, about hip-hop, about our times, the list of which included: Scott Poulson-Bryant, Alan Light, Joan Morgan, and Ann Powers. They deconstructed hip-hop, rock, pop, and other parts of American culture in ways that were brilliant, exciting, uplifting, and very much personal.

With all this going on in my life, I also officially moved to New York City in August 1990, to an old prewar building in Uptown Manhattan. I lived with two roommates—a man and a woman—recommended by some mutual friends. We were all young, all artists, all on our own, determined to survive and to win. One of the people who recommended me as a roommate was a recent City College graduate named Adera Gerima, whom I'd met while I was still at Rutgers. She was born in America of parents from Ethiopia, East Africa. I was immediately taken with her natural copper-brown beauty, her wild, flowering afro, and her broad pearly white smile.

There was only one small problem: Adera had a man, nearly forty years old, living with her in her Fort Greene, Brooklyn, apartment. I found this out when she invited me and others over to her home for a reading of poetry and other kinds of literature. While there, I met her next-door neighbor Fiona, a dope fiction writer, and several other writers, including some folks somehow connected to the Dark Room Collective, a tribe of talented young Black wordsmiths based in Boston—Sharan Strange, Patrick Sylvain, Janice Lowe, John Keene, and Tisa Bryant. We New York and Boston writers had different tastes and sensibilities: to them we were too overtly political and blunt in the NY; to us the Boston folks were too focused on the craft at the expense of being bold and fearless with their words. But amidst the differences, youthful egos, and mad real tensions there was mutual respect, on some level.

I was so happy to be in the middle of a flourishing Black literary scene, in New York, in America. We read to each other in each other's homes, and did poetry readings together. I became friends with fellow young New York City poets, too—asha bandele, Lorena Craighead, Tony Medina, Willie Perdomo, and Sabah as-Sabah. By now, Ras Baraka had graduated from Howard University, and he joined us, too. We rented vans and drove to read and to perform our poetry in various states. Many of us young writers would crowd the pioneering Black literary agent Marie Brown's tiny office on Broadway at Houston in Greenwich Village, just to soak up her wisdom and her thoughts on how best to get published.

As with everything else in my life, I was in a hurry. When it was suggested that there was no new Black literary scene happening, I immediately produced a massive reading at New York University with thirty-five poets, including the folks from Boston's Darkroom Collective. And when I saw that we were being left out of anthologies and conversations, I talked Ras into coediting *In the Tradition: An Anthology of Young Black Writers*, even though we had no publisher. I wrote and faxed writers around the country to solicit their poems and pieces of fiction.

I encountered dynamic young Black writers like Kupenda Auset, Tamara Jeffries, and Valerie Boyd in Atlanta; Andrea Wrenn and Ira Jones in St. Louis; Charlie Braxton in Mississippi; and Ruth Forman, Lisa Teasley, and Michael Datcher in Los Angeles. There was a movement afoot, and I was in the middle of it. I was young, Black, and an artist in early 1990s New York City, which was a great thing to be.

And I was smitten with Adera, despite her live-in boyfriend.

My girlfriend and the bathroom door

Nobody said
this life would
be easy—that it
would take
shooting hot hate
into our blue veins
to smother the
archaic wails
of people
sprinting from
steel gangplanks
to iron waters
to cotton trees

ADERA WAS born in Harlem and raised out in Queens. She was genuinely sweet, very much the girl-next-door type. She was all about Black people and the Black community, and often wore African clothing and jewelry. And like me, she was a writer.

I schemed on how to get through to Adera, to let her know she would be better off with me than her much older boyfriend. I had to play it cool, but by the fall of 1990, not only had she dumped her boyfriend, but I was now living in her Brooklyn apartment in the heart of Fort Greene, a magnet community for writers and other artists. We were the young dynamic couple, and the envy of others in our growing literary and artistic circle. We continued to host readings in our apartment and hung out with a host of other young writers.

One day early in our relationship, Adera hit me with some news: she was pregnant. The only thing was, it was by her ex-boyfriend, from prior to our dating. Devastated, I thought that our relationship was over before it had begun, but the pregnancy didn't last. We stayed together, which surprised her, but before this woman my longest relationship had lasted only a few months and I wanted this one to be different.

Around this time I sensed that Adera's friends did not like me. I thought them pretentious and elitist; they thought me rude and crude. One by one I began to cut them off from her, or her from them, and my tirades became more frequent. Even when friends came around that I did not mind being with, I could sense their trepidation—and I had the feeling that they had been talking about me behind my back. This made me feel small and insecure.

Finally, the situation came to a head one summer day in July 1991. Adera and I had spent much of the day arguing, and as we were returning from the laundromat, she ran ahead of me to our apartment building. I caught up with her at the front door, dropped the clothes at her feet, went inside, and slammed the door behind me. She eventually brought the clothes into the apartment, set them down, and started back outside. Enraged, I grabbed her by the seat of her shorts and pulled her back into the apartment. We struggled in the kitchen, the dining area, and the bathroom, and as we moved toward the living room, I shoved Adera into the bathroom door. Her face bruised, and she began to cry. I tried to calm her down as we wrestled on the living-room floor. When she let out a high-pitched yell for help, I jumped to my feet, suddenly aware of what I was doing. Shaking with fear and exhaustion, I watched Adera run barefoot out of our apartment into the street. I stood there trembling.

What should I do? I couldn't move. Should I close the door or leave it open? What if someone had heard us and called the police? What if Adera had run straight to the station house and was coming back to have me carted off to jail?

She did come back, without the police. We talked quietly, and knowing that I had nowhere else to go, she allowed me to continue shacking up with her for about another month. But clearly the relationship was over. Adera told me I needed to get therapy for my anger and violent tendencies.

Sam Anderson, my boss at the New School, referred me to a therapist named Martha Wingate. She was an older Black woman, which was good because I wanted to learn, as a young man, directly from a woman. I was embarrassed, ashamed, and guilt-stricken. I felt like a failure, like I had let everyone down. And I believed in my heart, as I made my way around New York City, that every single person I crossed paths with knew what I had done to Adera.

Several weeks after that incident, after I had moved out of Adera's apartment, my anger got the best of me again. I was downtown in Greenwich Village when I saw her. When Adera did not respond to me in the way that I thought she should, I screamed at the top of my lungs, in broad daylight, "You Black heffa!" and every other kind of derogatory thing I could say about her. It was instantly clear that she was both disgusted and resigned that I was abusive, and she got away from me as fast as she could. A few days later I received an order to appear in court—I was now the subject of a restraining order and had to stay away from her.

After that, I doubled down on my efforts to get help. Therapy was excruciating and uncomfortable, but I took my appointments with Martha Wingate seriously. I talked at length about what I had done to Adera, to other women, to other people generally, but I also talked about my mother, my childhood, all the violence I had known in my life. I also talked with women of my generation, especially the ones I met through my activism and literary work, including quite a few who had attended Spelman, the historic Black women's college in Atlanta. I was told to read things like Pearl Cleage's book *Mad at Miles*, the writings of bell hooks, Audre Lorde, and many other Black women writers. Doing so, it dawned on me for the first time that I had barely ever read anything by women writers of any race—except Emily Dickinson's poetry and the few women writers I discovered in English courses at Rutgers, like Zora Neale Hurston. It also dawned on me that I knew little to nothing about women's history, about anything women had done outside of what we males were taught: they were caretakers, they were sexual objects. Here I was raised by women, shaped by women my entire life, yet completely ignorant of women and girls. It was inevitable, given my journey and mis-education, that I would come to hurt women.

In *Mad at Miles*, Cleage takes on Miles Davis, an American and an international cultural icon who had written boastfully in his own autobiography that he had beaten his then partner, the Oscar-nominated actress Cicely Tyson. I struggled through Pearl Cleage's book, painfully aware that she was not only talking about Miles Davis and his abuse of women, but about men like me.

My reading made me think about all the times I had disrespected a girl or woman in some way:

The teenage girl we called "Whorey Dorey" on the streets of Jersey City, because we thought she had had sex with every boy in the 'hood. The many times I raced through my grammar school hallways and grabbed and squeezed and smacked girls' behinds, with no remorse whatsoever for sexually objectifying them. The too-many-to-count girls I had sex with in college, many of whom with names that I could not recall, not thinking twice that I saw them as nothing more than a part of my college experience. The time two other college boys and I tried to "run a train" on a college girl in the dark after I had had sex with her, but it not happening because she resisted, loudly. The one night another college girl and I had sex in a drunken stupor and my not even thinking or knowing if she had consented. The fight I had with Teena Dyer inside RU's Paul Robeson Cultural Center, after sexing her and dissing her over and over, and us swapping punches until my shoulder popped out and she cursed me as I fell to the floor in pain, stepping right over me. The time I became so angry at Piper in the Educational Fund Office at Rutgers that I picked up a stapler and threw it right at her head. The time Akosua Busia, one of the stars of the film version of *The Color Purple*, came to Rutgers to speak, and how I attacked her viciously during the question-and-answer session for betraying the Black man, in spite of the fact that I had not read the book nor seen the film. The fateful day I pulled my knife on Shelley Rodgers in the Paul Robeson Cultural Center of Rutgers, effectively getting myself kicked out of college.

I was twenty-five years old and knew I had to make a change. But I had no clue what to do other than to write. I had already done some freelance work for *Essence*, the Black women's magazine, so I asked my editor, Audrey Edwards, if I could write about what had happened with Adera. Ms. Edwards was taken aback, though she supported me on it.

I called the essay "The Sexist in Me," and Audrey Edwards pushed me hard, demanding more honesty, more rewrites. I was so afraid of writing something like this, of having it in a publication read by millions of women around the world. At the same time, I kept hearing my mother's voice from my childhood, saying: "The truth shall set you free." My mother also always said, "A liar is a thief," and told me to "not be like your father."

But this left me in a horrible situation. Throughout my life, my mother—and society in general—had told me what I should *not* be, but rarely did anyone say what I *should* or *could* be. A few older Black men—such as my boss, Sam Anderson—had served as role models here and there, and I had read Malcolm X's autobiography several times, digging endlessly for new lessons on manhood. But I never developed any consistent or constructive means of defining—or of redefining—manhood for myself. I was ignorant, but I didn't know that I was ignorant. I was suffering from a condition called "male privilege." After spending all those many years screaming about racism, I had never thought about other forms of oppression and discrimination because they didn't touch my life. Or so I thought.

I remembered the numerous kitchen conversations my mother and Aunt Cathy had had while my cousin Anthony and I were growing up. Yet it had never crossed my mind that I was contributing to the reality that men—most of us, at least—were no good.

When "The Sexist in Me" appeared in the "Brothers" section of *Essence* in September 1992, the response was immediate and electric. I described exactly what had happened on that day I pushed Adera into the bathroom door, how easily I had joined the ranks of abusive men in America. For the first time I admitted that I was sexist—socialized to be so since I was a boy. I said that what I did to Adera was inevitable, given the path that I had traveled. I discussed how this confession was a necessary first step, but that I could not stop here, that I not only had to challenge myself, but also other men and boys, especially if they were using the "b" word habitually.

I was stunned by the response. Floods of mail poured into *Essence* about my essay, much of it supportive. I received graphic letters from women who had been battered, beaten, stabbed, even shot by a boyfriend or husband. Women told me about being sexually assaulted by their fathers, uncles, cousins, or brothers; rape survivors wrote, too. I lost some male friends and some male supporters, and there were both women and men who told me straight up that they would never forgive me "for putting my hands on a woman," regardless of what I said or did.

My editor told me that Adera had reached out, too, wanting to write her own piece, but was politely rejected, as the magazine did not want to turn this into a back-and-forth. It surprised me that Adera did not try to write something elsewhere about what had happened, but I also imagined what it must have felt like for her, as the victim and survivor of violent and abusive behavior. I longed for the day when I could tell her in person how sorry I was, but I knew that day was not coming any time soon.

Now fully aware of my ability to hurt others, I soldiered on toward a new and different version of myself, to challenge the cycle of pain once and for all. I did not quite know how to go about this, but I knew that I had to try. But I remained sad that this difficult life lesson had come at Adera's expense. In time my life would become dedicated partly to writing, speaking, and organizing around the need to end violence against women and girls. In time I would come to question and challenge images of women and girls in every form of American pop culture, including my beloved hip-hop. Feminists bell hooks and Gloria Steinem helped me through the process, and I participated in numerous workshops, conferences, and even one-on-one sessions, all focused around the need to redefine manhood toward peace, love, and a different and healthier way to handle conflict and anger. Adera would personally accept my apology a decade later, but I knew that would never be enough. I had to commit myself, as a man, to helping to rid the world of sexism and gender violence. And that I could never put my hands on a woman again. And I have not.

24

MTV's *The Real World*

it smells like distorted childhoods
and diapered friendships and parents
who fed us Watergate and Vietnam
and ronald reagan and saturday morning
cartoons without giving us a love we could
grip and suck on when the earth
was burning in our direction

B Y THE end of the summer 1991, my writing career had taken
off in new and exciting ways. As I became more and more involved in the literary scene—in New York City and around the
country—poetry and its offshoot, the spoken-word movement, exploded nationwide. Living in Harlem made me long for Brooklyn, a
place I never thought I'd live. The BK bubbled with an artistic energy
reminiscent of the Harlem Renaissance of the 1920s.

Around that time, the Puerto Rican poet Tony Medina became
one of my best friends. The Medina, as we called him, was born in the
Bronx borough of New York City the same year that I was born, 1966.
Both his father and mother had addictions at the time of his birth,
and they left him in the hospital, a ward of the state, until his *abuela*,

his grandmother, finally came to get him. One of the most well-read human beings I've ever met, Medina was able to move effortlessly from Shakespeare and Chaucer to Sonia Sanchez and Jayne Cortez. He served in the military for a couple of years after high school, married and divorced, and settled back in New York with a college degree and stacks and stacks of his poems—he was incredibly prolific for one so young. We also shared a great love of the literary and cultural legends, and we went through the roof when we learned that in Paris, France, in February 1992, there would be a major conference called "African Americans in Europe," on Black artists like Richard Wright, James Baldwin, Josephine Baker, and others who had emigrated from the United States to France to work. Tony and I immediately set about getting our passports and raising the necessary funds for plane tickets and lodging. Young, wild, and free, we imagined ourselves to be like Langston Hughes, exploring the world when he was in his twenties.

I continued contributing news articles and music reviews to various publications, as well as bios of artists for record labels, including artists such as Usher and Kris Kross, for whom I also provided media training. The first bio I wrote was for the Columbia Records R&B group Joe Public, a band out of Buffalo, New York. One day in November or December of 1991, while I hung out with Joe Public and their publicist, Chrissy Murray, at Ellen's Stardust Café in Manhattan's Times Square, I noticed a group of Muppet-sized but incredibly loud young Black women wearing even brighter colors than Joe Public and myself. One of the young ladies, in particular, wore an eye-patch and a T-shirt and jeans covered with condoms. I learned that they were members of a new all-girl group called TLC. The one with the patch went—appropriately enough—by the name Left Eye.

As we returned to conversation at our table, a White woman named Tracie Fiss passed her business card to each of us and said she did casting for MTV. After glancing at Tracie's card for a moment, I stuck it in my pocket and sort of forgot about it. But then I looked at it again later that day, and the next day, and decided to call her. Tracie seemed thrilled that I did, and told me to make a short video of myself describing who I was, what I did, what I loved to do, what I did for fun, etc., and to provide some pictures of myself. The photos part was easy but I didn't own a video camera. I called my old college mate David McKnight in Jersey City. David agreed to use his video camera to film me. We knocked it out in no time and I sent my stuff to Tracie. I never thought about being famous or rich or that the show—whatever it was—might be a hit. I simply thought that perhaps I could book a few speaking gigs from the visibility, just as I remembered Sister Souljah always getting speech opportunities each time she appeared on television, especially national television. I never really watched MTV because my mother and I could never afford cable when I lived with her, and there was no cable at Rutgers for our dorm rooms. I knew, vaguely, that MTV started in the early 1980s, and I recalled that one of the members of the Monkees had something to do with it. I did know that MTV refused, initially, to play Michael Jackson's videos until his record label told the fledgling network that it would pull all its other artists unless the network aired MJ content . . . or so the story went. I knew that MTV's *Yo! MTV Raps* was hugely popular and made stars of cohosts Fab Five Freddy, Ed Lover, and Dr. Dre.

I eventually sent Tracie a short video about myself. All I knew was that the video I sent was for a new kind of programming—part documentary, part soap opera—and that it would be called *The Real World*.

Meanwhile 1991 turned to 1992 and Tony Medina and I continued on our grind to get all our paperwork for our Paris trip. Ignorant to the ways of passports, I paid a rush fee just in time for our trip to Paris, the first week of February. And I got called for an interview for *The Real World* with Jonathan Murray, cocreator of the concept along with Mary-Ellis Bunim. Jonathan, I learned, came from a documentary background while Mary-Ellis previously worked primarily in soap operas. They partnered to form Bunim-Murray Productions, and the idea of "a reality show" came to be. Murray asked me youth-oriented questions about sex, about partying, about how I would get along with people different than me. In all honesty, I gave them the answers that I thought they wanted to hear because getting on the show seemed like a cool thing. But going out of the country for the first time in my life, to Paris, excited me even more.

When I received the call informing me of my selection as a "cast mate" on the first season of MTV's *The Real World*, I could not believe it. Fortunately, taping for *The Real World* would begin the day after my return from Paris. That trip was only the second time I had ever been on a plane in my life. Two years earlier, I flew for the first time when college students brought me up to Vermont to cover their student protest for one of the publications that I wrote for at the time. I remembered my complete terror when the plane lurched from the ground. But for this Paris trip I felt no such thing. It felt natural, like it would be one of many trips that I would take on planes, just as I heard my mother and my Aunt Cathy say my Aunt Birdie was doing when I was a boy, to strange and faraway places.

We had found a hotel in Paris, the same one where Langston Hughes allegedly stayed in the 1920s—but by the time Tony Medina and I landed, got our luggage, and caught a cab to central Paris, I had quickly realized that the taxi fare would swallow half of the $100 I had with me. And when we got to the hotel, it looked like it had not been upgraded since the 1920s, when Hughes had been there. With its peeling walls, enormous roaches, and paper-thin, twin-bed mattresses, it brought to mind a New York City dump of an apartment. And there was no heat.

But Tony and I did not care. We had made it to Paris and intended to have the time of our lives. Neither one of us could afford to attend the conference itself, so we showed up around the periphery of the venue where luminaries such as Danny Glover and Henry Louis Gates were present. At one dinner we got to go to, a drunk Medina repeatedly referred to the writer Elizabeth Alexander as "Lizzy," which irked her to no end. Tony Medina thoroughly enjoyed rubbing it in to what he called "the teacup mantelpiece poets," those young Black and Latino writers who preferred the academic style of poetry to our raw and direct political poetry.

At some point during one night of drunkenness and cigarettes and jazz in the Pigalle district, Tony realized that he had lost his bag, which contained two or three of his poetry manuscripts. Our evening of merriment and pleasure screeched to a halt as we searched for the bag, though we didn't find it until the next day. But we now faced an even bigger problem—our hotel. Tony and I had run out of money and decided to sneak out of the hotel without paying. We found a new hotel and stayed there for one night, but when we told Willie Perdomo that we had skipped out of our previous hotel without paying, he told us the story of a young James Baldwin. Baldwin had been arrested and jailed for stealing bedsheets from a Paris hotel, and Perdomo assured us that we would suffer the same fate if we did not get back to that first hotel with payment.

Scared, Tony and I thought fast as we hung around the conference that day. We met the Detroit poet and literary scholar Dr. Melba Joyce Boyd, her son and daughter, and her sister and nephew. They immediately took a liking to our rebel spirits, especially when we blabbered out how we got to Paris, and our misadventures since being there. Fortunately, Tony got the idea to sell copies of his first poetry collection, *Emerge and See*, at the conference, to raise money for us to eat and to pay for another hotel room. With the enthusiastic assistance of Dr. Boyd, her son, her daughter, and her nephew, we did just that. The books flew from our hands. In that frenzy, a Dutch woman and her son asked to buy a copy of Tony's book. Surprised, we gladly took their money and struck up a convo with them. Soon thereafter the mother invited us to stay at her Paris home for the duration of our trip. Tony and I could not believe it, and gladly accepted. We took the money that we'd made, went back to the first and second hotels, and paid our debts. On the way to the Dutch family's home, we stopped at a bookstore where East St. Louis poet Eugene Redmond was participating in a reading with the elderly Colombian poet Arnoldo Palacios.

Based in Paris, Palacios was crippled with tuberculosis. Mad stressed by our Paris trip, Tony and I got into an argument right there at the tiny bookstore and began throwing punches at each other, knocking over the old South American poet in the process. Eugene Redmond proceeded to tell everyone he encountered at the conference what the two hot-headed, young New York poets did. Embarrassed, Tony and I patched things up fast, apologized profusely, and continued on, since we counted on each other for survival in this foreign country.

By the end of our trip, Tony and I figured out a way to get into the school cafeteria of the Sorbonne: we simply bought meal tickets from French students on the street. We dined on long rolls of bread and something called "couscous," which looked like the grits my mother made me as a child, but tasted very different.

Like so many American writers before us, we fell in love with Paris. I vowed to come back, to live there one day, to learn the French that I'd flunked my first semester at Rutgers. When Tony and I landed back at JFK we got a not-so-friendly reception: Airport security directed us to follow them to separate rooms and heavily interrogated us about who we were and the reasons for our trip. They told us to empty our bags and to remove some of our clothes. We suspected that it might relate to the politics of our poetry. Either that, or—as occasionally happened—they mistook Tony for a Middle-Easterner. Undaunted, we went about our business after leaving that airport, more determined than ever to be very serious poets and political voices like the writers we admired.

◆

The next day, Sunday, February 16, 1992, I showed up at 565 Broadway, in the Soho section of Manhattan, to meet my new "roommates," and to begin shooting MTV's *The Real World*. Our building neighbors included the renowned dance and artistic couple Geoffrey Holder and Carmen de Lavallade.

When I walked in, it felt like I'd won the grand prize of a game show. I had been living in a dumpy room in a prewar building uptown in Harlem, and now I was moving into this four-thousand-square-foot duplex loft with six other young people.

I met my roomies, each of us selected from among five hundred applicants: Norman Korpi, the visual artist; Eric Nies, the model; Heather B., the rapper; Julie Oliver, the dancer; Becky Blasband, the singer and musician; and Andre Comeau, the leader of his own rock band. Eric arrived first, Becky second, and I was the third person to show up. The seven of us were slated to be there until Monday, May 18, 1992. We all had signed contracts that paid us $1,300 at the beginning of taping and $1,300 at the end of taping. One thing that I had noticed on the paperwork bothered me: the producers would be able to use their footage from this period "in perpetuity throughout the universe," or something like that. That seemed like an awfully long time, and a great distance, but I signed the contract anyway.

Given my background as an activist and writer, I had already thought long and hard about the images of Black folks in popular culture. There was no way I was going to go on MTV shufflin' and jivin' and saying and doing things that would embarrass the Black race, or me. I intended to be myself, a twenty-five-year-old Black man in America.

A child of American television, I grew up on reruns of shows like *Gilligan's Island*, *The Brady Bunch*, and *Star Trek* and took note of how the stars of those programs were forever typecast, forever doing reunion shows and specials, no matter how old they got. I vowed that I would never become one of those people, permanently stuck in a TV box. To me, that would be as oppressive as the ghetto my mother and I had escaped when I was a boy.

Our new digs were impressive: there was a big fish tank, Warhol-like pop art, forest-size plants, multi-hued art deco furniture, and a cool, spiraling staircase to our bedrooms. Behind a wall we also knew that there was a control room where the production team monitored what we did, and decided what was camera-worthy.

I never gave any thought to what I was wearing, or to my style—none of us did; we were just ourselves. For me, that meant my high-top fade twisted into baby dreads; colorful T-shirts sporting some message or other; white cowrie shell necklace whose roots trace back to Western Africa; super-baggy jeans or overalls, sometimes worn with a necktie; and a fly thrift-shop suit jacket to top everything off.

At our first sit-down as a group, Heather B.'s pager beeped, and Julie, the youngest of the bunch at nineteen—and fresh off a plane from Birmingham, Alabama—innocently yelled out, "Do you sell drugs? Why do you have a beeper?" The camera caught me making a face at Julie's racist comment, but nevertheless, Eric, the hippest White dude there, became my roommate. He was "a wigger," as young White males deep into hip-hop were called. I also learned quickly that two pets were along for the ride: Gouda, Norman's black dog the size of a small horse, and Smokey, Heather's cat. I still had a debilitating fear of dogs and also had a flashback to how much I hated an old girlfriend's cat.

One night early on, Heather, Julie, and I went out to dinner to get acquainted, and Heather and I attempted to school Julie about racism and her beeper comment. At one point, Julie said I seemed angry or bitter, and I told her I had every right to be. Little did I know, those first interactions would lead to periodic flare-ups on racial issues over the next three months.

One day, Becky and I got into it, and at the end of the bickering I called her the b word. Another time, Eric and I had a falling out, and I wrote him a letter talking about race and racism in a way that he clearly did not understand. On another occasion Norman and I got into a shouting match about racism. There was the accusation from Julie, after we had had an off-camera argument, that I had thrown something at her (a candlestick), which was not true. And there was a moment when Julie and I went outside in front of the building and had an explosive back-and-forth about race and racism. Somewhere in all these beefs with my White cast mates, I proclaimed that "Black people cannot be racist" because "racism equals race plus power." I was frustrated and alienated at times, especially as Heather B., the only other Black cast mate, became best friends with Julie, and I wound up avoiding the loft as often as possible, spending more time in my Harlem apartment than anywhere.

During this three-month window of taping *The Real World*, February through May of 1992, I got wind of a new Quincy Jones venture called *Vibe* magazine, which would focus on hip-hop and urban culture. I got a small record review in this test issue, but Jonathan Van Meter, the young, White, openly gay editor in chief, saw something bigger for me. He had read my clips, including a piece that I had written for *Urban Profile* magazine called "Ghetto Bastard." In it, I talked about not only my inner-city roots in New Jersey, but also how I narrowly escaped a beat-down from a group of Jersey guys outside the Palladium on West 14th Street in Manhattan. First chance I got, I broke north, almost got hit by a car, and jumped into the first yellow cab that I found. This was in 1991, when I thought I had finally escaped my past in New Jersey.

Jonathan asked me if I was interested in writing a two- to three-thousand-word feature article on Treach and Naughty by Nature. I eagerly agreed to do it, and when I got a chance to sit down with the group, especially Treach, I was taken aback by how similar our lives had been growing up in the ghetto. Then and there I decided that I would write about hip-hop from the perspective of what the genre meant for Black men, how it had saved us and empowered us when we were searching for meaning in our lives. Once the piece was finished, a decision was made to put a solo black-and-white image of Treach on the magazine's cover shot by famed celebrity photographer Albert Watson.

I cried when I received the news. After almost six long years of freelance writing, covering everything from things like the City College stampede after Puff Daddy's basketball game and concert, to school science fairs, to sitting in the wrong seat at City Hall for mayoral press conferences, to random sporting events, I had scored my first cover story for a major publication. I tried to get the MTV folks to follow this part of my life, but I received a lukewarm response. They did feature me teaching at NYU mentoring a younger Black male named

Morris Staton, and reading poetry at the Nuyorican Poets Cafe; so at least they documented a small part of my life as a writer and activist.

Near the end of the taping of *The Real World*, on Wednesday, April 29, the city of Los Angeles erupted in violence at the acquittal of the cops who had viciously beaten Rodney King about eighty times with a baton—on videotape, no less. We sat in front of the television mesmerized by the scenes occurring in America's second-biggest city. I did not know what to say or feel since I was around mostly White people, but my insides churned at the rank injustice. By the time the police, the U.S. Army, Marines, and National Guard restored order, the riots had caused 53 deaths, 2,383 injuries, more than 7,000 fires, damage to 3,100 businesses, and nearly $1 billion in financial losses.

Rob Fox, one of the directors of *The Real World*, eased next to me as I watched the news, and told me that he wanted to produce a documentary for MTV about Los Angeles—from the perspective of young people—after the rebellion. And furthermore, he wanted me to be the host and the writer. Unbeknownst to me, Rob had listened closely to everything I said during the taping of *The Real World*, and he felt that I would be the perfect face for the report. So soon I found myself shuttling back and forth between New York and Los Angeles for the remainder of 1992, my very first trip to California.

I got to experience Los Angeles on the ground, live and direct. Gang bangers in East and South Central L.A. introduced me to parts of the city in a way that would otherwise not have been accessible. The day that we drove through "The Jungle" was no joke—armed gang members were patrolling the infamous area. A wheelchair-bound, gunshot-victim Crip gang founder named Mike Concepcion helped us to navigate South Central. We also enlisted the support of the rapper Ice-T, since he knew those same streets. We made sure to include a young Asian from Koreatown, given the tensions between Black residents and Korean store owners, and a young White guy working for a new program called Teach for America. *Straight from the 'Hood* won numerous awards when it aired in 1993, and even kicked off MTV's "Free Your Mind" national campaign.

Before any of this transpired, though, MTV's *The Real World* premiered on Thursday, May 21, 1992. I was so hyped about being on a television show that I persuaded my mother to allow me to get her cable for a few months so she could watch it, too. Leading up to the show's debut, the entire cast had done interviews with every media outlet you could name—*Time, Newsweek, USA Today*, and *Entertainment Tonight*—and I began to feel that we were about to be a part of something bigger than us, something bigger than any of us could ever imagine. The show became an instant hit for Generation X and was rumored to have inspired the mega-hit Gen X sitcom *Friends*. Our show captured things that we had never considered as we taped, such as Norman coming out as gay; Julie's friendship with a homeless woman; the antiwar protest some cast mates participated in; and, yes, the many conversations on race. The opening voice-over for the show, done by us all, encapsulated the spirit of it: "This is the true story of seven strangers picked to live in a loft and have their lives taped, to find out what happens when people stop being polite and start getting real."

We had been warned that we would not be able to go to a mall or walk down a street the same way again, and sure enough, everywhere I went I received star treatment. I met one teenager named Tyree on a New York City corner, who I befriended for years and watched evolve into the famous DJ Drama. In Los Angeles one night a group of excited young women literally raced by rap star LL Cool J to talk with me. Unbelievable. And, regularly, people would say bizarre things to me, like "I really love your character," and it wasn't clear if they knew I was being me or actually playing someone else.

As the episodes progressed, I got concerned about my portrayal. The producers did include my relationship with my girlfriend at the time, and they did include the younger Black man I was mentoring at the time, but still viewers talked constantly about my heated arguments. That first one, with Becky, so appalled my mother that she called me as soon as the show was over, telling me to never again call a White woman the b word. It shook my mother to the core that I had said something like that on national television. My mother had survived the vicious racism and segregation of America's pre–Civil Rights era, and her memory chip logged what happened to Black men who disrespected White people, especially White women, in any way.

But that was nothing compared to the heated reactions to my famous argument with Julie. I came across as a Black man with a chip on his shoulder, screaming at the top of my lungs at this poor young White woman from Down South, calling her a "racist." Nothing in my life, not even getting kicked out of Rutgers or getting jumped in Newark, New Jersey, prepared me for the extreme reactions to my "character" on *The Real World*.

The vast majority of Black folks generally sided with and supported me, arguing that I spoke for them and that they had never witnessed anyone like me on television. Many of them told me that they had never heard someone articulate the notion of racism so bluntly and that Black people could not be racist. On the other hand, the vast majority of White folks found me terrifying, or considered me a bully, or even a monster. And they called me a racist. Even White people who worked at MTV shunned me, perhaps afraid that I would snap on them at any moment. I worried that I had been branded and stereotyped with the label of "angry young Black man," and that it would stick with me forever.

September 1992 came, and my *Vibe* cover story hit the stands and sold out immediately. When Quincy Jones mentioned my name in media interviews about the writers for his new publication, it blew me away. And when *The Real World* seven attended the 1992 MTV Video Music Awards on September 9, the crowd went wild for us. MTV gave us Hershey's Kisses to toss to our "fans," and you would have thought we were the second coming of the Beatles the way they lost their minds and fought over those candies. My personal highlight was seeing Nirvana perform, as I was a huge admirer of lead singer Kurt Cobain. His lyrics spoke directly to my lifelong sense of alienation and confusion.

Just two years before, at twenty-four, when I had moved across the Hudson River from Jersey to New York City, I wrote in my diary that I wanted to be remembered as one of the best writers of my generation. Now I was fully immersed in the new poetry movement, a star writer at Quincy Jones's *Vibe* magazine with an offer to be a full-time staff writer, and I enjoyed the free publicity of the MTV machine thanks to our little reality show that could. The future looked promising for me and I dreamed of book deals . . . of writing movie scripts . . . of settling in Hollywood . . . of hosting my own TV show.

For the first time in my life, all things seemed possible, and I was not about to let these opportunities slip away.

25

Vibe and Tupac Shakur

I write 'cuz I wanna be free *before* I die, knowhatahmsayin'?

THAT SPRING, *Vibe* officially launched as a full-fledged publication with staff and permanent office space given the massive success of the test issue the previous fall. Among others, the original team included Jonathan Van Meter, Diane Cardwell, Rob Kenner, Michaela Angela Davis, Hilton Als, Emil Wilbekin, Alan Light (who I helped convince to leave *Rolling Stone* and take the music editor position at *Vibe*), and three staff writers: Joan Morgan, Scott Poulson-Bryant (he gave *Vibe* its name), and me. Many on the staff had attended Ivy League or other elite institutions, whereas I attended Rutgers, a state school. Or they had a journalism pedigree I simply did not have. I vowed to myself that I would out-work and out-write everyone there; I would not be the token ghetto dude in the building. Everything my mother taught me about hard work kicked in, and I did not intend to let her—or myself—down. I was mad nervous at our first staff meeting, as folks went around the table introducing themselves and talked about their vision for *Vibe*. I knew that no one on the original team of *Vibe* had been through what I had in life.

When the topic turned to hip-hop mogul Russell Simmons, I

learned that he chose not to partner with Quincy Jones on *Vibe* because he opposed Q's decision to hire Jonathan Van Meter as the editor in chief. I wondered if this was about Van Meter himself, or if Russell Simmons did not think a gay White man was the right person to lead a hip-hop magazine. According to reports, Simmons was concerned that there were not enough straight Black males on staff at *Vibe*—a fact as I looked around at the original team—and the assumption was there would not be any shared experiences with the rap artists we'd be covering. I respectfully disagreed with this notion because a generation before James Baldwin, an openly gay Black man, captured the spirit of the Civil Rights Movement better than any writer had, or could. And I knew quite a few gay writers of my generation, out or not, who were writing religiously, and brilliantly, about hip-hop culture.

Additionally, by getting to know my cast mate Norman Korpi, who announced his gayness on MTV's *The Real World*, I began to understand and empathize with the gay community in a new and different way. Jonathan gave me this one incredible opportunity to write full-time for a magazine, a decision that some of his White friends questioned because of the manner in which MTV depicted me on *Real World*. Jonathan ignored their belief that I did not like White people. I maintained great loyalty to him for having my back as he did.

My first pitch was to write a piece on a young rapper and actor named Tupac Amaru Shakur. I explained to the group that his name was rendered 2Pac; that he had just been in a film called *Juice*; that his mother, Afeni, had been a member of the Black Panther Party and had been in jail just weeks before he was born on June 16, 1971. He had never really known his dad, but his stepfather, Mutulu Shakur, was a Black activist and Black Liberation Movement member who has been a "political prisoner" for years. Tupac had studied at the prestigious Baltimore School for the Arts and had subsequently moved to the Bay Area, where his mother had become a crack addict. Like so many young Black men in America's ghettos, Tupac took to the streets, spending time with drug dealers and hustlers, who were like family to him. Somewhere in the midst of this he found his way to the rap group Digital Underground, first as a dancer and roadie, then finally as a rapper himself. Tupac's music was a cross between Public Enemy and N.W.A.

No one had real interest in who I was talking about, or if they did, they were not into why Tupac Shakur should be considered for a cover story, or a feature article even. The air was sucked out of me, but I did not care. I wanted to write about hip-hop and Black men in a way that humanized us and put our lives in context. I thought about this as it related to my own life, especially coming off *The Real World* experience of being regarding mainly as "the angry Black male." I thought White people and elitist Black folks condemned hip-hop because they did not understand poor, working-class Black and Latino folks, or did not want to. Poor, working-class African Americans, Latinos, and West Indians created hip-hop and built it into the major economic and cultural force that had given rise to *Vibe*. I did not intend to participate in a slick repackaging of the culture—my culture—minus voices like Tupac's, which needed to be heard.

Instead of Tupac, I was given an assignment to write a cover story on the hottest new rapper in America, Snoop Doggy Dogg. While I held on to my Tupac folder—determined to write about him in the future—I dived into the saga of Snoop Dogg.

I flew to Los Angeles to interview Snoop, Dr. Dre, and others who worked with Snoop. At the time, Snoop faced murder charges—his bodyguard, McKinley Lee, had allegedly shot Phillip Woldermarian, a member of a rival gang, while Snoop allegedly drove the vehicle from which the gunfire erupted. (O.J. Simpson's attorney Johnnie Cochran defended both men and they were acquitted.) The violent nature of the case made Snoop the most popular new music star, of any genre, in years. With his molasses-thick Southern drawl, infectious storytelling reminiscent of Slick Rick—who had been a huge influence on Snoop's style—and his open gang affiliation, Snoop made for a compelling cover story. I spent some of my most interesting time with Snoop in the recording studio during the making of what would become his hit single "Gin and Juice." He drank gin and juice while scratching random lyrics down on a pink legal pad. David Ruffin, Jr., son of the late Temptations front man, sang the contagious hook, and Snoop's cousin, Daz Dallinger, of Tha Dogg Pound, chimed in, too.

The Snoop article was on the cover, and it sold out. By now, *Vibe* was getting really popular. We thought of it as the *New Yorker* for urban America, because of the quality of the writing, editing, and photos in the book each month. Writers such as Cristina Verán, Amy Linder, dream hampton, Michael Gonzales, and Bobbito Garcia appeared in the magazine's pages, and photographers as talented and distinguished as Dan Winters and Dana Lixenberg shot the images that graced our covers. I even received a subpoena to testify as a witness at Snoop's trial because of statements he had made to me when I wrote my article, but Time Warner's lawyers stepped in and I never heard from the court folks again. I felt invincible and thought that I was moving away from the typecasting and negativity of my *Real World* "brand."

Shortly after I finished my Snoop cover, Jonathan and Diane asked me if I still wanted to write about Tupac Shakur. So in the spring of 1993, I met Tupac for the first time at the historic Jack the Rapper music conference in Atlanta, Georgia. The event took its name from Jack Gibson, the longtime radio personality who got his start in the late 1940s–early 1950s and who launched WERD, the first Black-owned radio station in America, in Atlanta. Considered to be the father of Black radio, Gibson, and other pioneering African-American radio personalities like Daddy O and Jocko Henderson, wove rhymes into their shows, a sort of early hip-hop.

In the center of a room buzzing with celebrities, pseudo-celebrities, and groupies—both male and female—there was Tupac Shakur, surrounded by a gang of admirers. When Karla Radford, our CEO's assistant, introduced me to Tupac, saying "Hey wassup, you need to meet my friend Kevin Powell from *Vibe* magazine," Tupac looked at Karla, then in the direction of me, and smiled that wide toothy grin of his. "Yo, wassup! You my man from that MTV show! Yo dog, I had your back on that show, like for real!"

There I was, mad nervous about approaching Tupac, and it turned out he was a fan of mine—he happily agreed to do an interview with me.

There was something about Tupac Shakur. No one would call him the best rapper, not even close, but he had great rap moments, was a superb actor, and had a kind of dynamic charisma that cannot be taught to anyone. I would follow Tupac everywhere he went for the next two and a half years: Atlanta, Los Angeles, and New York. But it all began with that first cover story: "Is Tupac Crazy? Or Just Misunderstood?" I wasn't happy with the photo Diane Cardwell picked for the cover—it featured Tupac posing in a white straitjacket. I found that image and the headline to be offensive and stereotypical, but the powers that be at *Vibe* won, and the issue flew off the newsstands.

In the piece, I described Tupac as a James Dean–like figure for the hip-hop generation, and I put his biography in context using quotes from his mother, Afeni Shakur. During one of our interviews, I had gotten the weirded-out feeling that Tupac knew he would not live long. He had said to me, "I want you to be Alex Haley to my Malcolm X." Of course, I thought, *What if I want to be Malcolm X, too?*

Shortly after the first Tupac cover, I was rudely awakened to how cruel the magazine business could be. Jonathan Van Meter had a heated disagreement with upper management over a proposed Madonna–Dennis Rodman cover, and he left the magazine. His pals like Diane Cardwell and Hilton Als departed with him. Alan Light, our music editor, became the new editor in chief. I liked Alan a lot, but for the first time I began to wonder why all the editors and copy editors at *Vibe* were White, and why White photographers shot every single cover image shot. Even our Black photo editor—who I respected but found to be timid when it came to issues of race—once suggested to me that Black and Latino photographers lacked the technical competence to shoot covers for our magazine. In spite of my success at *Vibe*, I began to sulk, even as I piled up one cover story after another.

As fellow Black staffers came to me to complain about our lack of power at this ostensibly Black publication, I became bolder and louder in my criticisms of management, and disrespectful to my editors, Alan Light and Rob Kenner, who were both White. It did not help that tension existed between me and Danyel Smith, the woman who had been my first music editor at *San Francisco Weekly*, and whom I also helped recruit to *Vibe*. I had wielded my star power on a project involving a cross-country road trip, all expenses paid, documenting our generation, Generation X. I got my friend Radcliffe Bailey hired to sketch art from the experience, and Danyel's husband Carl Posey to photograph the entire journey. While Radcliffe and I drank and enjoyed ourselves, Carl got nervous about starting the work. Carl and I argued repeatedly, and when we got to Los Angeles, I picked a fight with him and threw him off our RV. Danyel and I became distant after that, and I never got any music assignments that were not about male rappers—I was passed over for pieces that I really wanted to do, such as on female acts like En Vogue and TLC.

By then, Tupac had become so famous that it did not seem to matter. After being charged with sexual assault in New York City in 1994, he gave me—and by extension, *Vibe*—an exclusive jailhouse interview from Riker's Island. In that prison conversation Tupac recounted detail by detail not only what happened in a hotel room with a woman he'd met at a Manhattan club, but also how he did not try to stop his "friends" from having sex with the woman after he'd done so. Maintaining his innocence, Tupac said he was not guilty of sexual assault, but of not helping the woman. Given how much I witnessed first-hand women of every type fawning over Tupac in public, how much he spoke of his love for his mother, for women in general, I believed him, I believed that he did not sexually assault or rape anyone—and many other women and men felt similarly. But given my own developing consciousness around sexism, and given how real sexual violence was against women in America, in the male-dominated entertainment and sports worlds, I thought it was important that Tupac admitted his role of using the woman as a sex toy then discarding her. He was clear, and very apologetic.

Tupac also spoke very passionately about the night in November 1994 that he got shot five times in the lobby of a recording studio in New York City's Times Square. As he had done in recounting the night of the alleged sexual assault, Pac took us through each scene of that evening. As I sat across from him at a long table in Riker's Island, you would not have known that besides myself there was his publicist, his lawyer, our *Vibe* photographer Dana Lixenberg, prison officials, and correction officers. Tupac spoke fast, nervously, and used the phrase "woo-de-woo" a lot, to accent or punctuate things he really wanted clear on my tape recorder. It was the most incredible and most surreal interview I had ever done in my life.

While in jail Tupac also released a sensitive, moving tribute to his mother called "Dear Mama." Tupac spoke about mothers like mine. That single, coupled with his behind-bars conversation with me, created a massive spotlight on Tupac. He was now perhaps the most famous—and infamous—Black man in America. We changed the names of several individuals Tupac mentioned in the piece, for legal reasons and, presumably, because they, or their associates, had threatened folks at *Vibe*. We had to run a response to the interview with many of the figures properly named, so that they could dispute publicly Tupac's allegations. And so in addition to its widespread popularity, *Vibe* suddenly became one of the hotbeds of an East Coast–West Coast battle that would come to include Tupac and Death Row Records founder Suge Knight, The Notorious B.I.G., and Bad Boy Records founder Sean "Puff Daddy" Combs. I did what any serious journalist would do and documented everything that happened.

After Tupac's release from prison in fall 1995—around the time of Louis Farrakhan's Million Man March in Washington, DC—some people thought he would show up in the nation's capital. I was there, although by this point I was no longer in awe of Minister Farrakhan. I had come to regard him, as well as the Reverend Jesse Jackson and the Reverend Al Sharpton, as political opportunists, or what Dr. King called "manufactured Black leadership": classic and articulate manipulators of Black misery and Black ignorance. To me they were purveyors of sound bites for the media, ambulance and crisis chasers with no real plan of action and uninterested in building and sustaining institutions or organizations that served the needs of Black America holistically. Farrakhan and Jackson were like father figures who had disappointed me greatly, as my own biological father had done. I resented them both for doing things in the name of Black folks and the Black community that seemed to suit their needs and agendas. Sharpton had a track record, dating to his youth minister days, of working for anyone or anything with a paycheck, and there had been articles and many conversations about him wearing wiretaps to spy on his fellow Black activists. He brought a circus atmosphere to every single thing he did and that was neither leadership nor activism, not to me.

Yet I went to the Million Man March out of racial solidarity and obligation. I cannot lie: I was greatly moved by the sight of thousands upon thousands of Black men and boys, from all over America, walking the streets of Washington, DC, to the United States Capitol Building. I heard Black men referring to each other as "brother" in a way I had not since my days of youth activism as a Rutgers student. People were talking about jobs and other opportunities that might come from this march. There were chants supporting the building of a national movement.

But I had great reservations, too. The oft-repeated rationale—that Black men had to take their rightful place in the household—was sexist. I had been raised by a single Black mother, and I knew Black women were capable of raising boys to men, because my mother had done so. I also cringed at the use of the word "atonement" over and over, as if Black men had to do more atoning than any other group in America. And I was irritated when the mighty crowd was asked to make donations to the march, and baskets were passed as if we were at one of those church revivals I had come to despise as a child.

Tupac's name came up several times, and some people asked me directly if he would be coming, but Suge Knight had whisked him from prison to Los Angeles to begin recording what would become *All Eyez on Me*. In any case, I thought I was done with Tupac—my Black consciousness and activist spirit wanted no part of this East Coast–West Coast madness. It was tribal warfare and, worse, a terrible example of Black-on-Black hatred. But when Rob Kenner approached me to do an exclusive cover story on Death Row Records that would feature Suge Knight, Dr. Dre, Tupac, and Snoop Dogg on the cover, I could not turn it down. I ended up on the set of Tupac's $600,000 "California Love" video in a remote desert area outside of L.A. Suge Knight was marching around the *Mad Max*–like scene, but there was no Tupac in sight. Eventually, someone directed me to Tupac's trailer. I knocked on the door, and a person on the other side pushed it open, releasing a powerful gust of marijuana smoke. There he was: big eyes shining brightly, childlike smile still as broad as an ocean, massive exposed muscles developed during his prison stint. Clearly this was not the same Tupac who, only ten months earlier, while in jail, had told me that he had stopped smoking weed, that he was not a gangsta, that "thug life is dead."

From that day in November until his death late the following September, Tupac seemed to me to be a replica of the character he played in *Juice*. Hearing his new album and listening to his television interviews shocked me. It pissed me off that he escalated the tensions between East Coast and West Coast rappers (born on the East Coast, Tupac's loyalties had wavered back and forth until he signed to Death Row Records in October 1995). When I asked Tupac what was going to come of the East Coast–West Coast rift, he said, "It's gonna get deep." (And he was right—first Tupac was blown away, then The Notorious B.I.G., and both murders remain unsolved all these years later.)

A few weeks after the video shoot I spoke to Tupac again. Apparently, much had changed in Tupac's mind since our last conversation about a year before. He told me how angry he was, and with everyone. But he said that he could trust Suge Knight and the Death Row family to protect him from his enemies. I remember hanging up the phone after that interview, on December 2, 1995, and feeling sick. Tupac had displayed a side of himself, a darker, more menacing side, that made me think, *Damn, maybe I never really knew him.* I didn't want to speak to Tupac Shakur anymore. I guess a part of me knew it was only a matter of time before he would get his wish and be gone from us forever. I never stopped following Tupac's life, though, and whenever I heard someone mention his name, I listened as carefully as I had in 1992.

Tupac was me, and I was him, ghetto children from birth, living until it was our turn to die. So, in a way, the "new" Tupac made me feel as if I had lost a friend, and that I couldn't do anything about it. He was gone.

Around that time I also spoke with Snoop Dogg in person—he was more paranoid than ever—a nervous Dr. Dre, and finally Suge Knight, who gave me the most bizarre interview of my career. In his overly air-conditioned office with red carpet and gigantic Death Row logo in its center, Knight kept his very big dog Damu (which meant "blood" in Swahili) with him the entire time and lectured me sternly about the questions that he did not like.

As I got into my rental car that night, I was shocked to see Faith Evans, The Notorious B.I.G.'s wife, in a car. Why was she there? Was Tupac having an affair with Biggie's wife, as he claimed? Was she simply there to record a track with Tupac? I decided to leave Faith out of my piece to avoid adding more fuel to this fire. A few days later I spoke with Tupac by phone and he was short, tense, and mumbled things about M&M peanuts of different colors not going together, so why should East Coast and West Coast go together? I sighed to myself a few times as I listened to Tupac's rant. This was a year after he had admitted his many flaws, vowed to be a better person, and even said that he should have stopped the men in his hotel room from sexually assaulting a woman there. The woman charged him with the attack, which he adamantly denied, saying that the sex was consensual. I hung up the phone from that latest conversation with Tupac Shakur not knowing what to believe or what to do.

The subsequent story, "Live from Death Row," became an instant bestseller and fueled speculation that an all-out East Coast–West Coast war was about to start, in spite of the fact that I ended the article by calling for peace and intervention by Black leaders like Louis Farrakhan and Ben Chavis. I did not know what else to say even though I had my great doubts that these Black leaders could help in any way.

◆

My own life began to unravel rapidly. My live-in girlfriend of several years, Peggy, moved out while I was away on a business trip, leaving me utterly devastated. I started drinking liquor more than I ever had. The alcohol became a way to cope with the constant stress and pressure of being a full-time journalist with a high profile. I had rented this brownstone garden apartment at 11A South Elliott Place as a sign of my so-called baller status shortly after landing the *Vibe* gig: star writer, nonstop parties, and a beautiful singer by my side. When Peggy left it felt as if I could hear the walls talking to me, the loneliness and isolation were that devastating.

One day, in May 1996, I got into another heated exchange with employees at *Vibe*. Previously, the magazine leadership had ignored or downplayed my outbursts, supposedly because of my value to the publication. Along the way I had threatened, intimidated, and bullied people, had run up a ridiculous $5,000 cell phone bill that they paid off, and committed other transgressions. This time, though, I found myself raging at about three different employees, to the point where I had to be restrained physically. This came on the heels of my taking the lead in publicly bashing *Vibe* for still not having a Black editor in chief, or many other editors of color for that matter. Keith Clinkscales, the *Vibe* CEO, a Black man I'd worked with since he owned *Urban Profile* magazine, asked me to sit down with him and Alan Light, the editor in chief. Also present was Rob Kenner, the senior editor and the best editor with whom I ever worked. Rob did not speak and could not look at me. Keith and Alan summarily fired me and told me to leave *Vibe* immediately. They cited my insubordination, my threatening behavior. In that moment I felt that my life was over and I wanted to disappear, to die; I cried hysterically in front of them. They told me that I would receive some sort of severance package, and that was it. Gone was my *Vibe* career and the *Vibe* cover stories; gone was my hosting and producing HBO's "Vibe Five" TV segments; gone was the follow-up to the screenplay I had written and sold to HBO, never to be produced; and gone was my rubbing elbows at swank V.I.P. "industry parties" with major pop culture figures like Tommy Hilfiger and Grammy-winner Toni Braxton.

I escaped New York City and spent the summer of 1996 in Atlanta, Georgia. Even though the Olympics were happening at that time, I didn't care, and barely left my hotel room. Deeply depressed, I felt like an abject failure, and drank heavily. My face, my neck, my stomach all became bloated and I lost all sense of myself. I only communicated with a few people, including my friend Radcliffe Bailey, who lived in Atlanta. I did manage to participate in the National Black Arts Festival there that summer, and even helped to curate the literary component, but being around quite a few other artists who also abused alcohol did not help. I felt myself sinking.

In September 1996, and back home in New York City, I heard that Tupac Shakur had been shot in Las Vegas for a second time, after attending a Mike Tyson fight with Suge Knight and their entourage. Wanting to do something, I foolishly called *Vibe* to offer my services, but they rejected me. Determined to get to Vegas, I phoned Nathan Brackett at *Rolling Stone*, and sure enough they flew me there. In Vegas, I linked up with my colleague Allison Samuels from *Newsweek*, and phoned Kidada Jones, one of Quincy Jones's daughters, and Tupac's most recent girlfriend. Given that almost a week had passed since his shooting, Kidada assured me that Tupac would pull through. Many people around the country believed this because Tupac had become a sort of mythic superhero, able to survive a horrific childhood and young adult life, all his legal issues, his time in prison, and the shootings.

On Friday, September 13, 1996, while watching Spike Lee's *Malcolm X* biopic in my hotel room, I got the call from Allison telling me that Tupac Shakur had died. I made my way to the hospital and into the University Medical Center of Southern Nevada lobby with Allison and some other folks, but could not get any farther. Tupac's music blared everywhere as SUVs, Hummers, and other vehicles cruised back and forth in front of the hospital. A loud gasp went up with the announcement of Suge Knight's arrival. Karen Lee, Pac's publicist, had personally warned me to stay away from the hospital, for fear of someone recognizing me and trying to hurt me as some twisted revenge for Tupac's murder. I hung my head low as Suge walked by, and didn't see even a single scratch on him, though there were reports that he, too, had been shot during the attack on Tupac.

That night, Allison Samuels and I drove to the intersection of Flamingo Road and Koval Lane, the site of Tupac's shooting. As she called in her story, I stared at that intersection, wondering how there could be no witnesses in such a well-lit and heavily traveled area. I called my homegirl Tracy Carness in Los Angeles, one of my closest friends, someone who had worked on the set of *In Living Color* during one of Tupac's many incidents, and who was in the circle of young Hollywood that knew his genius, but also his endless problems. Tracy's first words to me, before we could even exchange greetings, were "Kevin, he's dead. I can't believe he is dead." Neither could I. Tupac was, in a phrase, a "bad nigga," which scared a lot of people, and excited just as many. I placed myself somewhere in the middle. He had not scared me, but I had feared for him. I loved the fact that he threw up his middle finger anywhere and anytime it suited him. In his mind, he was given this world and this world gave him—and those who looked like him—the middle finger all the time. Tupac Shakur exacted revenge on White people, on snobby Black folks, on the rich, on anyone without sympathy for the oppressed and voiceless on this planet.

When I got back to New York City, I filed my story and it ran on the cover of *Rolling Stone*, my last one ever on Tupac Shakur. After it ran, I got a call from a man named Billy Garland who claimed to be Tupac's biological father. I met Garland a few weeks later in Jersey City, my hometown. In our interviews, Tupac had adamantly denied knowing his father, and I did not believe that Garland was his father until I saw him in person. The moment I met him, I knew he was Tupac's dad. He had the tall, lean body, the flat-footed walk, the girlish eyelashes, the long nose, and, yeah, the bushy eyebrows.

I had mixed emotions about the meeting. While I was glad to meet Garland—Afeni Shakur had referred to him in my first *Vibe* article as "Billy"—I also knew how long it had taken him to reconnect with his son, and then only after he had seen Tupac in *Juice*. What would have been different about Tupac's life had Billy been there? Did Billy only become interested in his son once he became famous and, presumably, rich? Did Billy realize that Tupac had spent his entire twenty-five years searching for father figures in the form of teachers, street hustlers, fellow rappers like Ice-T and Chuck D, and men as different as Suge Knight and Quincy Jones?

I didn't ask Billy Garland any of these questions but sat and talked with him for a few hours in his apartment, about his life, Tupac's life, and his absence from Tupac's universe. Billy showed me pictures of himself with Tupac, the letters Tupac wrote him from prison, the many cards he received since his son's untimely death. Tupac barely knew this man, as I barely knew my father. Was Billy Garland one of the damaged souls from the Civil Rights era, an ex-Panther and now a broken-down warrior trying to get a grip on his life via his dead son? He even asked me if he should sue Afeni Shakur for half of the Tupac Shakur estate, which I found to be appalling. This man had contributed little to his son's life, and now he wanted to reap the benefits of the money a dead rapper as iconic as Tupac would bring.

But for some reason, I could not be angry with Billy Garland. A part of me understood exactly where he was coming from because he was a Black man in America with nothing to show for his life except a tiny apartment and a dead, famous son. Billy had lived a hard life in the 1970s and 1980s. Men like Billy Garland, Tupac Shakur, and me, for that matter, did not get blueprints about how to live. The world threw us into deep water and told us to swim, although we didn't know how and were too terrified to learn.

Sitting there listening to Billy Garland made me think of my own father, of how my mother crossed paths with him in Jersey City just a year or two before Tupac died. How my father pretended to be interested in seeing me, but told my mother that he had no pen or pencil when she offered to give him my number. My father did give my mother a picture of my "brother," a boy named Michael, to pass along to me. I kept the photo for a while, hoping my father would contact me, since my mother found a pen and gave him my number. But he never called, and one day in a state of rage and despair at my father, I ripped Michael's photo to shreds. Shortly thereafter I wrote an open letter to my father, which *Essence* magazine published, and I broke down reading it in public at the National Black Arts Festival in 1994, utterly distraught that he betrayed and dissed me a second time.

I left Billy Garland's house and made my way into the breezy October evening. And as I walked, I realized that after all those years at *Vibe* making a full-time salary—plus benefits and a 401(k) plan—I had little money to my name, and little to show for my hard labor. I had blown every single dime, some of it supporting my now ex-girlfriend Peggy. She was a singer who never had a steady paycheck, so I covered every single expense for her life, in addition to mine, wasting and partying hard, saving nothing. Desperate for another opportunity, I phoned a White male editor at *Spin*, since *Rolling Stone* had made it clear there was no position there for me. With more than a hint of sarcasm, he told me that "We do not have time for any superstar writers," and hung up on me. Confidence shattered, I endured the endless references to Kevin Powell as "yesterday's news," that I "had fallen off." People who'd once invited me to everything no longer returned my calls. I had gone from my heyday of conducting the final interview with the late great writer Audre Lorde and the *New Yorker* pursuing me to write about hip-hop icons like Ice-T to begging random publications to give me a record review to write. I was poor once more, and I was desperate.

And I sank deeper and deeper into depression, drank more than ever, and learned the crushing news that *Vibe* would only give me $7,000 as a severance package after I had spent four years giving everything I could to build the magazine into a cultural juggernaut. Flabbergasted, I had no choice but to accept the money. The few speaking gigs that I scored saved me, enabling me to cover my rent and to pay other bills. Broken and broke, a thirty-year-old has-been, I sold my entire CD collection—more than a thousand—for pocket money. I got about $500 for them, though they were probably worth at least four times that.

On a March night in 1997 I was awakened by Karla Radford calling me. "Kevin, Biggie is dead," she said. "They killed him. At our *Vibe* party. I cannot believe this. I just saw him alive—"

I was shocked, flabbergasted, numb. First Tupac, now The Notorious B.I.G. These two former friends had been twisted into rivals, and now they were dead. As for me, well, I seriously feared for my own life. Terrified of going to the West Coast ever again, I drank more and more, bracing myself for the violence. When Biggie's funeral procession, winding its way through his native Brooklyn, made it to my neighborhood, I refused to go out. I could not accept that both he and Tupac were dead. I woke up depressed, moved through the days depressed, and went to sleep depressed. When my landlord on South Elliott Street and I got into it, he immediately moved to evict me after five years in that brownstone basement apartment.

With no money for rent and no security for a new apartment, I decided I needed to head back uptown, back to Harlem. I was leaving Brooklyn after being pushed to the edge of darkness; I was filled with depression, and despair. And I wanted to die—

26

Suicide

the words like gunshots blasted into
the skin silencing the nightmares of a
generation . . .
and someone will fanzine you
and call you a tragic genius
and bury you in mtv heaven

A ND SO I drank liquor, beer, wine—anything readily available
or handed to me—the way that I had eagerly drunk white or
chocolate milk as a child. I drank when I woke up in the mornings, I drank in the middle of the day, I drank liquor to force myself
to sleep at night. When I had no liquor, I drank things like Nyquil.

In that Harlem room above St. Nicholas and 155th Street, the landlord's kindness to me did not matter. It did not matter that he accepted
my rent late, which was often, or that he, an incredible cook, would
prepare meals daily for both himself and me. It did not matter that he
saw me as a son, talked with me about life, his, mine, this gentleman,
this middle-aged gay Black man referred to me by a mutual friend. It
did not matter that he looked out for me in a way many older men
in my life, straight or gay, never had. I appreciated his sympathy, was

humbled by his humanity, but kept my distance at times, unable to fully accept anyone's generosity and concern, as I was so ready to die.

Across the street I could hear Black males playing boom boxes, sputtering fanciful rhymes about Harlem days and Harlem nights into the 3 A.M. air. These Black men thought this rap game would be their ticket to ride. Little did they know that I heard them—me, Kevin Powell, who helped to build *Vibe*; me, Kevin Powell, Tupac's biographer, who rose so high, and who fell so low, back into the gutter with them. Through gulps of liquor I would cry and think of Nirvana's Kurt Cobain, how, pushed to the brink, he blew his brains out. But I did not want to do it with a gun. I hoped to get struck by a bus or car or truck, hoped someone would push me from the edge of a subway platform. I thought of taking pills so that I could die peacefully in my sleep. I thought of getting a knife one last time in my life. This time I would pull it on myself, and use it to slit both my wrists, then my own throat. I had no desire and no reason to live, even as I worked odd gigs. I had talked my way into curating the Rock and Roll Hall of Fame's first-ever exhibit on hip-hop history, the first-ever in America. I wrote a couple of low-paying cover stories for Russell Simmons's *One World* magazine, doing profiles of Chris Rock and Lauryn Hill. I did speeches whenever I could book them, and even put together a speaking tour that included myself and the rapper Common and DJ Drama. I was able to conceal how bad my drinking had become.

But that hip-hop exhibit, those writing opportunities, and those public lectures were but momentary lifts to my completely devastated self-esteem. I hated life and I hated myself. I hated and resented my many peers suddenly landing jobs in something called the dot-com revolution. I did not understand, did not want to, but heard stories of companies called start-ups giving massive salaries to people like me with media and pop culture expertise. Except I never received a single call or offer. There were a few trips to Los Angeles, to audition to tape pilots for entertainment news programs, but each one stalled. I could not catch a real break. Feeling trapped, and with no reason to exist and no purpose whatsoever, I dated women here and there, had sex here and there, smoked cigarettes and cigars, and haunted strip club after strip club, across the country, between speaking gigs. At the start of one doomed relationship I showed the woman my private parts then apologized while smiling like a perverted kid; talked my way into living with her for a spell; sometimes walked her to the subway for work in the mornings and then scrambled back to her apartment to sleep and cry; and I often came home stinking of after-hours bars I frequented as she grabbed me by the collars, wondering if I was also cheating on her. Fact was I was cheating on myself. No matter, she kicked me out and that was how I landed in that room in Harlem—

During one road trip I traveled with my friend Radcliffe Bailey to the National Association of Black Journalists convention in Tennessee, and gamely ignored all the panels and presentations, made my way to the open bar each day, and on a boat ride one night got so drunk that I raced to the front of the ship and screamed as loudly as possible, "It is about time Black folks rode a boat voluntarily!"—thinking I had made some profound statement about slavery.

I was bitter. I was angry at professional Black people because I felt they were too afraid to hear a young Black man like me talk about racism and about my intense feelings of isolation and alienation. I was angry at professional White people because I felt they were afraid to recognize me as a whole human being. I felt I was as good a writer as any White male writer of my generation, yet White men I'd worked with at *Vibe*, and even mentored, passed me by in the media, writing not just about hip-hop, but anything they wanted. I thought it was the ugly and evil combination of racism, power, and privilege, but I still desperately believed someone would give me one more shot as a writer at a magazine or newspaper.

Eventually I moved back to Brooklyn, to Clinton Hill, where I lived in a basement apartment, beneath a nice young couple, their children, and the woman's mother. They had no idea who I was or what I did, other than that I wrote, lectured at colleges, and appeared to be a decent human being. They had no idea about my escapades in that underground apartment, the faceless women who came and went, the irresponsible sex, the inability to commit to any long-term relationship for fear of being abandoned, as my father abandoned me, as Rutgers had discarded me, as MTV and *Vibe* had discarded me, as I had discarded myself.

I confronted two different Black male writers—my peers—at different times, within months of each other, for writing articles that attacked me, my writing, and my character. The police showed up at the brownstone, looking for me after one of the writers filed charges against me because I took his eyeglasses from his face and smashed them to the ground. I did not pay taxes—stopped completely—and did not care. I took a road trip with my Uncle Lloyd to South Carolina after it became clear that he had destroyed himself, his marriage, and his family. I looked at Uncle Lloyd—a man I had once worshipped as one of the only positive male figures in my bleak life—and was terrified that I, too, would become a broken and destroyed man like him.

I stupidly pursued being a music executive, wasting money that I did not have on producers and singers, desperate to regain some semblance of the credibility and the clout that I had once enjoyed at *Vibe*. But the first singer I represented up and quit after I had moved her from Down South to Brooklyn, paid for her apartment, gotten her a job, and covered her basic bills. Prompted by misplaced rage I wound up in a club fighting an old colleague from *Vibe*, punching him as he punched me, biting and chomping him as we tussled on the floor. I had nowhere else to put my self-hatred and my rage except into the hurting of another human being who had done absolutely nothing to harm me.

In the aftermath of our bout a young Black male came up to me in that club in disbelief, telling me that he'd just heard me deliver a speech on the state of Black males in Brooklyn, that he had believed in me, and here I was living, hypocritically, the opposite of what I had preached. I never saw that young man again, did not know him, but the look of disappointment on his face would trouble my soul for a very long time—

Haunted by that young man's words, I continued working with an activist friend, April Silver, in creating something we called "Hip-hop

Speaks," which eventually included activists like Rosa Clemente, DJ Kuttin Kandi, and Ras Baraka. It was one more desperate effort for me to find my way. We helped to organize rallies, meetings, and teach-ins in Harlem, and those gatherings gave me some relief from the crushing depression. But my spirit was barely able to breathe for long before I fell back into darkness. I suffered from a debilitating fear that my entire life had been a sham and that I should save everyone the trouble by dying.

◆

On September 10, 2001, at Syracuse University in upstate New York, I gave a speech to first-year students. Those young people were unaware of the walking disaster I was. Next morning, I rose and prepared to catch a flight back home to New York City. April Silver mentioned she thought one of the World Trade Center buildings was on fire; then, a beat later, she told me to turn on the television in my hotel room.

As soon as I did, I saw a plane smash into the Twin Towers. Trapped, once more, this time in this hotel room in Syracuse, I didn't sleep for twenty-four hours, watching the news until I was ready to vomit. The next day I took the longest train ride of my life back to New York. When I arrived at Penn Station, I saw no one on the streets of the city in the middle of the day. I walked with my luggage to Union Square, and saw the pictures being passed around of loved ones, described then only as "missing." I spent weeks circling Greenwich Village and Union Square, amazed by the growing number of flyers of friends, family members, husbands, wives, mothers, fathers. I did not know what to do, how to help, so I did nothing except write this poem that November:

September 11th

Might it be, as my mother said to me on this ugly, sinful day,
That the world is on its last go-round?
Hijacked wild birds strip the sky of its innocent morning breath
Steel towers crumple like playing cards on an uneven metal table
Unrehearsed screams we dare not hear leap from windows

Into the open, bottomless palms of God
I cannot stand to watch life reduce
Itself to powdery dust and soot lathering the devil's inflamed
mouth
But I am fixated on the television anyhow:
Is this what slavery was like?
Is this what the holocaust was like?
Is this what famine is like?
Is this what war is like?
Is this how you felt, dear mother, when King and the two Kennedys
were killed?
I want to stitch up the sky, deny humans the right to fly
Cry until my tears have washed hatred
From the mildewed underarms of history
And I want to say to the firemen
Ah, yes, the firemen:
Your husband, your father, your brother, your uncle, your friend
Thank you for speeding to the end of
Your time and thank you for showing us that
Courage is a soul so unselfish it would
Scale a collapsing building to liberate a stranger
Even as your blood relatives wonder if you are alive—
From the remains of this madness
I detect a heartbeat called life
From the remains of this madness
I smell an aroma called love
From the remains of this madness
I embrace a body called humanity
From the remains of this madness
I construct a dream called hope
From the remains of this madness
I will ride the wings of the deceased
Into the clouds, scribble their names on the sun,
Erect a memorial to the moon, chant the blues

For New York City, then resurrect a world
Where a new-born rose will jut through the broken concrete.

◆

Somewhere in the midst of my sadness around this tragedy, I decided to quit drinking alcohol forever—ashamed and embarrassed by the drinking binges that had stretched into half a decade. Cold turkey. And I started to rise up once again.

I rose as I celebrated the one hundredth birthday of Langston Hughes—my literary hero—at the University of Kansas in Lawrence, Kansas, and was startled when an elderly White woman said to me, after hearing my Aunt Cathy poem about her emotional breakdown, "I am Aunt Cathy, too." And I rose by giving speech after speech, in suburbs, ghettos, backwater towns, growing, slowly, painfully, from the "race" man I once was into someone who drew connections between race and gender and class, who echoed the poet Sonia Sanchez's words that we were all sisters and brothers, no matter who we were. I rose as I tried to find my way as a writer once again, as a speaker, as an activist, writing books, inching closer, though carefully, to engaging with communities in New York City (though I was still terribly frightened of being discarded and dissed again).

I rose to a different and deeper kind of consciousness when I learned of the vicious and senseless murders of Shani Baraka and her partner, Rayshon Holmes, in August of 2003. Shani, the sister of my friend Ras Baraka; Shani, the daughter of the famous poets and activists Amiri and Amina Baraka. Killed dead by the husband of her older sister, a community activist, ironically, and an unapologetic batterer; he who had been attacking and beating this older sister nonstop, threatening to take her life at any moment. Shani had spent time at this home of the older sister and the abusive husband, and had been warned to stay far away by her parents, by her brothers, especially since the older sister had finally moved out. Then one day when Shani and Rayshon came there to retrieve some of Shani's belongings, thinking the husband was not there, he appeared and instantly shot and murdered her, then shot Rayshon, too. Two human beings dead, because they were women, because they were lesbians, because they were two women in love with each other. At the tragically sad funeral I cried like I had never done in my life, and felt as if I was going to plummet through the church pew, into the earth, with Shani and Rayshon. The entire church wailed and moaned in a sorrow song. Ras said Shani was the best of all the children and then he collapsed into his brothers' arms, unable to say any further words of a painful and traumatic eulogy. It was then and there at the funeral of Shani and Rayshon that I resolved I would speak even louder about violence against women and girls, even louder about the violence and hatred aimed at gay people, that I would be an ally and supporter for the rest of my life. Shani and Rayshon were dead but I had to rise—

And still I rose when, in late August 2005, Hurricane Katrina mangled a region and a people. I watched as President George W. Bush flew his plane past those people back to the White House, a house that Black slaves had built. I was not shocked by President Bush's reckless disregard for the survivors of Katrina. He and his administration had dragged us into one war after another and had tortured political prisoners. Here was a president who had been a draft dodger of the Vietnam War and as much of a drunk as I had been. He allowed his administration to openly spy on everyday Americans in the name of national security and the fight against terrorism, and this was a president who said there would be no child left behind, then left millions of kids behind because of his twisted notions of school reform and the addition of ruinous "testing." The explosion of the national debt, bailouts and breaks for the super-rich, and Bush's unapologetic embrace of the most extreme right-wing ideas and policies awoke in me a spirit of activism long dead, because *I* had been dead for so long, emotionally, spiritually. Katrina was the match that lit my fire and I knew I had to do something to help—

I could not bear to watch the images of people—my beautiful Black people—screaming for help, from rooftops, from floating mattresses. So April Silver and I jumped into relief mode and rallied hundreds and hundreds of people in New York to fill two trucks' worth of goods, donations that we immediately shipped to the Gulf Coast. Along with my friends Shannone Holt and Cynical Smith, we boarded a plane to Baton Rouge and then drove ourselves right into New Orleans as the last few folks evacuated, thanks to the help of Louisiana native and friend Renee Lapeyrolerie.

We saw the discarded clothes, the abandoned homes, a shoe here, a boot there. We saw the half-eaten pieces of fried chicken, the cups and cans and bottles of water and soda. We saw the water everywhere, the washed-out city. We felt death pushing down on us, sparking another wave of depression and fear in me. We drove from New Orleans to Houston, stopping along the way to speak with, to help, and to film the survivors of Katrina. Several of us created something called Katrina-on-the-Ground, which brought more than seven hundred college students to the Gulf Coast in the spring of 2006, to do relief work in New Orleans, Mobile, Alabama, and Biloxi, Mississippi. We trained them in Selma, Alabama, at the youth camp site of Rose, Hank, and Malika Sanders, because we wanted them to have a sense of history and of historic purpose. I gave a year to that relief effort, spending my own money. The blues returned with a vengeance when I finally realized that while I had worked to rescue others, I began to sink again, incapable of separating myself from other people's suffering. Yes, Katrina nearly drove me back to drinking, but I resisted, instead writing poetry—

Katrina

Here
I am
My lawd
On top of this roof
Can't nobody hear my cry
I said
Here I am my lawd
On top of this roof

Can't nobody hear my cry

My lawd

I am thirsty

My lawd

I am hungry

My lawd

I am lonely

My lawd

I need your help

Because they keep passing me by

I said I need your help, my lawd

Because they keep passing me by

I did nothing, my lawd

I have nothing, my lawd

I need something, my lawd

Because Ka-tri-na—

Done broken the levee

Ka-tri-na—

Done made my load heavy

Ka-tri-na—

Done made me ready

For that long walk to you

Ka-tri-na—

Done made me ready

For that long talk with you

My lawd

I am coming—

To get my due

My lawd

I am coming—

To cash my check

Here I am, my lawd

Here

I am—

27

Running for Congress

what is it to be locked away
     in the imagination of kidnappers—
an unwanted and unappreciated spoil of war?

IT WAS while I was spearheading Hurricane Katrina relief efforts in Selma, Alabama, in March 2006, that I first contemplated running for Congress back home in Brooklyn. I did not know what else I could do to help people, given how much the complexities and frustrations of Hurricane Katrina relief efforts weighed on my mind. I thought that if I ran for office and won, it would provide me with a national platform to help Katrina survivors and the other forgotten Americans in George W. Bush's America. With wars overseas coupled with financial and political suffering in our country, Mr. Bush and his Vice President Dick Cheney seemed to be running two governments: the one we knew and a separate, more sinister one in which they did as they pleased.

In 2004, I had reported for BET at the Democratic National Convention in Boston and the Republican National Convention in New York City. There in Boston, I had witnessed a tall, dark-complexioned woman named Michelle Obama hit the stage to introduce her hus-

Can't nobody hear my cry

My lawd

I am thirsty

My lawd

I am hungry

My lawd

I am lonely

My lawd

I need your help

Because they keep passing me by

I said I need your help, my lawd

Because they keep passing me by

I did nothing, my lawd

I have nothing, my lawd

I need something, my lawd

Because Ka-tri-na—

Done broken the levee

Ka-tri-na—

Done made my load heavy

Ka-tri-na—

Done made me ready

For that long walk to you

Ka-tri-na—

Done made me ready

For that long talk with you

My lawd

I am coming—

To get my due

My lawd

I am coming—

To cash my check

Here I am, my lawd

Here

I am—

27

Running for Congress

what is it to be locked away
            in the imagination of kidnappers—
an unwanted and unappreciated spoil of war?

IT WAS while I was spearheading Hurricane Katrina relief efforts in Selma, Alabama, in March 2006, that I first contemplated running for Congress back home in Brooklyn. I did not know what else I could do to help people, given how much the complexities and frustrations of Hurricane Katrina relief efforts weighed on my mind. I thought that if I ran for office and won, it would provide me with a national platform to help Katrina survivors and the other forgotten Americans in George W. Bush's America. With wars overseas coupled with financial and political suffering in our country, Mr. Bush and his Vice President Dick Cheney seemed to be running two governments: the one we knew and a separate, more sinister one in which they did as they pleased.

In 2004, I had reported for BET at the Democratic National Convention in Boston and the Republican National Convention in New York City. There in Boston, I had witnessed a tall, dark-complexioned woman named Michelle Obama hit the stage to introduce her husband, "my babies' daddy, Barack Obama." The writer asha bandele had already mentioned Obama to me when he began his run for a United States Senate seat in Illinois that year. That night in Boston I sat transfixed as Obama addressed many of the things that I had been speaking about for several years on the lecture circuit across America: that we were a nation of many faiths; that there was just one America; and that we needed to figure out how to build bridges to each other. After delivering his keynote address, Barack Obama received a standing ovation, and almost immediately there was chatter of him running for president.

I also covered the Republican National Convention in New York City, but that was the polar opposite of the DNC conclave. Nearly lily-White, it felt unwelcoming, sterile, toxic, as if folks like me did not belong there. I could feel White folks eyeballing me, trying to figure out if I was down with them or just one of those liberal media "spies." There were numerous demonstrations and rallies against Mr. Bush and the Republicans throughout the week. Upon leaving Madison Square Garden every night of the convention, I felt like I needed to take two or three showers to wash away the nasty feeling built up from hearing all kinds of vitriol from one right-wing speaker after another.

Two years later, I received a call from *New York Daily News* columnist Errol Louis inquiring about my political ambitions. I had been talking with political operatives about the possibility of running for Congress, and I learned instantly that gossip travels fast in that scene. Several days after, I was stunned when I received calls from some political operatives informing me that Louis had written a devastating piece about me in the *Daily News*. Among other things he compared me to a wife-beater, brought up my fights and arrests in New York City, and essentially deemed me unfit for public office. I had done years of work around ending violence against women and girls—with writings, forums, and workshops, throughout America—but this writer mentioned all my good work only in passing. After reading the article, I called him to ask why he had written the article in the way he had, given my public acknowledgments through the years of my shortcomings, and the fact that I dedicated many years to work on gender violence prevention. He coldly told me that I was not ready for political office, that he was not going to lose any sleep over my feelings, and that he hoped his pen could derail my political career.

Depressed once again, I opted not to run for Congress in 2006 against the incumbent in my Brooklyn district—a Black man named Ed Towns. Towns had held the position since the Reagan years of the 1980s, and owned the dubious distinction of being one of the great embarrassments in Congress when it came to attendance, voting record, and introduction of bills—none of which dissuaded his constituents from returning him to office every two years.

The one thing that provided temporary relief from the vicious *Daily News* attack was a cover story I did on the comedian Dave Chappelle for *Esquire* in May 2006. I had known Dave since the early 1990s when I was on MTV and at *Vibe*, and he was the teenaged comic Whoopi Goldberg affectionately referred to as "The Kid." In fact, when *Chappelle's Show* was slated for Comedy Central, Dave phoned me to ask if I would be the narrator for a spoof he was doing on MTV's *The Real World*. Wanting to keep great distance from that past, I politely declined. But I was pleasantly surprised *Chappelle's Show* became such a huge hit, and when Dave did a block party in Brooklyn, this time I joined him there, and on stage too, when he requested I write about the entire day and night. It was magical and the concert included Kanye West, Lauryn Hill, Dead Prez, John Legend, Erykah Badu, and Jill Scott. Nothing ever came of my handwritten notes of the evening until Chappelle abruptly quit the Comedy Central show and his publicist asked me to write the only profile interview for a print publication that he would be willing to do. I agreed, thinking it would be a coup for me to make some extra cash, land a coveted *Esquire* cover story, and possibly give some new life to my lagging literary career.

For *Esquire*, I spent several weeks following Dave in New York City, in Los Angeles, and in his home farm area of Yellow Springs,

Ohio. There were days when Dave eagerly answered my questions, and there were days when he said he no longer wanted to do the article. In Los Angeles I rode with him and others to the Grammy Awards in February 2006, where Chappelle, ironically, introduced the reclusive and confounding soul legend Sly Stone to the crowd.

We then went to an afterparty I was not expecting, at Prince's posh Cali home. The gates were purple, with his famous logo combining male and female symbols etched in deliberate places. Inside there were celebrities like Mariah Carey and Jamie Foxx, food and drink flowed, and there in the darkened music room we were told that Morris Day and The Time would be the special musical guests. It was at that very moment that I, standing alone, met Prince. I looked at him and he looked at me. And he said to me, "You're the writer, right?" Stunned he even knew who I was I said "Yes" but could get no other words from my mouth. I turned my head in embarrassment and shyness, and when I spun back around to say more to Prince, he was gone. I never saw him again that night.

After the Grammys and the Prince party, Dave had had enough of Hollywood and announced that he was ready to charter a private jet and head home to Ohio. He chain-smoked the entire flight, which drove his publicist Carla and me crazy. When Dave finally nodded off, we stole the remainder of his cigarettes so we did not have to inhale any more secondhand smoke. In Ohio, in the dead of winter, I spent a long and miserable week meeting Dave at his favorite local coffee shop, or not, depending on his mood. Some days I was a journalist asking him questions about his life, and other days I was his therapist, telling him that he should return to his Comedy Central show (he had quit during the making of season three). Chappelle felt betrayed, and he felt that he had betrayed people, but by the time the *Esquire* cover story hit newsstands in May 2006, it was barely noticed, because Dave had already done interviews on *The Oprah Winfrey Show* and *Inside the Actors Studio*. I had written what I thought was one of the best articles I had ever written and I was distraught, but it seemed there was Chappelle fatigue. Additionally, I had had some pretty intense disagreements with a White male editor at *Esquire*, Mark Warren, about race and certain racial elements I thought critical to the Chappelle cover story. *Esquire* and other mainstream publications had long been criticized for not hiring Black writers and Black editors, and I walked away thinking part of the reason why was that these mostly White male staffs had no clue how to relate to Black men like me as equals. I never again heard from Mark Warren, or anyone else at *Esquire*.

So I moved on by renewing my interest in politics. My speaking engagements picked up at colleges and universities around the country, and over time I would wind up visiting every American state at least once. These trips reinforced for me that all people were my sisters and brothers, which I had first learned from the poet Sonia Sanchez. I was still deeply critical of racism, of White privilege and power in America, but I no longer blamed every single White person for the system of racism. I felt that Americans of every race, culture, and creed needed to be educated, or re-educated, about history, whether it was American history, or their own family histories. Such an education was crucial if we were ever to be serious about one human race, one human family.

By 2008, with Barack Obama's presidential campaign at full steam, I decided to run against the incumbent congressman in my district in the September Democratic primary in Brooklyn, New York. I assembled a team of folks—both young people and steely political veterans—and I got a crash course in bare-knuckle politics. I had had experience in voter education, voter registration, and get-out-the-vote work, and I had campaigned and fund-raised for others. But doing this for myself was difficult, and I found it hard to spend so much time on the telephone begging for donations, endorsements, and support. A constant stream of random folks showed up at our campaign office proclaiming to have access to large numbers of voters, or magical powers to sway some person or entity who could push me toward victory. I loved walking block after block in the Fort Greene, Clinton Hill, Bed-Stuy, Canarsie, East Flatbush, Midwood, and East New York sections of Brooklyn, but even then there was no escaping the subculture of political hustlers of varying stripes: suited and slick-talking real-estate developer types; political operatives angling for positions and payments from my campaign in exchange for advice and "connections"; the lords of the underground, the streets, and the housing projects who were absolutely positive they could deliver "the ghetto vote" for me. I encountered these and others in a congressional district with nearly half a million residents, with groups as diverse as the Hasidic Jews in Williamsburg, the White voters in Fort Greene and Clinton Hill, and the Blacks and Puerto Ricans in East New York. The entire borough of Brooklyn has nearly three million residents, more than one hundred spoken languages and ethnic groups, and is as close to representing the mosaic that is America as any area in the nation. With few resources, we brought energy and enthusiasm to our campaign and put a spotlight on the ineptitude of Congressman Towns and his dismal legacy.

But Errol Louis at the *Daily News* struck again. This time, he invited me on his local radio show to discuss my campaign. Even though I was reluctant after what he'd previously written about me, I decided to go on his program anyway. My closest advisers—particularly Marisa King-Redwood and Lauren Summers, both of whom served as my publicist at different points in my life—coached me, but the moment we went live, he seemed to do everything he could to paint me as some sort of monster. I stayed calm, answered each and every question, and I felt like I won that round of the battle. But shortly thereafter, he assailed me *again* in his column. I felt like he had some sort of vendetta against me—something that went far beyond my running for Congress.

I thought my reputation might be helped by the summer 2008 major fund-raiser in New York City I had planned, with Dave Chappelle as the headliner. I asked Dave personally, and he agreed. We created the invitations, set up a host committee, did extensive email blasts and phone calling to get donors to commit. Chappelle had all but become a recluse in the two years since I had interviewed him for *Esquire*, so there was quite a media buzz about his attendance. I checked in with Dave regularly, and his publicist Carla too, and everything appeared fine.

On the night of the event, Wednesday, July 9, 2008, over seven hundred people packed Eugene, a Manhattan nightclub. Chris Rock showed up and told me that Jerry Seinfeld was doing his best to make it, too. I could not believe my luck. But then my luck changed—Dave Chappelle called me to say that he had missed his flight and would not be able to make it after all, right during the 7 P.M. hour when the doors opened. I panicked—some donors had paid up to a thousand dollars expecting to see Chappelle. I did not know what to do, and the event producers and my consultants thought one idea was to ask Chris Rock and to get him to replace Chappelle. Rock, there with his wife, Malaak, refused, saying he did not believe in doing such a thing, out of respect for other comedians.

We stalled the restless crowd as long as we could—about an hour—then finally I had to suck up my fears and frustrations and tell the people the truth: Dave Chappelle was not coming. The audience listened politely, but you could feel the deflation of the nightclub. People headed for the exits, while others angrily demanded refunds.

That night we raised over $50,000—the most I had ever raised to that point at any fund-raiser—but we had to pay a good chunk of it back in refunds (some people even threatened to sue me for false advertising). I was devastated. The next few days the media blasted me and my campaign as a sham and a fraud. I never regained momentum from what happened, and Dave Chappelle avoided me for a long time after that, never offering an honest explanation as to why he did not show up.

After losing the congressional primary race by a wide margin, I swore that I would never run again. I did not feel supported as a progressive candidate, even in allegedly liberal New York City with its overwhelming Democratic Party majority. Being publicly attacked from so many angles caused me great pain. The divisions created by political campaigns in Brooklyn—especially in the Black community—proved to be a bitter pill to swallow. The number of times I was slyly offered a different political seat reinforced how corrupt the whole system was. It was clear that much of it had nothing to do with democracy.

Moreover, voter apathy was disheartening. White, Black, Latino, Asian, male or female, straight or gay, able-bodied or disabled, Christian, Jewish, Muslim, or some other faith, or atheist—what these residents had in common, time and again, was a complete lack of interest in politics, in politicians, and in voting. I was told, "You are just like the rest of them," or "I don't vote and I don't care," or "What are *you* going to do for *me*?" Where my advisers told me to spend only two to three minutes on each voter, I had found myself unwilling to do that: I would sit with some voters for ten, fifteen, thirty minutes, even an hour, listening to their concerns, their criticisms, their vision for what political leadership should be.

I found myself delivering resources, services, and information on the spot, asking elected officials and faith leaders if they themselves had a directory of resources for the city of New York or, minimally, for the borough of Brooklyn. No one did, so the seeds were planted for BK Nation—the BK stands for "Building Knowledge"—an organization I eventually cofounded to be a clearinghouse of information that was so desperately needed. American politicians like Ed Towns sat in office for decades, appealing to those they knew would vote consistently, such as older voters and people who were organized in their respective communities and made their voices heard. And those politicians rarely, if ever, provided consistent information, resources, and services to the people of their district. Citizen ignorance meant more power for the people in political office, without any accountability.

I also closely followed Barack Obama as he made history on his way to becoming the first Black president of the United States. His victory was thanks in no small measure to the record number of young multicultural Americans who voted for the first time. But I also knew Obama's win was the result of a very savvy marketing campaign, with catchy phrases like "yes we can" and "hope," remixed from the presidential aspirations and slogans of Jesse Jackson in the 1980s.

Much was also sampled from the short-lived 1968 presidential bid of Bobby Kennedy, except Bobby had been speaking fearlessly and bluntly about poverty, oppression, and creating concrete solutions in the years before his fateful campaign. So something felt askew to me, like Barack Obama was not quite who we were told he was; that he was more an uber-popular brand, like the iPhone, rather than a visionary or innovator like the Bobby who emerged after his brother John was assassinated. Besides, no one person had ever changed America before, so it was surreal to me that people now believed this man could if we put him in the White House—

No matter, on Tuesday, November 4, 2008, though still reeling from what had happened during my campaign, I held an election-night party. In the middle of it, one of my former "consultants" handed me a large yellow envelope, which contained papers suing me for nearly $20,000 that he claimed I owed him. The man and his agency had done barely anything for my campaign. Shortly thereafter, a fraternity brother (I had been initiated into Alpha Phi Alpha, the oldest Black fraternity in America, in March 2008) claimed that I owed him $10,000 for car service and security expenses. Running for office left me penniless and distraught.

A few months later, in March 2009, while still sorting through the wreckage of my congressional race, I got a call I never expected to receive: a request from a producer to appear on *The Oprah Winfrey Show* during a segment relating to the sensational allegations that the R&B singer Chris Brown had brutally beaten his then-girlfriend Rihanna during Grammy weekend in February.

While I would not address the Chris Brown–Rihanna situation per se, I was invited to talk about male violence against women in general. What an incredible opening to use one of the biggest platforms in America to set straight a record that people like the *Daily News* columnist twisted. After so many years of consistency and of transparency, it hurt me deeply that my life could be reduced to that one incident with my girlfriend without regard to my efforts to make amends and to be an ally to women and girls.

The prospect of appearing on *Oprah* terrified me because I could not be certain about the questions that I would be asked or how I would be portrayed. I desperately wanted to avoid being branded "a woman beater" for the rest of my life. I decided to do it because I had faith in Oprah's sense of fairness. After a great pre-interview, during which they told me that I would be flown to Chicago to sit with Oprah, I learned that the interview would take place via Skype from my home in Brooklyn. A bit deflated, I nevertheless decided to make the most of the opportunity. That March morning I sat nervously in front of my computer talking about manhood, about gender violence, about the changes that men needed to make, about the things women and girls could do. By the time of the broadcast seven hours later, I had passed out from sheer exhaustion, but right after it aired my BlackBerry started buzzing with mad text messages. In a daze, I realized that people who had seen me on *Oprah* were giving me overwhelmingly supportive feedback. I cried tears of joy, thanked God for the opportunity, and called Oprah's producer to say the same.

Emboldened by that appearance, and by the wave of support that followed, I began considering a run for Congress a second time. However, given the war-like nature of politics, I had reservations. But a 2008 campaign worker named Gregory strongly encouraged me to try again. He sat with me one day and laid out a masterful plan for victory in 2010. Sold, I trusted Gregory even though I did not know him well, and off we went, into a new year and a new campaign. In short order, Gregory signed on as my campaign manager, bringing along his acquaintance Josh to serve as the field director. My friend Horatio—a Black man—became the deputy campaign manager. Given that both Gregory and Josh were White, I wanted at least one Black man besides myself in a significant position on the leadership team. Horatio had already worked with me on an initiative called Black and Male in America, which staged monthly workshops in Brooklyn and a national conference in 2007.

As 2010 began, things seemed better. I became more comfortable making fund-raising calls, and with no competing presidential campaign, it seemed like an ideal time for a congressional campaign like mine. Enthusiastic young volunteers joined the team, a multicultural army of college students, social-justice activists, and friends. Congressman Towns refused to debate me as he had during the previous campaign, ducking and dodging our public criticisms of his record, his legacy, and his lack of vision. Thanks to Twitter and Facebook and a creative team, we hammered home the obvious flaws in his performance as a congressman, and even passed along his campaign office number so the electorate could phone in their displeasure directly.

To counter us, Towns sued to get me off the ballot. Our entire campaign leadership team, and key volunteers who participated in the petition process to get me on the ballot, wound up in court. This ate up two weeks of our campaign and thousands of dollars in lawyer fees. Around this same time, the *Daily News* ran an article exposing my IRS issues. The piece got the numbers wrong, but the damage was done. Forced to write a blog for the *Huffington Post*, I laid out the details of my financial state, how I got to that point, everything—a truly humbling experience. Although we won the court case and remained on the ballot, my campaign was sunk. Labor unions, Black churches, and so-called progressive organizations like the Working Families Party, which had avoided me all along, did not respond to my calls for campaign help, or made excuses as to why not, just as they had done in 2008. It was mad deep how various groups like these, as well as certain wealthy, well-connected individuals, all played the same shell game: We will support and donate to you if this one or that one supports and donates to you.

I was further dejected when in early August 2010, Gregory abruptly left the campaign, and a few days later Josh also walked away. A week or so later, in the midst of some joking in the campaign office to lighten the mood, Horatio quietly packed up his stuff and announced his departure. I followed Horatio to a Brooklyn bus stop in Bed-Stuy and pleaded with him to stay on through the primary one month later. He would not look me in the eyes and, like Gregory and Josh before him, wouldn't give me a clear reason for quitting. In the pouring rain, I walked back to our headquarters and slumped to the floor in tears. I felt profoundly betrayed by people I had trusted the most.

To make matters worse, I was disrespected, maligned, and verbally abused even more in the 2010 campaign than in 2008 by residents in the Congressional district. Sadly, some of the foulest things said to me, online, offline to my face, were from Black folks, many of them much older than me. I was called a celebrity seeker, an opportunist, and ugly, unprintable names purely because I had the audacity to run against Ed Towns. We never knew who these people were but suspected their allegiance to Congressman Towns, to the way things were. One Black Brooklyn "journalist" threatened to fight me if I did not do an interview with him, and it was later revealed he was on Mr. Towns's payroll as a "consultant." It was so disappointing, so hurtful, so spiritually draining that I thought long and hard about leaving Brooklyn, and New York City, for good after the campaign.

One month later, on Election Day, I campaigned near Starrett City, a massive housing development in Brooklyn, with some supporters, including friends from my home state of Jersey. Late in the afternoon, Congressman Towns and his own "posse" showed up. It was a hostile situation and both sides traded insults and menacing stares. A few fast-talking Towns supporters even attempted to move me away from my friends to pretend that we were down with each other. Moments later I stood face-to-face with Mr. Towns, and we talked.

Here was a man in his seventies in a silly Kangol hat, a man old enough to be my father, who had swept into office in the 1980s as a beneficiary of the Civil Rights Movement and Black activism; but who did not help Black New York shake off the catastrophic effects of the 1980s crack cocaine scourge and Reagan-era social policies. Meanwhile, Black leadership in New York, rather than nurture and prepare the next generation of Black voices to succeed them, had done exactly what their White forerunners had done: they dug in their heels to keep hold of power and became leaders of what I called "a ghetto dictatorship." The community-first values of the Civil Rights era had been replaced by the post–Civil Rights era values of me-first, career first. They wanted to control and dominate a building, a block, a housing project, a district, a church, a community center, an organization, by any means necessary.

You saw this pattern with old-school Black political leaders nationwide, too. Ghettos existed wherever there were Black city council members or alderpersons. Ghettos existed wherever there were Black state senators and assemblypersons. And ghettos existed in most of the congressional districts represented by Black House members. Forty-plus long years of Black political representation, and in record numbers, and yet it seemed our communities were worse off than even before the Civil Rights Movement.

Systemic racism, of course, had done a number on these communities from coast to coast, too, from how financial institutions had treated urban areas, to the deterioration of public schools with White flight in the 1960s and 1970s, to loss of factories and other job incubators, to the often combative relationship between our communities and local police. And the more recent gentrification of urban areas had widened the economic gap across America. Brooklyn had become besieged with gentrification, with White folks moving into longstanding Black and Latino neighborhoods under the pretense of "development." This was happening on Congressman Towns's watch, and he was saying and doing nothing. Much of my years in New York City had been spent in Brooklyn and it was shocking to see the transformation of that borough, of people priced out and pushed away, evicted under mysterious circumstances, or straight up told their Brooklyn was in the past. If a leader had any vision, she or he figured out some way to help the people to help themselves, to make sure there were equal opportunities for all. You did not retreat to what is safe, secure, and predictable.

Ed Towns, however, basically had turned his back on Brooklyn— on the Black community. Congressman Towns knew that he would win that night, but I could also see in his tobacco-brown eyes that he knew his political power was waning. After years of gentrification,

Brooklyn's residents—especially the new White inhabitants—were asking pointed questions about the leadership in their new 'hoods. Ed Towns had to go—he knew it, I knew it, Brooklyn knew it.

Outside Starrett City, I simply wished Congressman Towns and his family luck. The betrayal by Gregory, Josh, and Horatio stung me for months and months. I never confronted them, and I never heard from them again, but I could not escape the belief that they had duped me into running for Congress a second time, only to set me up for this huge fall.

28

Love, a many splintered thing

i have this need to feel you
make love out of the sweat
itching our palms give
you to your mother so that she
can give birth to you

MET HER in Brooklyn, in April 2001, a couple of weeks before my thirty-fifth birthday, and I saw her backstage at a traveling circus in Coney Island—a multicultural-themed extravaganza with animals, acrobats, and special effects straight outta the Dirty South. My friend Colette, a publicist for the circus, invited me there, and I checked out a woman performing tricks atop one of the elephants; I asked Colette if I could meet that elephant lady afterward. But Billie was there in my path: big, beautiful brown eyes, curly natural red-brown hair, dots of freckles about her nose, lush, full lips, and a sleek, athletic body. Billie was part of the circus troupe that replicated classic Black dance moves like the jitterbug and the lindy hop. She gave me a look, smiled shyly, and pointed her finger at me and said, "Aren't you that guy from MTV?"

Ten years younger than I and from Oakland, California, Billie was a professional dancer, conceived in the poverty of the Mississippi Delta by two teenage parents who never married and did not really like each other. By the second day of our acquaintance, we were lovers, but since she was traveling with the circus—she was on her way to South Africa—I cut her off, thinking that this could not last. But even though Billie was out of the country, I could not get my mind off her. I sensed that I knew her from a previous lifetime and that we had met in this life to fall in love with each other.

I had felt extremely connected to a woman like this once before, nearly a decade earlier. Her name was Mona, and she was a recent graduate from Oberlin College. In my heady days of MTV and *Vibe*, Mona had schooled me on gender issues, feminism, and why she thought pretty much every single man walking the earth was a natural disaster. I fell in love with Mona, wrote her love letters, and was disheartened that my love was not reciprocated. We had sex once, the only time that I ever cheated on a woman; at the time I was living with Peggy, the singer. Guilt-stricken, I came home unable to even look my girlfriend in the eye, vowing that I would never cheat on another woman. In the years between Mona and Billie, I dated, thought I had fallen in like a couple of times, but genuinely believed that I was doomed to be single for the rest of my life.

Billie called me after the September 11 tragedy, and we instantly reconnected, embarking on a back-and-forth, long-distance relationship between New York City and Oakland. We could not get enough of each other. Neither one of us could say for sure what love or, for that matter, self-love was. We made it up as we went along. We dated for a while, made love, argued. I felt that she tended to worship everything White people said or did, and it made me uncomfortable. My positions about Blackness and race in America disturbed her in turn.

During breaks from our relationship, which stretched from 2001 to 2011—ten long years of love, hate, compassion, anger, engaged love-making, and sheer indifference—we parted ways, dated others, got our feelings hurt a few times, and always reunited. I desperately wanted to return to Billie after dating a singer and bartender with a master's degree who duped me into believing that we were made for each other. I had spent so many years dogging women out, especially during my college years and right after, that I went to the other extreme as I learned about sexism in this male-dominated world. I did not want to be the "typical" man. In time, I learned that the singer never fully disconnected from her previous boyfriend. After unprotected sex in the summer of 2004 she announced that she missed her period *and* spilled the beans that she had been having sex with her ex, too. Humiliated, I did not want to break out like my father did, but the notion that I might be sticking around for someone else's baby traumatized me. I stayed and two weeks later she informed me that her period arrived and that she was not pregnant. She promptly kicked me to the curb and went back to her ex-boyfriend.

Confused, beat down, and snake-bitten, I returned to Billie. We even talked of marriage, of a life together, of children, but I was so emotionally unstable, my life so wildly unpredictable, that I could not make that final commitment.

Billie was a feminist, determined to make something of her life, and she did not want to wind up like her mother, unmarried, with children, and dependent on a man. Her mother dressed like a character in a hip-hop music video and dated a much younger man, a former drug dealer, a guy who wouldn't even speak to me. I suspected that his dislike related to my role as an activist—I was a dude who cared about community, while he sold substances that helped to destroy our communities. I always felt nervous at the house that Billie's mother shared with her boyfriend because I knew the ghetto world too well: at any given moment someone could drive by and blast us all, or roll up into the house and murder us, just for being there. Sure enough, I learned that, right after one of our rare visits, a rival drug cartel had shot at the boyfriend, barely missing.

By mid-2006, on the heels of Hurricane Katrina, I was living

in an apartment in Downtown Brooklyn. I begged Billie to move to New York City to marry me. But when she arrived in July 2006, the thought of marriage, of lifelong commitment, terrified me, and I acted out in every way imaginable to turn her off, to convince her that this would never work. Eventually, she left, and we rarely spoke over the next four, long years.

Billie called me in October 2010, a month after my second congressional campaign defeat, when I was feeling betrayed by so many people I had trusted. Contact with Billie reconnected me with a sense of the possibility of trusting others again. She was familiar, comfortable, someone I urgently needed after the revolving door of strange and random people during my two Congressional campaigns. We talked as if no distance separated us, not time, not geography. She told me that she'd recently been living in Atlanta, but that the man she'd been dating had turned out to actually be married with children and Billie was one of several "side chicks." Embarrassed, she reached out to me because I, a pro-feminist man, could give her sound advice. While I did my best, it was clear that she was angry and filled with a desire for revenge.

This was not the Billie I had known, but I pushed the thought from my mind. We talked regularly right into 2011, when, once again, she agreed to move to New York City in the spring, if I was serious about getting married.

Completely broke after my congressional campaigns, I pulled my few coins together and put down $2,500 on an engagement ring for Billie, while the real possibility of losing my apartment hovered above my head and speaking gigs at colleges and elsewhere dried up because of the terrible economy and my being removed from that scene for years as I ran for Congress. For the first time in my life, bankruptcy loomed large.

Almost from the moment that we agreed to move toward marriage, I felt a shift in Billie's energy toward me, and she talked to me as though I were dumb or no-good. And once in New York City she began complaining about the "junk," the "clutter" in our home.

Dumbfounded, I wondered if her treatment of me mimicked the mixed signals—and the downright venom—that I had sent to her for so many years. Did I—and perhaps, other men—push her to this?

I sucked it up and worked my tail off that summer, commuting to Virginia via bus to teach at George Mason University, crashing with friends because I could not afford a hotel room. I was trying to do whatever I needed to do to ensure that Billie and I survived, fulfilling a promise I had made to her when I convinced her to move to New York, but it backfired on me. Everything I did seemed to fall short of her expectations.

Our relationship became so terrible that I slept on the sofa. Whenever I asked Billie if she liked me in any way, she stared at me and then averted her eyes. One night, after waking up in a state of frustration and misery, I woke Billie up to confront her about our dysfunctional relationship, but she blew me off. Then it happened: out of my mouth came that phrase, the one I had not uttered since the early 1990s on MTV. I called Billie the b word, adding the word *stupid* before it. Stunned, Billie fell silent.

From the moment I said those words, I wished that I could scoop them from the air and swallow them whole. But I could not. The damage was done, and I knew it. It did not matter how much I apologized. It did not matter how well Billie knew my history of challenging myself and men and boys on sexism, on misogyny. It did not matter how many times Billie and I had discussed the ways of men and boys. Nor did it matter that I had allied myself with women and girls. I had fallen backwards, woefully backwards, into an abyss, acting like the men my mother had warned me not to become.

I pleaded with Billie when she started packing her bags the next day to return to California. I begged her not to leave me, and she grudgingly agreed to attend therapy with me, but nothing improved. In late July 2011, she announced that she was leaving me for good.

Not knowing what else to do, I escorted Billie to Newark Airport in Jersey, in a cab driven by an old Puerto Rican man whose service I had used for about a year. We did not speak on the ride across the

Brooklyn Bridge and through the Holland Tunnel. Nor did we speak much when we finally got to Newark Airport. I felt compelled to take her, to ride with her, because of some faint hope that she might change her mind and agree to work things out with me. No such luck. We checked her bags, and we walked slowly to the security checkpoint. When I could go no further with her, she turned to me and said, "I hope you get yourself together." Disheartened, I stood there as Billie showed her I.D. to the airport personnel, put her items in trays, took off her shoes, and marched through the security machine. She looked at me, waved, and I continued to watch her as her petite figure became smaller and smaller and eventually disappeared.

Back in the taxi, I sunk into the back seat of the car and bawled loudly, unable to hold back the tears and mucus falling from my eyes and nose. I howled as if I lost my life through Billie's rejection and departure. My body shivered with icy recollections of what I might have done, recently, through the years, to push Billie away for good, to turn her against trusting men, against trusting me. In that moment, I did not want to be, did not want to live. I pushed back the depression stitched to the edges of my soul, not certain how long I could hold back the floodwaters of sadness. The driver cleared his throat, visibly uncomfortable with the scene: "I know this is none of my business, but if someone can make you feel like that, you really should not be with them."

He was right. Billie was gone, and there was nothing I could do about it. The walls had closed on me with our relationship and one year later my financial misadventures closed on me, too. After trusting my fraternity brother Marcus to be my financial adviser and confidant for three years, he dissed me by sending an email to complete strangers calling me, more or less, an economic disaster, and indicating that he would sue me for thousands of dollars in back pay if I ever reached out to him again. The only thing I could surmise was that he did this because I dared question, finally, how he was handling my apartment situation, my mounting debts, and other financial problems.

A week or so later I tore a meniscus in my left knee as I played basketball to work out the overwhelming stress and grief in my life. Luckily I didn't need surgery, as I had had no medical benefits since my days at *Vibe*. A month after that, in May of 2012, I crashed my bicycle just one block from my building, ripping and dislocating my right shoulder from its socket. "What did I do to be this black and blue," I whispered to myself as I lay in a Brooklyn hospital bed in the most unbearable pain of my life. I had no clue how I was going to pay this medical bill.

Shortly thereafter I filed for bankruptcy and relived every poor financial decision of my life, plus people suing me left and right, including for debts tied to my two Congressional races. I ate peanut butter and jelly sandwiches and drank water much of that summer of 2012, spent time in New York parks listening to street musicians, and I kept to myself, not really wanting to be bothered. I was recovering from those two injuries, from Billie, from my shattered trust in friendships, again, because of Marcus, my fraternity brother.

◆

One day around that time, another Alpha Phi Alpha fraternity brother of mine, Dorsey Spencer, who was working at the American University in Nigeria, emailed to ask if I wanted to come to Africa to speak to the students. He said they did not have much money for a speaking fee, but that they could at least get me there. I didn't care what they wanted me to do, what the topic would be, nothing. The God I believed in very deeply had answered my prayers and I would finally go to Africa, as I had always dreamed of doing. Overcome with emotion in that moment, I thanked Dorsey profusely, repeatedly. He had no idea why.

The trip came at a time when I needed it more than ever.

29

Africa

what will we call this new-born baby?
let us call him ra—god of the sun
let us call her isis—mother of creation and the universe
let us baptize this new-born baby with a red
thunderbolt from shango

I **FELT LIKE** I had won the grand prize on some game show. I told everyone I could I was going to Africa. Having gotten the immunization shots required, I educated myself as best as I could on the political situation in Nigeria, and I was on my way.

For years Africa had tugged mightily at my spirit, calling me home to visit her, to spend time in the geographical space where all of civilization was born. When I was a college student at Rutgers University, I digested as many books and documentary films as possible about Africa. In fact, my introduction to the continent was through my work, as a first-year student, in the anti-apartheid movement. But what I knew of Africa was largely through the often negative, destructive media images that depicted Africans as violent and warring factions or as starving people in famines.

Learning of Africa through the movement to liberate South Africa had transformed my thinking, begun the process of washing away an entire early life of profound self-hatred, and, for the first time in my life, given me a land base with which to connect. Except for Native Americans, the original "owners" of this land, every people in our nation come from somewhere, be it voluntarily as immigrants or through barbaric force and free labor, as was the case with my African ancestors. As I evolved as an activist and writer and I encountered so many Africans from Africa studying in America, or permanently living in America, or Americans of different races and cultures who had visited Africa, or lived or worked there for extended periods, I felt a profound sense of guilt that I had not gone. Part of it was the expensive cost of getting there, and part of it was my inner conflicting emotions.

Yes, somehow I was subconsciously afraid to make the journey, afraid of what I might feel once I arrived, afraid that I would be so pulled emotionally by the experience that I would not want to return home to America. And afraid that because my ancestors were centuries removed from there I would be a foreigner in the most uncomfortable and unpleasant ways. But in the aftermath of my failed Congressional campaigns the desire to go had grown so enormous, so great, had so filled the belly of my spirit that I determined that I couldn't put it off any longer. But I had no idea how I was going to get there until this free trip was offered by my fraternity brother at the American University in Nigeria.

Still, in the days before my trip, I also felt some shame in going, since Hurricane Sandy had just caused great destruction to New York City and New Jersey, where my mother had no heat or hot water for several days. I offered her a hotel or my Brooklyn apartment, but she refused. Before I left, I gave her some money and batteries for her flashlights, as she requested, but she would not budge.

My mother has never been on an airplane, never left America, never even been off the East Coast, so through my various travels, she experiences these trips with me. I laughed to myself when I heard my mother say things like "We not no Africans, we don't know nothing about no Africa, we Americans." Because in her own way she is saying the American South, New Jersey, New York, America, is all we know since our ancestors were captured, kidnapped, and stolen from Africa to work for free throughout the Americas.

So for people like my mother, our lives did not begin in Africa. But, as has been said many times, a tree without its roots cannot stand. So goes it for us who are of African descent, in America, in Canada, in the Caribbean, in Latin America, in Europe, in Asia, wherever we are on the planet. I was absolutely clear that I was an African, long before this trip. Likewise clear that I am an African American, which means, as Amiri Baraka stated so compellingly in his landmark book *Blues People*, those of us born here in the United States maintain many of the traits and cultural nuances of Africa, but are, in fact, a completely different group, too.

But when I hear the South Carolina Geechee dialect of my mother and many relatives from that state's Low Country, or think of the many beliefs or superstitions and sayings passed from generation to generation, or watch how we praise God in our churches and are seemingly possessed by holy spirits, it is abundantly clear to me that Africa is all up in us, even if we've been conditioned to believe that it is not.

On Thursday, November 8, 2012, I landed in Africa for the first time in my life. The plane was packed, mostly with Nigerians traveling from either England or America back home to what many Black folks across the globe call "the motherland." I smiled as I watched and listened to the Nigerian passengers talk in some of the several hundred languages spoken in Nigeria, including English. I especially looked into the eyes and faces of the elder passengers, as you could see the recent history of Nigeria etched in their soulful expressions, the contours of their skin, the elastic motions of their hands.

One of my seat mates was a young man who was also heading to Yola, Nigeria, and who did tech work for the university's library. His name was Nas (short for Nasir, like the rapper), and he gave me great insight into Yola. He told me to go with an open mind, not to judge, to know that Yola was a very simple place. Nas made me think of Nneka, the dynamic Nigerian singer I had seen perform in Brooklyn two weeks before. Indeed, if anyone had voiced what was happening in present-day Nigeria as Fela once did, it was she, Nneka.

Representatives of the American University in Nigeria greeted me after I'd passed through customs in Abuja, the de facto seat of the Nigerian government since there was much violence and chaos in Lagos, the actual capital city. They were incredibly kind and respectful, would not allow me to carry any of my bags myself, and put me in a vehicle to a hotel where I would get a nap for a few hours before flying, one last leg, to Yola. On the ride to and from that hotel I noticed many things: the police and security forces everywhere, with guns pointing at the ground; the numerous motorcycles, called *okadas*, which served as "taxi rides" in and near the airport; the swarm of cabdrivers hustling for riders and fares; the many people, male and female and all ages, walking or waiting along the roads of Abuja, quite a few balancing buckets or wood or boxes very skillfully upon their heads; the burning sight and smell of garbage here there everywhere as I would learn that many poorer Nigerians simply did this because it takes too long for garbage disposal to happen by the government; the cross-section of outfits, from traditional African attire worn by women and men, to the many dressed as if they were straight outta Compton or Brooklyn in America; and the rhythm and energy of Nigeria—slow, methodical, the people moving as if the world must wait upon them, this cradle of civilization responsible for the beginning of the entire human race.

At my hotel I phoned my mother to let her know that I had made it to Africa, then passed out. I was shocked awake from a short nap right before noon by the loud ring of the phone announcing that it was time to go to the airport for my flight to Yola. I went on an airline called Arik, which billed itself as "the wings of Nigeria." As much as I'd flown, I had never seen two Black pilots and an all-Black flight crew until there in Africa.

The next day it was quite magical to wake up at sunrise for the first time on the African continent. I thought about the significance of this: I do not care where you are from, I think everyone of every race, culture, and ethnicity should make it a point to connect with their roots and know their history as much as possible, and also to visit their country of origin at least once. To me there is no greater way to fall in love with yourself as a human being, to truly understand the greatness of humanity and our human connections, than to know who you are and where you come from. In fact, just before my trip here to Nigeria, I learned from Gina Paige of African Ancestry that my mother's side of the family is from Guinea-Bissau, and that we share genetic ancestry with two groups in that nation today: the Brame and Balanta people. I chuckled when Gina told me that people from that area had much to do with rice, because in the Low Country of South Carolina, where my family is from, rice is a staple. And my God did my mother cook a lot of rice as I was growing up.

I also thought about the Black pilots and flight crew, and how important it was to see positive role models as we grew up, who looked like us, so that we could know what is possible for us to accomplish. Many young Black men I'd encountered back home in America's ghettos only aspired to be three things: rappers, athletes, and hustlers in some form. Why? Because that is what they see daily in our communities, where so-called successful men are often missing in action. It is also what the American media machine pushes to us more than anything else in the form of sports, entertainment, and news coverage of our 'hoods.

In Yola, the poverty was devastating. Thoroughly devastating. Garbage was everywhere, as were wooden shacks serving as makeshift homes or tiny stores, and children in high numbers during school hours either begging for money or trying to sell anything, from black-market gas in canisters, to sugarcane, to bottles of water at a local outdoor marketplace; jumbo flies and other creatures crawled on the different meats, fruits, and vegetables being sold to the residents. I asked Francis, my driver and an employee at the university, how he, a native of Yola, had survived this. "Education," he said, plain and simple. Grimly, he added that without an education the future for these children would be the streets. Same for me in America, I said to Francis. I looked at the children, and the many adults grinding on the streets, too, with a mixture of love and sadness.

These are my people, all of them. . . .

During a full day with the students at the American University in Nigeria, I gave a speech on leadership, and had a lengthy interactive dialogue with students on the state of Nigeria and our world. Nigeria has Africa's largest population; in fact, it's the biggest Black community on the planet, and has a vast potential. The young people wanted answers; they were anti–political rhetoric and anti-corruption, and we talked much about a new Nigeria where there would be no corruption and no Nigerian-on-Nigerian violence. This made me think a great deal about America, my America, and the work I wanted to do in the coming years with BK Nation.

There is no denying that Nigeria has produced some of the smartest people and most passionate human beings on the planet. I was particularly impressed with a twenty-year-old Muslim named Faridah Ibrahim, who was the university's student government president. I told Faridah that one day she would be president of Nigeria. That was how powerful she was. When Farida spoke, everyone listened attentively, even if they did not agree, even if her points made them uncomfortable. Her particular gripe was the level of student apathy, the lack of participation, which I recognized from my own college student days and Congressional campaigns. It is always just a dedicated few who do the work to make change happen in our world. Those who are leaders must meet people where they are, not the other way around.

Another young Muslim woman stood up and proclaimed her dream for Nigeria: "Nigeria is one people." She envisioned a united Nigeria, which would have many different groups and states (the three largest being the Yoruba, the Ibo, and the Hausa people). Thanks to the carving up of Africa by European colonizers centuries ago, many African nations still suffer because artificial boundaries force disparate groups to coexist. In the latter part of the twentieth century, after many nations declared independence, civil wars and mass genocide took place, as in Rwanda. It is not enough to say Africans are simply corrupt and killing each other senselessly. This is rooted in the history of the exploitation of this great continent, which continues to this day, albeit in different forms. Nations like Nigeria, where oil is big business, are rich in natural resources, but the wealth, as elsewhere, is hoarded by the one percent at the top.

The Nigerian students were keenly aware of all of this. They spoke forcefully about morally bankrupt Nigerian politicians and preachers, just as many of us said this about unethical Black American leadership. The students noted that many of these leaders were complicit with multinational corporations in exploiting and undermining Nigeria. Likewise there were heated student debates about a rebel group called Boko Haram, which stood for "Western education is forbidden" in a combo of the Arabic and Hausa tongues. I was warned not to travel too far from Yola for fear of being kidnapped by Boko Haram, erasing a road trip to Cameroon I was considering. I have lectured at colleges and universities in America for about twenty years, but rarely have I encountered students so able to name elected leaders and state their political positions, and to pinpoint the leaders' moral and spiritual failures in serving their people as eloquently as these Nigerian young women and men.

Indeed, the female students were agitating for sexual equality, and Muslims and Christians both readily expressed their disdain for the old ways of viewing women and girls. One young lady stated, "We are not pieces of furniture, nor are we baby-making machines." In a nation in which polygamy is normal and quite a few men have as many as four wives, that was a profound statement of resistance and rebellion. So if there is to be a new Nigeria, led by folks like these young students, it will be co-led, unquestionably, by women. And how Nigeria went, I was reminded several times, would shape the future direction of the entire continent of Africa.

Even though there is widespread post-colonial political corruption, and huge disparity between the elite in politics and business and the poor, there is also in Nigeria mind-blowing resiliency and a unique ability to survive dire circumstances that I suspect many Americans could not handle. Nigerians live with a constant presence of armed military and police and random checkpoints. They adapt to having few of the basics of life. Some make traditional huts from mud and hay (a dying art in Africa) for their homes, and do not have running water. They live in a nation with no unifying language and cannot speak or understand each other as they travel from region to region inside their own country. And electric outages were a common, daily occurrence, any time of the day or night, something I had to adjust to quickly.

◆

A bunch of us decided to drive three hours or so to the Sukur Kingdom, which I had heard was over five hundred years old, atop a mountain that we could hike up and down. The idea reminded me of my readings on such kingdoms. Back when I was a college student, I would turn page after page in awe, as the history of Africa and the world unfolded before me. I was amazed to learn that we Black people had built kingdoms and magnificent societies, opened institutions of higher learning, and were inventors in those ancient times before slavery and colonization ravaged Mother Africa. While studying scholars like Ivan Van Sertima, the Guyanese historian, during my Rutgers years, I learned that while the Greeks and Romans had created civilizations in their own right, many of them had studied with ancient African sages and intellectuals.

I had acquired a deep sense of pride in who I was as a Black person from this more balanced portrait of history. But when a people do not know who they are, they will not like who they are or what they see, and will engage in self-hating, self-sabotaging, and self-destructive behavior. For the Black community globally, that means internalizing racism, referring to ourselves as "niggas," engaging in Black-on-Black violence, bleaching our skin to make it lighter or closer to that of our White sisters and brothers, and putting chemicals in our natural hair to make it appear to be straighter, curlier, so-called "good hair." And, yes, even in Africa I saw ads to make skin "brighter" as in whiter.

The ride to the Sukur Kingdom was very difficult, three-plus hours in a minivan dodging crater-size holes every few feet, for miles and miles. It was rough, bumpy, uncomfortable, and I often wondered if the vehicle would simply break down under the stress of this terrain.

But the trip was worth it. The sights and sounds of Nigeria unveiled themselves minute-by-minute, mile-by-mile: A family of seven, including a husband, wife, and children, miraculously riding together on a bicycle. The boy with the stick herding what seemed like one hundred sheep alone. The countless Nigerian women carrying babies strapped to their backs as they ducked and dodged fast-moving cars and fast-talking men along the roads. The folk songs of Nigeria altered by the steady and slow foot beat of people walking great distances because they had no automobile and no bike. The daring young men who rode recycled, souped-up motorcycles, their recklessness less about a fear of dying than about a love of living, creating a space in which their daredevilry brought them as close to freedom as they could get. The many police and military checkpoints along our route, where we were confronted by stone-cold Black men with dark, penetrating eyes, wearing helmets and pointing guns or rifles into our vehicle. I wondered what would have happened, at any given stop, if our van did not have the marking "American University in Nigeria."

At the foot of the Mandara Mountains, one of which we would climb to the Sukur Kingdom, a teenage boy was sleeping on the front patio of a seemingly abandoned building. He slept so peacefully, his shoes to his right, that I was reluctant to wake him. He jerked himself awake when he sensed my presence. He did not speak English and I did not speak his language of Hausa, but we nodded easily at each other. His name was Solomon and he was strikingly handsome, with a smile that could easily have landed him a contract as a model in another land. It turned out that Solomon was a prince in the village at the foot of the mountains, and was resting before taking a message to the king to whose mountaintop village we were headed.

I've hiked mountains in California, Hawaii, and the Colorado Rockies, so the Mandara Mountains, leading to the five-hundred-year-old Sukor Kingdom, were not enormously difficult, but the day was fire hot. The path to the top was rugged, with rocks everywhere. Several times I thought that I was going to roll or twist an ankle or simply fall flat on my face.

Our group was made up of about ten people, but as we climbed, we separated into small sub-groups. I was in the lead group with our Nigerian translators and the prince, Solomon. Green landscapes stretched all around us; snakes hissed as we passed bushes and trees. A herd of cows and of goats grazed along the trail.

My heart pounded as we neared the top of the mountain, and I ran up the rest of the way to the village. Children surrounded us, staring, pointing, giggling, and wondering who these strangers were. Women of the village also stepped up to have a look at us and to wave. The people in Nigeria always wave and bend their heads in acknowledgment of others, and I found myself doing the same to them throughout my trip. For me it said something about one's humanity if you recognized the existence of another human being with a greeting, even if just in passing. In this way Nigeria reminded me of how people in the American South always spoke to each other no matter what.

As I was taking photos and selfies of the children with my iPhone, two men crossed briskly before us, went to the other side of the village, and sat down. We were told the man next to a gargantuan and old baobab tree sitting in a plastic white chair was the king of the village. Similar seating was set up for us in front of him and we were summoned to greet the king, Hidi, and to be granted his permission to tour the village.

I thanked him for the opportunity to visit his kingdom, told him that I was from New York City, from America, that this was my very first trip to Africa, and how amazing it was to have read about African kings and queens and now to meet one in person. I asked for his blessing to tour the village and meet the people. King Hidi, who appeared to be in my generation, had come to power after his father died recently. The entire group talked through a translator, for about thirty minutes, and the king said that he was very happy that Barack Obama had been reelected president in America.

One of the king's men asked us for money. We did not know there was an admission fee to the Sukur Kingdom. The United Nations Educational, Scientific, and Cultural Organization (UNESCO) helped manage the kingdom and apparently took a cut of the entrance fees to the Sukur Kingdom. *Not cool,* I thought, *and so much for King Hidi's power.* But he clearly had some, just in a very old-school way: when I asked one of his aides how the king got up and down the mountain, he chuckled and said that the king's three wives carried him. To my pro-feminist male ears that reeked of terrible male privilege and an abuse of power.

The Sukur Kingdom had a population of 3,225 people, and it seemed that most of them were children. And most of the people lived in poverty and squalor. The farther inside we went, the more we saw unwashed children with wet or dried mucus on their noses and about their mouths, matted hair filled with red clay, and flies casually landing on their faces and bodies. In the traditional huts, a bed was a slab of rock with a very thin piece of cloth or a wooden plank atop it. Debris, litter, and garbage were everywhere, as were stray dogs and goats. A bull was tied near one of the huts.

My mind struggled to reconcile the image of the king sitting peacefully beneath the tree with that of the crushing poverty of his village. And it simply could not. Where did the tourists' fees go, if not to help the people of this kingdom? Were the king and his men gaming us in the same way? Why wasn't the king providing the basics for these children, some of whom may have been his and his three wives' children? I wondered why we, my people, any people on earth, hold on to traditions and cultures that are, in these modern times, so destructive to our very being.

Just as we were leaving, I saw, laying on the ground outside one of the huts, a gorgeous little girl with jet-black skin and pecan-colored eyes. She was folded in fetal position, writhing in pain on a mat, shaking. Flies dotted her body from head to toe. I asked what was wrong with her and was told that she had a mild case of malaria, that she had a severe headache too, and could not move. I wanted to hold her hand, to hug her, but I thought of the dire warnings to be careful in Nigeria, to not touch this, to not drink or eat that. So I looked her in the eyes and gestured at the little girl. And I prayed for her, prayed that she would not die an early death from this disease, prayed that she would heal very soon. And I felt that she heard me through her eyes, because she smiled at me, even as she was trembling. I placed my right hand over my heart and bowed my head to her, then waved goodbye.

◆

After eight days, I headed home. The Nigerians had taught me so much about history, culture, and tradition. Everyone, from the folks at American University, to the hotel workers, to the people at the Yola and Abuja airports, treated me so very kindly. There are all manner of facts and figures that can be cited about the ugly sides and corruption of this great African nation, but there is no denying the angelic soul of its people.

I want to be like them. That is not to say that I want to be Nigerian. I am an American, African American, with some great differences and great distances between this continent and the land where I was born. I am thinking of the reservoir of love and of resourcefulness, against all odds, that many a Nigerian embodies in this magical place. I reflected on how the hit Broadway show *Fela!* and the man, and his life, and his music, feel and sound totally different to me now that I've been to Africa, to his homeland.

But it was also true that Africa was always there inside of me. I just had to come "home" to understand how profoundly that was the case.

And to be reminded, too, that Africa was everywhere. In those stunning Nigerian faces I saw a friend from Brooklyn, or Chicago, or New Orleans, or Oakland. In their long strides along the lonely roads of Nigeria I saw my South Carolina kinfolk similarly walking, with stick in hand, in search of work, love, freedom, possibilities. In their radiant smiles and belly-up laughter I saw the joy on my own mother's face, on her lovely dark-chocolate face, as she navigates the world of racism and sexism and classism in America, even in her golden years. In the weathered brown-earth hands of African elders I saw the hands of an old Black woman or an old Black man on a stoop or porch in Barbados or Jamaica, at church in Brazil or Puerto Rico, on a milk crate in the West End of Atlanta or the Brixton section of London, the lines and contours of those hands telling more stories about her or his life than a million words ever could. In the dazzling creativity reflected in the Nigerians' huts made from the materials of God's mouth, in their ability to walk and balance anything on their heads, I saw the supernatural and grand birth of Negro spirituals, of the blues and of jazz, of rock and roll and soul and funk, of reggae and salsa and merengue, and of hip-hop. I had traveled far, across centuries and generations and a wide expanse of water with stories to tell, to get closer to myself than I'd ever been before.

For sure when I first arrived in Nigeria, the bright faces of the Nigerians who greeted us beamed and said to me, as they said to every Black passenger who passed, "Welcome home!" I paused, stunned, wondering if they knew that this was my first time. No, could not be, but I interpreted their words to mean just that. "Welcome home, Kevin Powell. You may have an Irish first name and a Welsh last name, born of the legacy of that very vicious and brutal trans-Atlantic slave trade, but you've finally returned to where you are from."

I did not cry as I'd thought I would—not outwardly—but many days later, back here in New York, I was exercising on a treadmill and decided to play the music from Steven Spielberg's film *Amistad*, about the uprising of abducted Africans on a slave ship. The first song in the film is titled "Dry Your Tears, Afrika." A captivating song, it is a mishmash of traditional African rhythms and European classical music. It is a call, a chant, a melancholy plea, and as I was stepping on that treadmill, finally the emotions of my trip to Nigeria burst from beneath the flesh, punctured the backs of my eyes, and I exploded into tears. And I cried and cried and cried. Cried for my first trip to Africa. Cried for the people of Africa. Cried for what I had witnessed there. Cried because I knew I would never be the same again, because of this journey "home." And I vowed, on that treadmill, that not only would the remainder of my life, no matter how long or short, continue to be dedicated to helping others, to public service in any and every way possible, but that Africa, now more than ever, would have a permanent place in that work.

Because Africa, however faint and distant, still, for me, was one of the homes that I'd been searching for my entire life.

30
Finding my father

sunset nails the lip of a building:
a shadow eyes
            an ashy windowpane.
an old man sits on his cane
regurgitating cups of lenox
and the savoy:
i drink his face it burps
southern clay and city welts

MY FIRST trip to Africa made me think a lot about my father. One day, a woman from Seattle by the name of Minty LongEarth sent me a private message on Facebook saying she admired my work, and that she helped people find their family roots, and would be glad to help me if I ever wanted to do a search. I could not believe her generosity of spirit, and gladly took her up on the offer. I couldn't give Minty much to go on. My mother and I did not know my dad's birthplace, his birth date, or even if he was still alive. Every now and again Minty hit me with a lead via Facebook, but they all turned out to be dead ends.

I had resigned myself to the fact that I would never find my father.

Then nearly a year after my Africa visit, in October 2013, I was randomly surfing on the Internet and stumbled across a different spelling of what could be my father's name—Elish, instead of Elize Cunningham. This was all it took—with that new spelling, Minty was able to find my father. I was excited and relieved.

Elish Cunningham was born and raised in a town called Laurens, in Laurens County, South Carolina, less than an hour's drive from Greenville, on March 11, 1932. But then Minty broke my heart: My father had died on February 19, 2002, eleven years before our discovery. I cried tears for a man I had met only three or four times when I was a boy, until he cut off my mother and me when I was eight. I cried because I would never get to speak with him again in person, to ask him how he met my mother, how he felt toward her, why he did not marry her after promising to do so, and why he disappeared from our lives.

Nevertheless, the more Minty told me about my father, about his family, going back into the late 1800s, the more curious I became. I wanted to visit his hometown, to see for myself what had made him who he was.

But before I went to Laurens County, I spent Thanksgiving Day, 2013, with my mother. As we always did, she and I ate mostly in silence. Now retired, after twenty-five years of laboring as a home health-care worker for the elderly, my mother had suddenly been thrust into being an elder herself, and I was all she had other than her senior citizen apartment and some meager savings. She walks with a limp now, her body worn down from years of work, since those early days, at age eight, of picking cotton in South Carolina. Ma was rushed to the hospital a few years ago, her first visit to one since she birthed me, when her high blood pressure made her so dizzy she could not stand or function. I cried profusely on that day at the hospital because the one constant in my life has been my mother. It was surreal for me to see my mother lying there, strapped to the bed, resignation in her eyes. I am thankful she recovered and is better.

At some point during our Thanksgiving meal I told my mother I was going to go to South Carolina to see where my father was born and raised. As forever happened when I brought up my father, her blood boiled. She screamed at me, telling me how betrayed she felt. I told her that my father, dead or alive, would never replace her in my life, that she would forever be both my mother and my father, but that I must take this journey for my own peace of mind, to find at last the other half of myself. When I added that my father was dead, I sensed, for a moment, that my mother softened, and I saw a distant look in her eyes, as if she traveled back to the 1960s, back to the time before I was born, back to that day, whenever it was, that they met.

I traveled south with my longtime friend Cynical, the filmmaker who'd traveled to the Gulf Coast with me to do relief work after Hurricane Katrina. When we arrived in Laurens County, we went straight to the cemetery where Minty had told me my father was buried, next to a church where generations of his family worshipped. I struggled through the grass and weeds to find my father's tombstone and grew frustrated as I saw his last name again and again, but no sign of him. I moved farther and farther back through the cemetery, until finally I found him. I screamed with relief and sorrow and dropped to my knees in front of the tombstone. I spoke to my father, telling him that I was happy I'd found him at long last. I told him about my life, about how much he hurt my mother and me, about my many days of wishing for a father, of the great trials and confusions of my life, of how I was a man now in my forties. And I told my father that I forgave him, that I held no grudges against him or his family, and that I only wished that I had spoken with him one time before he died. Then I walked away.

After the visit to the graveyard, Cynical and I went to my father's last known address, but no one answered when we knocked on the door. We had better luck at the next house. We banged several times because we heard children playing loudly. Still no answer. We nearly gave up, until an old woman finally opened the door. I asked her name, and when she told me, sure enough it was one of my father's sisters. When I told her who I was, the woman stood in disbelief, and then promptly bear-hugged me. I experienced an overwhelming sense of joy—for the first time since the 1970s I had met someone related to my father.

A three-day whirlwind of meetings ensued, with cousins, aunts, sisters, and brothers I either did not know existed previously, or only knew of faintly. I learned that my father had married only once in his life and had children born in the 1950s, 1960s, 1970s, and 1980s. Papa truly was a rolling stone, and no one was quite sure how many children, in total, my father had. He himself was one of eight children—four girls and four boys. I learned that my paternal grandfather was not Black, but half White and half Native American, and had been the product of a White man raping an Indian woman there in South Carolina. I also learned that my father's father had had a violent temper and a severe drinking problem, both of which he passed down to my father. My father had moved north, to New Jersey, in the 1950s. He always worked hard, always had money in his pocket, and always had an eye for women. His ex-wife told me that he was foul and disrespectful toward women. She cursed my father and his soul like my mother did any time I mentioned his name. I learned that he accepted paternity for some children and was suspected of fathering others. I learned that my father asked for me several times toward the end of his life, reminding family that he had a son up north. Because my father referred to me as "Cel-vin" with his slow Southern drawl, the entire family thought that was my name, and no one had a clue how to find me when he died. This was the reason that I was not included in the obituary list of his children, which saddened me.

Best of all, I learned that this family—my father's family—loved me. They welcomed me into their homes, into the family church, and into the entire community. My brother Michael Cunningham, whose photo my father had given to my mother back in the 1990s, had a brother who was killed tragically when they were children. Michael told me how happy he was to have a brother again.

But so much happened so fast over the course of three short days that I knew it would take time for me to process my feelings about these strangers, even though they told me that they loved me as if I had lived there all along. I could not quite understand how to return the love my father's family had given to me. I knew my mother's family tree—the Burrisons—their names, their faces, fragments of their life stories, because of the oral histories that had been handed around from kinfolk to kinfolk and generation to generation since I could talk and understand words. I could not discern how to return the love my father's family gave to me. I've had to be my own father my entire life; I've had to figure out how to be the man I so badly wanted my father to be.

When Michael's SUV led the rental car Cynical and I were driving to the entrance of the highway home, I returned his "I love you," but wondered if I would ever see him or any of them again, or if I even wanted to. The choice was mine.

◆

As Cynical and I headed north through the dark roads of North Carolina and Virginia and DC and Maryland and Delaware, to the morning dusk of New Jersey, I thought back to the many years I had traveled this same route on a Greyhound bus with my mother and Aunt Cathy and cousin Anthony, our lives packed into those cheap suitcases, with aluminum foil filled with fried chicken and hot sauce on Wonder Bread. I had come so far, yet I remained so close to the little boy with his face pressed against the expansive window of the Greyhound bus. I thought of my Aunt Pearlie Mae—my mother's oldest sibling and sister—the first to die in 2010, and how at the funeral my mother, my Uncle Lloyd, my Aunt Birdie, and my Aunt Cathy had each carefully selected the plot where they would be buried when their time came. I thought of my journey through life—through the ghetto, poverty, violence, abuse, Rutgers University, MTV, *Vibe*, hip-hop, Tupac Shakur, September 11, Hurricane Katrina, my campaigns for Congress, and my first ever pilgrimage to Africa. As a speaker, as an activist, as a writer, I have been to all fifty of these United States, and five of the Earth's seven continents, me the little boy once so terribly frightened of the world. I have witnessed people come and go, and

I've seen people live and die. I thought I would not make it to fifteen, to eighteen, to twenty-one, to twenty-five, to thirty, but here I stand, someone who challenges racism, sexism, classism, homophobia, religious hate of any kind, and the reckless disregard for the disabled.

As a young boy, I never thought that I would live to see a Barack Obama elected as president. Nor did I imagine that in the twenty-first century in our America, I would be in the middle of protests and organizing around the racial profiling murder of Trayvon Martin, or kneel on the front lines in Ferguson, Missouri, at the very spot where Michael Brown, a Black youth, was shot and killed by Darren Wilson, a White police officer. Or that so many women I know—of every race and of every age—would be the victims of some form of sexual violence in their lifetimes. Definitions of manhood, mine or any other male's, should not be based on the domination and exploitation of women and girls, ever, nor on the domination and exploitation of each other as men. With this awareness earned from a hardcore rites-of-passage I would wish on no one, I no longer take my life for granted, nor do I take the lives of others for granted. I am thankful for life, for my life, and I have found the strength, because of years and years of therapy, to forgive my father and my mother, and to also forgive myself. I've been damaged, I've been broken, I've been 'buked, I've been scorned, I've been unready for manhood, unready for my humanity. I've made so many mistakes in my life, hurt so many people, and hurt myself on far too many occasions. Out of that pain and trauma, I've found the will to live in a way that I did not think possible. Today and for the rest of my life, I believe in peace, I believe in love, I believe in therapy, I believe in healing, I believe in self-care, I believe in myself. And I humbly ask and pray that those I've disrespected or wounded in some way in my past life to forgive me, please.

I cannot say what the future holds for me, but I know that I want to live in a world in which life offers incredible opportunities to every human being. I want a world in which we treat every person with dignity, with grace, with class. I want a world where people who do have privilege and power and great wealth also have great humanity; that they come to understand privilege, power, and wealth are spiritually and morally empty without empathy and compassion for those who are not them. I want a world in which my story does not continue and multiply, from generation to generation, tragically. I see clearly that I am one of the lucky survivors—that I should have died several times, long ago. Today my life means nothing if I do not live it in service to others, if I do not help others, through my words, through my actions. I wake every morning without fear and I face the world anew. I no longer live with crippling self-hatred and low self-esteem. I value myself and what I have to contribute to this world. I cannot control how long I will live and I do not want to. But I can control how I live, what I do, what I say, what I write, how I treat people, and how I treat myself. This is why after years of alcohol abuse and neglect I am a vegan these days and will never drink liquor again. This is why I practice yoga and meditation; why I run marathons and hike mountains and why I marvel at every new day; and this is why I treat myself as a temple, not as the garbage can I once did. I truly believe that God—she—created us all to be equals, to be one human race, to be loved, honored, and respected, in spite of where and how we were born. She would have it no other way, and I hear her, louder and clearer than ever.

I know that my life, regardless of the troubles I have seen, has not been in vain. I can breathe, now, and I know, now, that my life matters. If we can withstand our many falls and mistakes and efforts to sabotage and destroy our own lives, if we can withstand oppression, discrimination, hatred, and abuse from others, from those who have power but no love for people, all people, then maybe, just maybe, we can come out of the harshness and magic of our life experiences as better human beings. I am doing my best now, more than ever, to be better. My mother raised me to be a man; time and again she has told me to do the right thing. Finally, I can say to my mother: You were right, Ma. I know what the right thing is, and I am doing it, Ma, I am doing it.

Acknowledgments

This, without question, is the hardest thing I've ever written in my life. While the writing and the memories are mine, there is no way I could have gotten through the journey of this memoir without the help, support, and editorial push of a few people. They include my Simon & Schuster editor Malaika Adero, as well as Judith Curr (you are such a class act, madam publisher), Albert Tang, Donna Loffredo, Jennifer Weidman (your legal edits rock J-Dub!), and Todd Hunter there at S&S. Thank you for believing in me, thank you for believing in this book. Additionally, I would like to thank, very deeply and very humbly, Michael Cohen, Tieler Giles, Kerry DeBruce-Burrison (you are the best graphic artist in America, period; thank you for the amazing cover design), Jessica Pinkney, Lisa-Erika James, Marisa King-Redwood (my publicist), Regina Brooks (my literary agent), and Tayllor Johnson (my assistant), all of whom worked in some way to get this book to the finish line. Michael Cohen, I am especially indebted to your editorial eye. Words cannot describe how grateful I am for your dedication to this project. I must thank my mother, my Aunt Cathy, my entire Burrison family tree, for there would be no me without any of you. I must also thank the people I've met through the many chapters of my life, who taught me, who challenged me, who loved me even when I did not know how to love myself. Finally, this book is for every human being who has survived and won small victories, even in the face of madness and darkness.

About the Author

Kevin Powell is the author or editor of eleven previous books. A poet, essayist, blogger, public speaker, marathon runner, skateboarder, hiker, bicyclist, and yoga student, Kevin's next work will be a biography of the late rapper and actor Tupac Shakur. Kevin is also an activist and philanthropist, and president and cofounder of BK Nation, a new American organization focused on civil and human rights, education, leadership development for young people, and holistic health and wellness. A native of Jersey City, New Jersey, he is a proud and longtime resident of Brooklyn, New York. Kevin has given speeches widely, in the United States and globally in places like Japan, the United Kingdom, and Nigeria, West Africa. He was the international ambassador for the Dylan Thomas Centennial Celebration in America in 2014 and has been a lecturer-in-residence at several schools, including Stanford University and Dillard University. Kevin's archives of his writings, speeches, and community work are housed at Cornell University as the Kevin Powell Collection. You can email him, kevin@kevinpowell.net, or follow him on Twitter, @kevin_powell.